UTOPIAN/DYSTOPIAN LITERATURE
A Bibliography of Literary Criticism

by
Paul G. Haschak

The Scarecrow Press, Inc.
Metuchen, N.J., & London
1994

British Library Cataloguing-in-Publication data available

Library of Congress Cataloging-in-Publication Data

Haschak, Paul G., 1948–
    Utopian/dystopian literature : a bibliography of literary criti-
cism / by Paul G. Haschak.
      p.   cm.
    Includes indexes.
    ISBN 0-8108-2752-2 (acid-free paper)
    1. Utopias in literature—Bibliography.   2. Utopias—
Bibliography.   I. Title.
Z7164.U8H38   1994
[PN56.U8]
016.809′93372—dc20   93-30232

Especially for Leigh Laney Kirtley

CONTENTS

PREFACE

Utopian/Dystopian Literature is the first book-length checklist in the English language devoted exclusively to the *general* literary criticism of individual Utopian/Dystopian plays, short stories, novels, novellas, and prose writing. It provides students with citations to criticism of major and minor Utopian/Dystopian works. It also provides citations to works that are partially Utopian in nature, and to works that, while not strictly Utopian, might be "read," in one form or another, as such.

Access to citations is simple enough. Writers of different nationalities and time periods are listed in an easy-to-use, alphabetical arrangement. In the back of the text are two convenient cross-references: a Title Index and a Critic Index.

American authors represented in this bibliography include Bellamy, Bradbury, Donnelly, Hawthorne, Howells, Le Guin, London, Melville, Poe, Skinner, Twain, and Vonnegut, just to name a few.

British authors include Amis, Bacon, Burgess, Butler, Chesterton, Forster, Golding, Hudson, Huxley, Lessing, Lindsay, Lytton, More, Morris, Orwell, Shakespeare, Shaw, Stapledon, Swift, Trollope, Wells, and Winstanley.

Continental writers include Cabet, Campanella, Capek, Chateaubrian, Cixous, Condorcet, Cyrano de Bergerac, Dante, Diderot, Doblin, Dostoevskii, Fenelon, Fourier, Herzl, Hesse, Jean Paul, Montaigne, Nabokov, Prevost, Rabelais, Sade, Verne, Voltaire, Werfel, Wittig, Zamiatin, and Zola, plus many, many others.

Ancient writers include Plato, Xenophon, Aristophanes, and Lucian.

Graduate, undergraduate, and high school students (and other true Utopians) will find this present volume most useful as a starting place for their own research. Students of science fiction (SF) and fantasy will find this volume useful, too, particularly in the areas where SF intersects with Utopia/Dystopia.

For the general reader, I recommend Marie Louise Berneri's *Journey Through Utopia* (1950). Also recommended for furthur study are Lewis Mumford's *The Story of Utopias* (1924), Frank E. and Fritzie P. Manuel's *Utopian Thought in the Western World* (1979), Chad Walsh's *From Utopia to Nightmare* (1962), A. L. Morton's *The English Utopia* (1952), Kenneth Roemer's *The Obsolete Necessity* (1976), Vernon

vii

Louis Parrington, Jr.'s, *American Dreams* (1947), Hoda M. Zaki's *Phoenix Renewed* (1988), and Robert C. Elliot's *The Shape of Utopia* (1970). For those interested in feminist Utopias, Nan Bowman Albinski's *Women's Utopias in British and American Fiction* (1988), Frances Bartkowski's *Feminist Utopias* (1989), and *Feminism, Utopia, and Narrative* (1990) edited by Libby Falk Jones and Sarah Webster Goodwin, are recommended.

For researchers seeking other bibliographic guideposts, please consult Glenn Negley's *Utopian Literature: A Bibliography with a Supplementary Listing of Works Influential in Utopia Thought* (1978), Gorman Beauchamp's "Themes and Uses of Fictional Utopias: A Bibliography of Secondary Works in English" (*Science-Fiction Studies* 1977, Volume 4, pp. 55–63), Arthur Orcutt Lewis's *Utopian Literature in the Pennsylvania State University Libraries: A Selected Bibliography* (1984), and Lyman Tower Sargent's *British and American Utopian Literature, 1516–1975: An Annotated Bibliography* (1979) and *British and American Utopian Literature, 1516–1985: An Annotated Chronological Bibliography* (1988).

Nota Bene: This checklist is a beginning to doing research. It is designed to be representative, not exhaustive. Never use it, in any case, as a substitute for real scholarship.

Entries for books and dissertations that are "multiples" have been shortened due to editorial concerns. **Full citations for these entries are available in the Appendix.**

Special thanks go to Barbara Tanner Brooks, Janice Riggs, Neley Bauers, Velta Carney, A. Rami Hijazi, Ralph Gabbard, Marilyn Moore, Philies Delone, and Lori Fairburn. Their good humor and their combined Herculean effort allowed me to complete the manuscript. Extra special thanks goes to Sheila Delacroix, a great librarian and an even greater person, for her support of this project.

LISTINGS

ABBEY, EDWARD

Good News

Dougherty, Jay. " 'Once More, and Once Again': Edward Abbey's Cyclical View of Past and Present in *Good News.*" *Critique* 29 (Summer 1988): 223–232.

Ronald, Ann. *The New West of Edward Abbey.* Albuquerque: University of New Mexico Press, 1982, pp. 210–238.

Tschachler, Heinz. "Apologie fur die Okalypse, Oder wie auch die Okologie das Abendland nicht vor dem Untergang Retten Kann: Ein Beitrag zu Edward Abbeys Utopischem Roman *Good News.*" In *Utopian Thought in American Literature,* 85–110.

ACOSTA, OSCAR ZETA

General Criticism

Saldivar, Ramon. *Chicano Narrative,* 90–98.

The Autobiography of a Brown Buffalo

Kowalczyk, Kimberly A. "Oscar Zeta Acosta: The Brown Buffalo and His Search for Identity." *Americas Review* 16 (Fall-Winter 1988): 198–209.

Padilla, Genaro M. "The Self as Cultural Metaphor in Acosta's *Autobiography of a Brown Buffalo.*" *Journal of General Education* 35, no. 4 (1984): 242–258.

1

The Revolt of the Cockroach People

Alurista. "Acosta's *The Revolt of the Cockroach People*: The Case, the Novel, and History." In *Contemporary Chicano Fiction*, 94–104.

Rodriguez, Joe. "The Chicano Novel and the North American Narrative of Survival." *Denver Quarterly* 16 (Fall 1981): 63–70.

Tonn, Horst. "Fiction and Politics in Acosta's *The Revolt of the Cockroach People.*" In *Missions in Conflict*, 195–202.

ADAMS, FREDERICK UPHAM

President John Smith

Parrington, Vernon Louis, Jr. *American Dreams*, 116–118, 188.

Pfaelzer, Jean. *The Utopian Novel in America, 1886–1896*, 118.

AE. See RUSSELL, GEORGE WILLIAM

ALBERTSON, RALPH

The Social Incarnation

Rooney, Charles J., Jr. *Dreams and Visions*, 104–105, 155, 181.

ALEXANDER, THEA PLYM

2150 A.D.

Sargent, Lyman Tower. "A New Anarchism: Social and Political Ideas in Some Recent Feminist Eutopias." In *Women and Utopia*, 3–33.

ALGER, HORATIO, JR.

General Criticism

Kenner, Hugh. *A Homemade World: The American Modernist Writers.* New York: Knopf, 1975, pp. 20–49.

Walden, Daniel. "The Two Faces of Technological Utopianism: Edward Bellamy and Horatio Alger, Jr." *Journal of General Education* 33 (Spring 1981): 26–30.

AMIS, KINGSLEY

The Alteration

Bradford, Richard. *Kingsley Amis,* 63–66.

Fuger, Wilhelm. "Streifzuge durch Allotopia: Zur Topographie eines Fictionalen Gestalttungsraums." *Anglia* 102, nos. 3–4 (1984): 367–376.

Garder, Philip. *Kingsley Amis.* Boston: Twayne, 1981, pp. 83–91.

Hutchings, W. "Kingsley Amis's Counterfeit World." *Critical Quarterly* 19, no. 2 (1974): 71–77.

MacKillop, I. D. "Armageddon Pier Staff: Second Decade Arms." *Cambridge Quarterly* 7, no. 4 (1977): 327–329.

Sutherland, John. *Bestsellers: Popular Fiction of the 1970's.* London: Routledge & Kegan Paul, 1981, pp. 242–244.

Russian Hide and Seek

Bradford, Richard. *Kingsley Amis,* 67–69.

Fuger, Wilhelm. "Streifzuge durch Allotopia: Zur Topographie eines Fictionalen Gestalttungsraums." *Anglia* 102, nos. 3–4 (1984): 382–390.

ANDERSON, COLIN

Magellan

Berger, Harold L. *Science Fiction and the New Dark Age,* 74, 76–77.

ANDREAE, JOHANN VALENTIN

Christianopolis

Bailey, J. O. *Pilgrims through Space and Time,* 25, 230.

Berneri, Marie Louise. *Journey Through Utopia,* 103–126.

Eurich, Nell. *Science in Utopia*, 120–134.

Mumford, Lewis. *The Story of Utopia*, 81–99.

Ross, Harry. *Utopias Old and New*, 74–80.

Walsh, Chad. *From Utopia to Nightmare*, 45–46.

Whitman, John Pratt. *Utopia Dawns*, 61–66.

AREVALO MARTINEZ, RAFAEL

General Criticism

Salgado, Maria A. *Rafael Arevalo Martinez*. Boston: Twayne, 1979.

White, Millicent Bolden. "The Utopian Novels of Rafael Arevalo Martinez: Structure, Themes, and Characters." M.A. thesis, University of North Carolina at Chapel Hill, 1981.

ARIAS, RON

The Road to Tamazunchale

Saldivar, Jose David. "The Ideological and the Utopian in Tomas Rivera's . . . *y no se lo Trago la Tierra* and Ron Arias' *The Road to Tamazunchale*." In *Missions in Conflict*, 203–214.

ARISTOPHANES

General Criticism

Berneri, Marie Louise. *Journey Through Utopia*, 45–51.

Ecclesiazusae

Barry, E. *Ecclesiazusae as a Political Satire*. Chicago: University of Chicago Press, 1942.

Bowra, C. "A Love Duet." *American Journal of Philology* 79 (October 1958): 376–391.

Dover, K. J. *Aristophanic Comedy,* 190–201.

Elliot, Robert C. *The Shape of Utopia,* 21–22.

Harsh, Philip Whaley. *A Handbook of Classical Drama,* 307–308.

Henderson, J. "Sparring Partners: A Note on Aristophanes' *Ecclesiazusae.*" *American Journal of Philology* 95 (Winter 1974): 344–347.

Murray, Gilbert. *Aristophanes,* 181–198.

Olson, S. D. "The Identity of the *Despotes* at *Ecclesiazusae.*" *Greek, Roman, and Byzantine Studies* 28 (Summer 1987): 161–166.

———. "The Love Duet in Aristophanes' *Ecclesiazusae.*" *Classical Quarterly* 38, no. 2 (1988): 328–330.

Pecirka, J. "Aristophanes' *Ekklesiazusen* und die Utopien in der Krise der Polis." *Zeitschrift, Wissenschaftliche, der Humboldt-Universitat, Berlin* 12 (1963): 215–220.

Reckford, Kenneth J. *Aristophanes' Old-and-New Comedy.* Volume 1, 344–353.

Spatz, Lois. *Aristophanes,* 132–133.

Strauss, Leo. *Socrates and Aristophanes,* 263–282.

Ussher, R. G. Introduction. *Ecclesiazusae.* By Aristophanes. Oxford: Oxford University Press, 1973, xiii-xlvii.

Young, S. *The Women of Greek Drama,* 162–170.

Lysistrata

Corrigan, Robert. *Comedy: Meaning and Form.* Scranton, PA: Chandler Publishing Company, 1965, pp. 356–357.

Dover, K. J. *Aristophanic Comedy,* 150–161.

Downs, R. B. "Greek Comic Genius: Aristophanes." In *Famous Books, Ancient and Medieval.* New York: Barnes & Noble, 1974, pp. 76–81.

Harsh, Philip Whaley. *A Handbook of Classical Drama*, pp. 292–294.

Henderson, J. Introduction. *Aristophanes' Lysistrata*. Oxford, England: Clarendon Press, 1987, xv-xli.

————. "Lysistrata: The Play and its Themes." In *Yale Classical Studies*, Volume 26, pp. 153–218. New York: Cambridge University Press, 1981.

Murphy, C. "Aristophanes, Athens and Attica." *Classical Journal* 59 (April 1964): 306–323.

Murray, Gilbert. *Aristophanes*, 164–180.

Quain, E. A. "Aristophanes: *Lysistrata, Birds, Clouds.*" In *Great Books: A Christian Appraisal; a Symposium on the First Year's Program of the Great Books Foundation*, edited by Harold Gardiner, 19–24. Old Greenwich, CT: Devin-Adair, 1949.

Reckford, Kenneth J. *Aristophanes' Old-and-New Comedy*. Volume 1, 301–311.

Semel, J. M. "Sexual Humor and Harmony in *Lysistrata.*" *LA Journal* 25 (September 1981): 28–36.

Solomos, Alexis. *The Living Aristophanes*. Ann Arbor: University of Michigan Press, 1974, pp. 181–190.

Spatz, Lois. *Aristophanes*, 91–102.

Stewart, D. "Aristophanes and the Pleasures of Anarchy." *Antioch Review* 25 (Spring 1965): 203–208.

Strauss, Leo. *Socrates and Aristophanes*, 195–213.

Vaio, J. "The Manipulation of Theme and Action in Aristophanes' *Lysistrata.*" *Greek, Roman, and Byzantine Studies* 14 (Winter 1973): 369–380.

Whitman, Cedric H. *Aristophanes and the Comic Hero*. Cambridge, MA: Harvard University Press, 1964, pp. 200–216.

Wilson, N. "Two Observations on Aristophanes' *Lysistrata.*" *Greek, Roman, and Byzantine Studies* 23 (Summer 1982): 157–163.

Young, S. *The Women of Greek Drama*, 153–161.

ARTAUD, ANTONIN

General Criticism

Knapp, Bettina L. "Antonin Artaud and the Mystics of Utopia." In *France and North America*, 123–131.

Rossner, Michael. "'La Fable du Mexique oder' vom Zusammenbruch der Utopien: Uber die Konfrontation Europaischer Paradiesprojektionen mit dem Selbstverstandnis de Indigenen Mexiko in den 20er und 30er Jahren." In *Literarische Vermittlungen: Geschichte und Identitat in der Mexikanischen Literatur*, 191. Tubingen: Niemeyer, 1988.

ASIMOV, ISAAC

"Breeds There a Man . . .?"

Ash, Brian. *Faces of the Future*, 170.

Patrouch, Joseph F., Jr. *The Science Fiction of Isaac Asimov*, 235–236.

The Gods Themselves

Moore, Maxine. "The Use of Technical Metaphors in Asimov's Fiction." In *Isaac Asimov*, 85–87.

Patrouch, Joseph F., Jr. *The Science Fiction of Isaac Asimov*, 263–270.

Watt, Donald. "A Galaxy Full of People: Characterization in Asimov's Major Fiction." In *Isaac Asimov*, 154–157.

Zaki, Hoda M. *Phoenix Renewed*, 67, 75.

ASTOR, JOHN JACOB

A Journey in Other Worlds

Neustadter, Roger. "Mechanization Takes Command: The Celebration of Technology in the Utopian Novels of Edward Bellamy, Chauncey Thomas, John Jacob Astor, and Charles Caryl." *Extrapolation* 29 (Spring 1988): 21–33.

Pfaelzer, Jean. *The Utopian Novel in America, 1886–1896*, 108–111.

Roemer, Kenneth M. *The Obsolete Necessity*, 47.

ATWOOD, MARGARET

The Handmaid's Tale

Atwood, Margaret. "A Feminist *1984*: Margaret Atwood Talks about Her Exciting New Novel." *Ms.* 14 (February 1986): 24–26.

————. *Margaret Atwood: Conversations*. Princeton, NJ: Ontario Review Press, 1990, pp. 200, 203, 214–217, 223, 231–232.

————. "There's Nothing in the Book that Hasn't Already Happened." *Quill & Quire* 51 (September 1985): 66.

Berkson, Dorothy. "So We All Became Mothers: Harriet Beecher Stowe, Charlotte Perkins Gilman, and the New World of Women's Culture." In *Feminism, Utopia, and Narrative*, 112–113.

Cowart, D. *History and the Contemporary Novel*. Carbondale: Southern Illinois University Press, 1989, pp. 76–119.

Cranny-Francis, Anne. *Feminist Fiction*, 141–142.

Davidson, Arnold E. "Future Tense: Making History in *Handmaid's Tale*." In *Margaret Atwood*, 113–121.

Fitting, Peter. "The Turn from Utopia in Recent Feminist Fiction." In *Feminist, Utopia and Narrative*, 144–145, 152.

Foley, Michael. "Satiric Intent in the 'Historical Notes' Epilogue of Atwood's *The Handmaid's Tale*." *Commonwealth Essays and Studies* 11 (Spring 1989): 44–52.

Freibert, Lucy M. "Control and Creativity: The Politics of Risk in Margaret Atwood's *The Handmaid's Tale*." In *Critical Essays on*

Margaret Atwood, edited by Judith McCombs, 280–291. Boston: G.K. Hall, 1988.

Fullbrook, Kate. *Free Women,* 187–190.

Heller, Arno. "Die Literarische Dystopie in Amerika mit einer Exemplarischen Erortering von Margaret Atwood's *The Handmaid's Tale.*" In *Utopian Thought in American Literature,* 185–201.

Jones, Dorothy. "Not Much Balm in Gilead." *Commonwealth Essays and Studies* 11 (Spring 1989): 31–43.

Kaler, Anne K. "A Sister Dipped in Blood? Satiric Inversion of the Formation Techniques of Women Religions in Margaret Atwood's *The Handmaid's Tale.*" *Christianity and Literature* 38 (Winter 1989): 43–62.

Kauffman, Linda. "Special Delivery: Twenty-First Century Epistolarity in *The Handmaid's Tale.*" In *Writing the Female Voice: Essays on Epistolary Literature,* edited by Elizabeth Goldsmith, 221–244. Boston: Northeastern University Press, 1989.

Ketterer, David. "Margaret Atwood's *The Handmaid's Tale*: A Contextual Dystopia." *Science-Fiction Studies* 16 (July 1989): 209–217.

Larson, Janet L. "Margaret Atwood and the Future of Prophecy." *Religion and Literature* 21 (Spring 1989): 27–61.

Malak, Amin. "Margaret Atwood's *The Handmaid's Tale* and the Dystopian Tradition." *Canadian Literature* 112 (Spring 1987): 9–16.

Rubenstein, Roberta. "Nature and Nurture in Dystopia: *The Handmaid's Tale.*" In *Margaret Atwood,* 101–112.

BACHELDER, JOHN

A. D. 2050

Parrington, Vernon Louis, Jr. *American Dreams,* 142–144, 147.

Pfaelzer, Jean. *The Utopian Novel in America, 1886–1896,* 102.

BACON, SIR FRANCIS

The New Atlantis

Achinstein, S. "How to be a Progressive Without Looking Like One: History and Knowledge in Bacon's *New Atlantis.*" *Clio* 17 (Spring 1988): 249–264.

Albanese, Denise. "*The New Atlantis* and the Uses of Utopia. *ELH* 57 (Fall 1990): 503–528.

Bailey, J. O. *Pilgrims through Space and Time*, 24–26.

Berneri, Marie Louise. *Journey through Utopia*, 126–137.

Bierman, Judah. "*The New Atlantis,* Bacon's Utopia of Science." *Papers on Language and Literature* 3 (1967): 99–110.

———. "*The New Atlantis* Revisited." *Studies in the Literary Imagination* 4 (April 1971): 121–141.

———. "Science and Society in *The New Atlantis* and Other Essays." *PMLA* 78 (December 1963): 492–500.

Birkner, Gerd. "Francis Bacon: *New Atlantis* (1672)." In *Die Utopie in der Angloamerikanischen Literatur*, 32–59.

Bloomfield, Paul. *Imaginary Worlds, or the Evolution of Utopia*, 77–93.

Bowen, Catherine Drinker. *Francis Bacon: The Temper of a Man.* Boston: Little, Brown & Co., 1963.

Crowther, James Gerold. *Francis Bacon, the First Statesman of Science.* London: Cresset, 1960.

Davis, J. C. *Utopia and the Ideal Society*, 105–138.

Demers, Patricia. "Bacon's Allegory of Science: The Theater of *The New Atlantis.*" *Journal of the Rocky Mountain Medieval and Renaissance Association* 4 (January 1983): 135–148.

Desroches, Rosny. "L'Utopie: Évasion ou Anticipation?" In *France and North America*, 83–92.

Eisley, Loren C. *Francis Bacon and the Modern Dilemma.* New York: Scribner's, 1973.

Eurich, Nell. *Science in Utopia,* 134–144.

Green, Adwin Wigfall. *Sir Francis Bacon.* New York: Twayne, 1967.

Hertzler, Joyce Oramel. *The History of Utopian Thought,* 146–153.

Jardine, Lisa. *Francis Bacon: Discovery and the Art of Discourse.* New York: Cambridge University Press, 1974.

Kaufmann, M. *Utopias,* 14–30.

Lachterman, David R. "The Conquest of Nature and the Ambivalence of Man in the French Enlightenment: Reflections on Condoriet's *Fragment sur l'atlantide.*" In *Man, God, and Nature in the Enlightenment,* 37–47.

Mumford, Lewis. *The Story of Utopias,* 106–109.

Pfeiffer, K. Ludwig. "Wahrheit und Herrschaft: Zum Sysematischen Problem in Bacon's *New Atlantis.*" In *Literarische Utopien von Morus bis zur Gegenwart,* 50–58.

Pons, Alain. "Science, Religion et Politique dans la *Nouvelle Atlantide* de Francis Bacon." In *Melanges Offerts a Maurice de Gandillac,* edited by Annie Cazenave and Jean-Francois Lyotard, 305–318. Paris: Pu de France, 1985.

Reiss, T. J. "Structure and Mind in Two Seventeenth-Century Utopias: Campanella and Bacon." *Yale French Studies* 49 (1973): 82–95.

Ross, Harry. *Utopias Old and New,* 64–67.

Simon, Elliott M. "Bacon's *New Atlantis*: The Kingdom of God and Man." *Christianity and Literature* 38 (Fall 1988): 43–61.

Vickers, Brian. *Francis Bacon and Renaissance Prose.* Cambridge, England: Cambridge University Press, 1968.

Wallace, Anthony F. C. *The Social Context of Innovation: Bureaucrats, Families, and Heroes in the Early Industrial Revolution, as Foreseen in Bacon's 'New Atlantis.'* Princeton, NJ: Princeton University Press, 1982.

Walsh, Chad. *From Utopia to Nightmare,* 46–47.

Weiner, Harvey S. "'Science or Providence': Theory and Practice in Bacon's *New Atlantis.*" *Enlightenment Essays* 3 (1972): 85–92.

White, Frederic R. *Famous Utopias of the Renaissance,* 207–250.

Whitman, John Pratt. *Utopia Dawns,* 45–50.

BALBUENA, BERNARDO DE

Grandeza Mexicana

Duran, Juan Guillermo. "Literatura y Utopia en Hispanoamerica."

BALLANTYNE, ROBERT MICHAEL

The Coral Island

Berger, Morroe. *Real and Imagined Worlds,* 55–59.

McEwan, Neil. *The Survival of the Novel: British Fiction in the Later Twentieth Century.* Totowa, NJ: Barnes & Noble, 1981, pp. 147–161.

Maher, Susan Naramore. "Recasting Crusoe: Frederick Marryat, R. M. Ballantyne and the Nineteenth-Century Robinsonade." *Children's Literature Association Quarterly* 13 (Winter 1988): 169–175.

Mannsaker, Frances M. "The Dog that Didn't Bark: The Subject Races in Empirical Fiction at the Turn of the Century." In *The Black Presence in English Literature,* edited by David Dabydeen, 114–117. Manchester, England: Manchester University Press, 1985.

Quayle, Eric. *Ballantyne the Brave: A Victorian Writer and His Family.* London: Rupert Hart-Davis, 1967, pp. 142–143, 146–147, 174.

Rose, Jacqueline. *The Case of Peter Pan; or the Impossibility of Children's Fiction.* London: Macmillan, 1984, pp. 78–79.

BAUM, L. FRANK

The Wonderful Wizard of Oz

Alex, Nola Kortner. *A Brazilian Oz?* Louisville, KY: Popular Culture Association, 1985. ERIC (ED 291098).

Baughman, Roland. "L. Frank Baum and the 'Oz books.' " *Columbia University Library Columns* (May 1955): 14–35.

Bauska, Barry. "The Land of Oz and the American Dream." *Markham Review* 5 (1976): 21–24.

Brotman, Jordan. "A Late Wanderer in Oz." In *Only Connect,* edited by Sheila Egoff, *et al.,* 156–169. New York: Oxford University Press, 1969.

Donovan, Ann. "Alice and Dorothy: Reflections from Two Worlds." In *Webs and Wardrobes: Humanist and Religious World Views in Children's Literature,* edited by Joseph Milner and Lucy Milner, 25–31. Lanham, MD: UP of America, 1987.

Erisman, Fred. "L. Frank Baum and the Progressive Dilemma." *American Quarterly* 20 (Fall 1968): 616–623.

Gardner, Martin, and Russel B. Nye. *The Wizard of Oz and Who He Was.* East Lansing: Michigan State University Press, 1957.

Hansen, Linda. "Experiencing the World as Home: Reflections on Dorothy's Quest in *The Wizard of Oz.*" *Soundings* 67 (Spring 1984): 91–102.

Hudlin, Edward W. "The Mythology of Oz: An Interpretation." *Papers on Language and Literature: A Journal for Scholars and Critics of Language and Literature* 25 (Fall 1989): 443–462.

Indick, Ben. "Utopia Allegory and Nightmare." *Baum Bugle* 18 (Spring 1974): 14–19.

Littlefield, H. M. *"The Wizard of Oz* Parable on Populism." *American Quarterly* 16 (Spring 1964): 47–58.

McReynolds, Douglas J., and Barbara J. Lips. "A Girl in the Game: *The Wizard of Oz* as Analog for the Female Experience in America." *North Dakota Quarterly* 54 (Spring 1986): 87–93.

Moore, Raylyn. *Wonderful Wizard Marvelous Land.* Bowling Green, OH: BG University Popular Press, 1974.

Remington, Thomas J. "The Niven of Oz: *Ringworld* as Science Fictional Reinterpretation." In *Science Fiction Dialogues,* 99–111.

Sackett, S. J. "The Utopia of Oz." *Georgia Review* 14 (Fall 1960): 275–291.

St. John, Tom. "Lyman Frank Baum: Looking Back to the Promised Land." *Western Humanities Review* 36, no. 4 (1982): 349–359.

Sale, Roger. "L. Frank Baum and Oz." *Hudson Review* 25 (Winter 1972–1973): 571–592.

Schumen, Samuel. " 'Out of the Frying Pan and into the Pyre': Comedy, Myth, and *The Wizard of Oz." Journal of Popular Culture* 7, no. 2 (1973): 302–304.

Starr, Nathan C. *"The Wonderful Wizard of Oz:* A Study in Archetypal Symbiosis." *Unicorn* 2, no. 4 (1973): 13–17.

Wagenknecht, Edward. *As Far as Yesterday.* Norman, OK: University of Oklahoma Press, 1968.

BEBEL, AUGUST

Die Frau und der Sozialismus

Asholt, Wolfgang. "Sozialistishe Irrlehren und Liberale Zerrbilder: Die Anfange der Anti-Utopie." *Germanisch-Romanische Monatsschrift Grundzuge* 35, no. 4 (1985): 369–381.

Maehl, William Harvey. *August Bebel: Shadow Emperor of the German Workers.* Philadelphia: American Philosophical Society, 1980, pp. 123–128.

BELLAMY, CHARLES JOSEPH

An Experiment in Marriage

Nydahl, Joel. Introduction. *An Experiment in Marriage,* v–xxviii.

BELLAMY, EDWARD

General Criticism

McCord, Sue Gordon. "The Utopian Consciousness in Edward Bellamy's Short Fiction." Ph.D. diss., University of South Florida, 1979.

Senescu, Betty Cobey. "The Utopia Within: Some Psychological Aspects of Edward Bellamy's Early Writing." Ph.D. diss., University of New Mexico, 1977.

Equality

Bowman, Sylvia E. "Bellamy's Missing Chapter." *New England Quarterly* 31 (March 1958): 47–65.

Gardiner, Helen Jane. "American Utopian Fiction, 1885–1910."

Nydahl, Joel. Introduction. *An Experiment in Marriage,* xii.

Parrington, Vernon Louis, Jr. *American Dreams,* 94–97.

Looking Backward, 2000–1887

Aaron, Daniel. *Men of Good Hope,* 92–132.

Abrash, Merritt. "*Looking Backward:* Marxism Americanized." *Extrapolation* 30 (Fall 1989): 237–242.

Bailey, J. O. *Pilgrims Through Space and Time,* 56–57.

Beauchamp, Gorman. "*The Iron Heel* and *Looking Backward:* Two Paths to Utopia." *American Literary Realism, 1870–1910* 9 (Autumn 1976): 307–314.

Becker, George J. "Edward Bellamy: Utopia, American Plan." *Antioch Review* 14 (June 1954): 181–194.

Bellamy, Edward. "How I Came to Write *Looking Backward.*" *Nationalist* 1 (May 1889): 1–4.

Berneri, Marie Louise. *Journey Through Utopia,* 243–255.

Bleich, David. "Eros and Bellamy." *American Quarterly* 16 (Fall 1964): 445–459.

———. "Utopia."

Boggs, W. Arthur. "*Looking Backward* at the Utopian Novel, 1888–1900." *Bulletin of the New York Public Library* 64 (June 1960): 329–336.

Bowman, Sylvia E. "Utopian Views of Man and the Machine." *Studies in the Literary Imagination* 6, no. 2 (1973): 105–120.

———. *The Year 2000: A Critical Biography of Edward Bellamy.* New York: Bookman, 1958, pp. 112–122.

Christensen, Bryce J. *Utopia Against the Family,* 4–5.

Coleman, Stephen. "The Economics of Utopia: Morris and Bellamy Contrasted." *Journal of the William Morris Society* 8 (Spring 1989): 2–6.

Collins, Gail. "Tomorrow Never Knows." *Nation* 252 (January 21, 1991): 58–61.

Conkin, Paul K. "Three Authors, Three Books, and Three Colonies: The Cooperative Commonwealth in America." In *France and North America,* 33–44.

Cooperman, Stanley. "Utopian Realism: The Futurist Novels of Bellamy and Howells." *College English* 24 (March 1963): 464–467.

Cornet, Robert J. "Rhetorical Strategies in *Looking Backward.*" *Markham Review* 4 (1974): 53–58.

Downs, R. B. *Books that Changed America.* New York: Macmillan, 1970, pp. 100–109.

———. *Molders of the Modern Mind: 111 Books that Shaped Western Civilization.* New York: Barnes & Noble, 1961, pp. 323–326.

Listings **17**

Dudden, Arthur P. "Edward Bellamy: *Looking Backward, 2000–1887.*" *In Landmarks of American Writing,* edited by Hennig Cohen, 207–218. New York: Basic Books, 1969.

Eastman, Max, Jacques Barzun, and Mark Van Doren. "Bellamy: *Looking Backward.*" In *New Invitation to Learning,* edited by Mark Van Doren, 414–427. New York: Random House, 1942.

Egbert, Nelson Norris. "Problems of Form and Content in Six Utopian Responses to Edward Bellamy's *Looking Backward, 2000–1887.*"

Elliott, Robert C. *The Shape of Utopia,* 111, 122, 146.

Forbes, A. B. "The Literary Quest for Utopia, 1880–1900." *Social Forces* 6 (December 1927): 179–189.

Fromm, Erich. Foreword. *Looking Backward, 2000–1887.* By Edward Bellamy. New York: Signet-NAL, 1960, v–xx.

Fuson, Ben. "A Poetic Precursor to Bellamy's *Looking Backward.*" In *SF: The Other Side of Realism: Essays on Modern Fantasy and Science Fiction,* edited by Thomas Clareson, 282–288. Bowling Green, OH: BG University Popular Press, 1971.

Gardiner, Helen Jane. "Form and Reform in *Looking Backward.*" *American Transcendental Quarterly* 2 (March 1988): 69–82.

———. "American Utopian Fiction, 1885–1910."

Hansen, Olaf. "Edward Bellamy: *Looking Backward: 2000–1887.*" In *Die Utopie in der Angloamerikanischen Literatur,* 103–119.

Harris, W. T. "Edward Bellamy's Vision." In *The American Hegelians: An Intellectual Episode in the History of Western America,* edited by William Goetzmann, 193–201. New York: Knopf, 1973.

Hicks, Granville. *The Great Tradition: An Interpretation of American Literature since the Civil War.* New York: Macmillan, 1935, pp. 131–163.

Howells, William Dean. "Edward Bellamy." In *Criticism and Fiction and Other Essays,* edited by Clara Kirk and Rudolph Kirk, 246–255. New York: New York University Press, 1959.

James, Max H. "The Polarity of Individualism and Conformity, a Dynamic of the Dream of Freedom, Examined in *Looking Backward*." *Christianity and Literature* 35 (Fall 1985): 17–59.

Jehmlich, Reimer. "Cog-Work: The Organization of Labor in Edward Bellamy's *Looking Backward* and in Later Utopian Fiction." In *Clockwork Worlds*, 27–46.

Ketterer, David. *New Worlds for Old*, 96–122.

Khanna, Lee Cullen. "The Reader and *Looking Backward*." *Journal of General Education* 33 (Spring 1981): 69–79.

————. "The Text as Tactic: *Looking Backward* and the Power of the Word." In *Looking Backward, 1988–1888*, 37–50.

Khouri, Nadia. "The Clockwork and Eros: Models of Utopia in Edward Bellamy and William Morris." *College Language Association Journal* 24 (March 1981): 376–399.

Kluge, Walter. "Sozialismus und Utopie im Spaten Neunzehnten Jahrhundert." In *Alternative Welten*, 197–215.

Kramer, Leonie. "Utopia as Metaphor." In *Utopias*, 133–143.

Kumar, Krishan. *Utopia and Anti-Utopia in Modern Times*, 132–167.

Levi, A. W. "Edward Bellamy: Utopian." *Ethics* 55 (January 1945): 131–144.

Martin, Jay. *Harvests of Change: American Literature, 1865–1914*. Englewood Cliffs, NJ: Prentice-Hall, 1967, pp. 220–223.

Matarese, Susan M. "Foreign Policy and the American Self Image: Looking Back at *Looking Backward*." *American Transcendental Quarterly* 3 (March 1989): 45–54.

Michaels, Walter Benn. "An American Tragedy; or, The Promise of American Life: Classes and Individuals." *Representations* 25 (Winter 1989): 71–98.

Morgan, A. E. "Diagram for a World that Might Be." *Christian Science Monitor* 37 (March 24, 1945): 8.

————. *Edward Bellamy.* New York: Columbia University Press, 1944, pp. 204–244.

Mott, Frank L. *Golden Multitudes: The Story of Best Sellers in the United States.* New York: Macmillan, 1947, pp. 165–171.

Mumford, Lewis. *The Story of Utopias,* 159–169.

Negley, G. R., and J. M. Patrick. "Edward Bellamy, 1850–1898." In *Quest for Utopia: An Anthology of Imaginary Societies,* edited by G. Negley and J. Patrick, 75–80. New York: H. Schuman, 1952.

Neustadter, Roger. "Mechanization takes Command: The Celebration of Technology in the Utopian Novels of Edward Bellamy, Chauncey Thomas, John Jacob Astor, and Charles Caryl." *Extrapolation* 29 (Spring 1988): 21–33.

Parrington, Vernon L., Jr. *American Dreams,* 69–97.

Patai, Daphne, ed. *Looking Backward, 1988–1888.*

Pfaelzer, Jean. "Immanence, Indeterminance, and the Utopian Pun in *Looking Backward.*" In *Looking Backward, 1988–1888,* 51–67.

————. *The Utopian Novel in America, 1886–1896,* 26–51.

Roemer, Kenneth M. "Contexts and Texts: The Influence of *Looking Backward.*" *Centennial Review* 27 (Summer 1983): 204–223.

————. "Getting 'Nowhere' beyond Stasis: A Critique, a Method, and a Case." In *Looking Backward, 1988–1888,* 126–146.

————. "The Literary Domestication of Utopia: There's No *Looking Backward* without Uncle Tom and Uncle True." *American Transcendental Quarterly* 2 (March 1989): 101–122.

————. " 'Utopia made Practical': Compulsive Realism." *American Literary Realism, 1870–1910* 7 (Summer 1974): 273–276.

Ross, Harry. *Utopias Old and New,* 143–154.

Sadler, Elizabeth. "One Book's Influence: Edward Bellamy's *Looking Backward.*" *New England Quarterly* 17 (December 1944): 530–555.

Sancton, Thomas A. "Looking Inward: Edward Bellamy's Spiritual Crisis." *American Quarterly* 25 (1973): 538–557.

Sanford, Charles L. *The Quest for Paradise,* 185–187.

Schiffman, J. H. "Edward Bellamy and the Social Gospel." In *Intellectual History in America,* Volume 2, edited by Cushing Strout, 10–27. New York: Harper, 1968.

————. "The Genesis of Edward Bellamy's Thought." M.A. thesis, New York University, 1951.

Schweninger, Lee. "The Building of the City Beautiful: The Motif of the Jeremiad in Three Utopian Novels." *American Literary Realism* 18 (Spring 1985): 107–119.

Seager, Allan. *They Worked for a Better World.* New York: Macmillan, 1929, pp. 97–116.

Seeber, Hans Ulrich. "Thomas Morus' *Utopia* und Edward Bellamy's *Looking Backward:* Ein funktionsgeschichtlicher Vergleich." In *Utopieforschung,* Volume 3, pp. 357–377.

Segel, Howard P. "Bellamy and Technology: Reconciling Centralization and Decentralization." In *Looking Backward: 1988–1888,* 91–105.

————. "Edward Bellamy's *Looking Backward* and the American Ideology of Progress through Technology." *OAH Magazine of History* 4 (Spring 1989): 20–24.

Shurter, R. L. "The Literary Work of Edward Bellamy." *American Literature* 5 (November 1933): 229–234.

————. "The Writing of *Looking Backward.*" *South Atlantic Quarterly* 38 (July 1939): 255–261.

Sloat, Warren. "Looking Back at *Looking Backward:* We Have Seen the Future and it didn't Work." *New York Times Book Review* (January 17, 1988): 3.

Spann, E. K. *Brotherly Tomorrows,* 176–190.

Staiger, Janet. "Future *Noir:* Contemporary Representations of Visionary Cities." *East-West Film Journal* 3 (December 1988): 20–44.

Strauss, Sylvia. "Gender, Class, and Race in Utopia." In *Looking Backward, 1988–1888,* 68–90.

———. "Women in 'Utopia.' " *South Atlantic Quarterly* 75 (Winter 1976): 115–131.

Suvin, Darko, "Anticipating the Sunburst—Dream and Vision: The Exemplary Case of Bellamy and Morris." In *America as Utopia,* 57–77.

Taylor, Walter F. *The Economic Novel in America.* Chapel Hill: University of North Carolina Press, 1942, pp. 184–213.

Thomas, John L. Introduction. *Looking Backward: 2000–1887.* By Edward Bellamy. Cambridge, MA: Harvard University Press, 1967, pp. 1–88.

Ticknor, Caroline. *Glimpses of Authors.* New York: Houghton Mifflin, 1922, pp. 112–121.

Trimmer, Joseph F. "American Dreams: A Comparative Study of the Utopian Novels of Bellamy and Howells." *Ball State University Forum* 12, no. 3 (1971): 13–21.

Wagar, W. Warren. "Dreams of Reason: Bellamy, Wells, and the Positive Utopia." In *Looking Backward, 1988–1888,* 106–125.

Walden, Daniel. "The Two Faces of Technological Utopianism: Edward Bellamy and Horatio Alger, Jr." *Journal of General Education* 33 (Spring 1981): 24–30.

Westmeyer, Russell E. *Modern Economic and Social Systems,* 78–93.

Whitman, John Pratt. *Utopia Dawns,* 105–110.

Widdicombe, Richard Toby. " 'Dynamite in Disguise': A Deconstructive Reading of Bellamy's Utopian Novels." *American Transcendental Quarterly* 3 (March 1989): 69–84.

———. "Edward Bellamy's Utopian Vision: An Annotated Checklist of Reviews." *Extrapolation* 29 (Spring 1988): 5–20.

Wild, P. H. "Teaching Utopia." *English Journal* 55 (March 1966): 335–375.

Wilson, R. Jackson. "Experience and Utopia: The Making of Edward Bellamy's *Looking Backward.*" *Journal of American Studies* 11 (April 1977): 45–60.

Winters, Donald E. "The Utopianism of Survival: Bellamy's *Looking Backward* and Twain's *A Connecticut Yankee.*" *American Studies* 21, no. 1 (1980): 23–28.

Ziemba, Margaret Mary. "Contrasting Social Theories of Utopia."

BENFORD, GREGORY

Timescape

Borgmeier, Raimund. " 'Science Fiction Comes to College': Gregory Benfords *Timescape* als SF-Universitatroman." In *Gattungsprobleme in der Anglo-Amerikanischen Literatur,* edited by Raimund Borgmeier, 239–253. Tubingen: Niemeyer, 1986.

Stone-Blackburn, Susan. "Science and Humanism in Gregory Benford's *Timescape.*" *Science-Fiction Studies* 15 (November 1988): 295–311.

Zaki, Hoda M. *Phoenix Renewed,* 55, 67, 74.

BERSIANIK, LOUKY

General Criticism

Arbour, Kathryn Mary. "French Feminist Re-visions."

The Eugélionne

Bartkowski, Frances. *Feminist Utopias.* Lincoln: University of Nebraska Press, 1989, pp. 133–158.

BESANT, WALTER

All Sorts and Conditions of Men

Neetens, Wim. "Problems of a 'Democratic Text': Walter Besant's Impossible Story." *Novel* 23 (Spring 1990): 247–264.

The Inner House

Abrash, Merritt. "Is there Life after Immortality?" In *Death and the Serpent,* 22–25.

BIRD, ARTHUR

Looking Forward

Pfaelzer, Jean. *The Utopian Novel in America, 1886–1896,* 99–100.

Roemer, Kenneth M. *The Obsolete Necessity,* 143, 145.

BISHOP, MICHAEL

No Enemy but Time

Zaki, Hoda M. *Phoenix Renewed,* 63–65, 67, 73.

BISHOP, WILLIAM

The Garden of Eden, USA

Parrington, Vernon Louis, Jr. *American Dreams,* 119.

Rooney, Charles J. Jr. *Dreams and Visions,* 66, 70, 71, 80, 105, 149, 151, 183.

BLANC, LOUIS

L'organisation du Travail

Berneri, Marie Louise. *Journey Through Utopia*, 215–216.

Kaufmann, M. *Utopias*, 143–158.

BLANCHARD, CALVIN

The Art of Real Pleasure

Nydahl, Joel. Introduction. *An Experiment in Marriage*, xxi–xxii.

BLISH, JAMES

A Case of Conscience

Amis, Kingsley. *New Maps of Hell*, 82, 102, 124, 138, 140.

Berger, Harold L. *Science Fiction and the New Dark Age*, 130–132.

Bradham, Jo Ellen. "The Case of James Blish's *A Case of Conscience.*" *Extrapolation* 16 (December 1974): 67–80.

Burgess, Andrew J. "The Concept of Eden." In *The Transcendent Adventure*, 73–81.

Ketterer, David. "Covering *A Case of Conscience.*" *Science-Fiction Studies* 11 (March 1984): 45–49.

McCarthy, Patrick A. "The Joyce of Blish: *Finnegans Wake* in *A Case of Conscience.*" *Science-Fiction Studies* 15 (March 1988): 112–118.

Parkin-Speer, Diane. "Alien Ethics and Religion versus Fallen Mankind." In *The Transcendent Adventure*, 93–104.

Stableford, Brian M. *A Clash of Symbols: The Triumph of James Blish.* San Bernardino, CA: Borgo Press, 1979, pp. 52–57.

BOCCACCIO, GIOVANNI

The Decameron

Jensen, Kirsten Grubb. "Aspetti Cortesi ed Utopistici nei Personaggi della Cornice del *Decameron* di Giovanni Boccaccio." *Revue Romane* 22, no. 1 (1987): 59–82.

Musa, Mark, and Peter E. Bondanella, eds. and trans. *The Decameron.* By Giovanni Boccaccio. New York: Norton, 1977. A Norton Critical Edition.

Sanford, Charles L. *The Quest for Paradise,* 13–14.

BOCCALINI, TRAIANO

Dispatches from Parnassus

Eurich, Nell. *Science in Utopia,* 122–123.

Manuel, F. E., and Fritzie P. Manuel. *Utopian Thought in the Western World.* Cambridge, MA: Belknap Press, 1979, pp. 151, 152, 292, 293.

BOND, DANIEL

Uncle Sam in Business

Rooney, Charles J., Jr. *Dreams and Visions,* 32, 119, 183.

BORGES, JORGE LUIS

General Criticism

Leddy, Annette Cecille. "Swift, Carroll, Borges."

Stabb, Martin S. "Utopia and Anti-Utopia: The Theme in Selected Essayistic Writings of Spanish Americans." *Revista de Estudios Hispanicus* 15 (October 1981): 377–393.

"Tlon, Uqbar, Orbis Tertius"

Aguilera Garramuno, Marco Tulio. " 'Tlon, Uqbar, Orbis Tertius,' O el Universo Creador a la Medida de Borges." *La Palabra y el Hombre* no. 29 (1979): 36–40.

Alazraki, Jaime. "Tlon y Asterion: Metaforas Epistemologicas." In *Jorge Luis Borges,* edited by Jamie Alazraki, 183–200. Madrid: Taurus, 1976.

Brivic, Sheldon. "Borges' 'Orbis Tertius.' " *Massachusetts Review* 16 (Spring 1975): 387–399.

Garcia Mendez, Javier. "Una Utopia de Borges." *Plural* no. 85 (1978): 56–60.

Hatlen, Burton. "Borges and Metafiction." In *Simply a Man of Letters,* edited by Carlos Cortinez, 131–154. Orono: University of Maine at Orono Press, 1982.

Hayes, Aden W. "Orbis Tertius and Orbis Novus: The Creation and Discovery of New Worlds." *Revista Canadiense de Estudios Hispanicos* 8 (Winter 1984): 275–280.

Irby, James E. "Borges and the Idea of Utopia." In *Jorge Luis Borges,* edited by Harold Bloom, 93–103. New York: Chelsea, 1986.

Isaacs, Neil D. "The Labyrinth of Art in Four *Ficciones* by Jorge Luis Borges." *Studies in Short Fiction* 6 (Summer 1969): 383–394.

Jaen, Didier T. "The Esoteric Tradition in Borges' 'Tlon, Uqbar, Orbis Tertius.' " *Studies in Short Fiction* 21 (Winter 1984): 25–39.

Lindstrom, Naomi. *Jorge Luis Borges: A Study of the Short Fiction.* Boston: Twayne, 1990, pp. 25–27, 148–149.

McMurray, George R. *Jorge Luis Borges.* New York: Ungar, 1980, pp. 56–61.

Mosca, Stefania. "Borges: Antiutopia." *Zona Franca: Revista de Literatura* 6 (March–April 1983): 29–33.

Stabb, Martin S. *Jorge Luis Borges.* New York: Twayne, 1970, pp. 100–106.

Sturrock, John. *Paper Tigers: The Ideal Fictions of Jorge Luis Borges.* Oxford: Clarendon Press, 1977, pp. 118–122.

Zaniello, Thomas. "Outopia in Jorge Luis Borges' Fiction." *Extrapolation* 9 (December 1967): 13–15.

Zlotchew, Clark M. "Tlon, Llhuros, N. Daly, J. L. Borges." *Modern Fiction Studies* 19, no. 3 (1973): 453–459.

BOUCHER, ANTHONY

Barrier

Walsh, Chad. *From Utopia to Nightmare,* 149.

BRADBURY, RAY

General Criticism

Mengeling, Marvin E. "The Machineries of Joy and Despair: Bradbury's Attitudes toward Science and Technology." In *Ray Bradbury,* 83–109.

Fahrenheit 451

Amis, Kingsley. *New Maps of Hell,* 107–113.

Berger, Harold L. *Science Fiction and the New Dark Age,* 39–41.

Colmer, J. *Coleridge to 'Catch-22': Images of Society,* 197–209.

Doxiadis, Constantinos. *Between Dystopia and Utopia,* 17.

Heuermann, Hartmut. "Ray Bradbury: *Fahrenheit 451.*" *In Die Utopie in der Angloamerikanischen Literatur,* 259–282.

Huntington, John. "Utopian and Anti-Utopian Logic: H. G. Wells and His Successors." *Science-Fiction Studies* 9 (July 1982): 122–146.

Johnson, Wayne L. *Ray Bradbury,* 85–88.

Mogen, David. *Ray Bradbury,* 105–111.

Ronnov-Jessen, Peter. "World Classics and Nursery Rhymes: Emblems of Resistance in Ray Bradbury's *Fahrenheit 451* and George Orwell's *1984.*" In *George Orwell and 1984,* 59–72.

Touponce, William F. *Ray Bradbury and the Poetics of Reverie.* Ann Arbor, MI: UMI Research Press, 1984.

Watt, Donald. "Burning Bright: *Fahrenheit 451* as Symbolic Dystopia." In *Ray Bradbury,* 195–213.

Zipes, Jack. "Mass Degradation of Humanity and Massive Contradictions in Bradbury's Vision of America in *Fahrenheit 451.*" In *No Place Else,* 182–198.

The Martian Chronicles

Gallagher, Edward J. "The Thematic Structure of *The Martian Chronicles.*" In *Ray Bradbury,* 55–82.

Johnson, Wayne L. *Ray Bradbury,* 107–118.

Mogen, David. *Ray Bradbury,* 82–93.

Rabkin, Eric S. "To Fairyland by Rocket: Bradbury's *The Martian Chronicles.*" In *Ray Bradbury,* 110–126.

BRADLEY, MARION ZIMMER

General Criticism

Hornum, Barbara. "Wife/Mother, Sorceress/Keeper, Amazon/ Renunciate: Status Ambivalence and Conflicting Roles on the Planet Darkover." In *Women Worldwalkers,* 153–163.

Russ, Joanna. "Recent Feminist Utopias." In *Future Females,* 71–75.

Wood, Diane S. "Gender Roles in the Darkover Novels of Marion Zimmer Bradley." In *Women Worldwalkers,* 237–246.

The Ruins of Isis

Arbur, Rosemarie. *Marion Zimmer Bradley,* 25–26.

Jones, Libby Falk. "Gilman, Bradley, Piercy, and the Evolving Rhetoric of Feminist Utopias." In *Feminism, Utopia, and Narrative,* 116, 119–122.

The Shattered Chain

Albinski, Nan Bowman. *Women's Utopias in British and American Fiction,* 164, 176, 177, 184.

Arbur, Rosemarie. *Marion Zimmer Bradley,* 27.

Schwartz, Susan M. "Marion Zimmer Bradley's Ethic of Freedom." In *The Feminine Eye,* 73–88.

BRANTENBERG, GERD

Egalia's Daughters

Moberg, Verne. "A Norwegian Women's Fantasy: Gerd Brantenberg's *Egalias Dotre* as *Kvinneskelig* Utopia." *Scandinavian Studies* 57 (Summer 1985): 325–332.

BRINSMADE, HERMAN H.

Utopia Achieved

Rooney, Charles J., Jr. *Dreams and Visions,* 112, 183.

BRONER, E. M.

A Weave of Women

Albinski, Nan Bowman. *Women's Utopias in British and American Fiction,* 170, 184.

Bartkowski, Frances. "Toward a Feminist Eros."

BROWN, CHARLES BROCKDEN

Alcuin

Axelrod, A. M. *Charles Brockden Brown: An American Tale.* Austin: University of Texas Press, 1983, pp. 99, 103.

Davidson, Cathy N. "The Matter and Manner of Charles Brockden Brown's *Alcuin.*" In *Critical Essays on Charles Brockden Brown,* edited by Bernard Rosenthal, 71–86. Boston: G. K. Hall, 1981.

Edwards, Lee R. Afterword. *Alcuin: A Dialogue.* By Charles Brockden Brown. New York: Grossman Publ., 1970, pp. 92–104.

Nydahl, Joel. Introduction. *An Experiment in Marriage,* xv–xvi.

Rice, Nancy. "Heritage: *Alcuin.*" *Massachusetts Review* 14 (Autumn 1973): 802–814.

Ringe, Donald A. *Charles Brockden Brown.* New York: Twayne, 1966, pp. 19–20, 22.

Warfel, Harry R. *Charles Brockden Brown: American Gothic Novelist.* Gainesville: University of Florida Press, 1949, pp. 81–86.

BRUERE, MARTHA

Mildred Carver, U.S.A.

Albinski, Nan Bowman. *Women's Utopias in British and American Fiction,* 49, 62, 68, 74, 109, 161.

Kessler, Carol Farley. "The Grand Marital Revolution: Two Feminist Utopias." In *Feminism, Utopia, and Narrative*, 70–71, 75–78.

BRUNNER, JOHN

General Criticism

Goldman, Stephen H. "John Brunner's Dystopias: Heroic Man in Unheroic Society." *Science-Fiction Studies* 5 (November 1978): 260–270.

Rasulis, Norman. "The Future of Empire: Conflict in the Major Fiction of John Brunner." In *The Happening Worlds of John Brunner*, 113–129.

Stand on Zanzibar

Auffret-Bouce, Helene. "*Stand on Zanzibar* ou l'art du Gerbage." *Études Anglaises* 41 (July–September 1988): 345–354.

Berger, Harold L. *Science Fiction and the New Dark Age*, 33–34.

Brunner, John. "The Genesis of *Stand on Zanzibar* and Digressions." *Extrapolation* 11 (May 1970): 34–43.

De Bolt, Joe. "An Introduction to John Brunner and His Works." In *The Happening Worlds of John Brunner*, 24–33, 38–39, 43–50.

Livingston, Dennis. "Science Fiction Models of Future World Order Systems." *International Organization* 25 (Spring 1971): 254–270.

Sargent, Lyman Tower. "Utopia and Dystopia in Contemporary Science Fiction." *Futurist* 6 (June 1972): 93–98.

BRUNO, GIORDANO

General Criticism

Horowitz, Irving Louis. *The Renaissance Philosophy of Giordano Bruno*. New York: Colman-Ross, 1952.

Singer, Dorothea Waley. *Giordano Bruno: His Life and Thought*. New York: Schuman, 1950.

Expulsion of the Triumphant Beast

Imerti, Arthur D. Introduction. *The Expulsion of the Triumphant Beast.*
By Giordano Bruno. New Brunswick, NJ: Rutgers University Press,
1964, pp. 3–65.

Riehl, Alois. *Giordano Bruno.* Translated by Agnes Fry. London: T. N.
Foulis, 1905, pp. 36–37.

BRUZOV, VALERIUS

The Republic of the Southern Cross

Walsh, Chad. *From Utopia to Nightmare,* 76–77.

BRYANT, DOROTHY

The Kin of Ata are Waiting for You

Albinski, Nan Bowman. *Women's Utopias in British and American
Fiction,* 172, 176, 183.

Pearson, Carol. "Coming Home: Four Feminist Utopias and Patriarchal
Experience." In *Future Females,* 63–70.

Sargent, Lyman Tower. "A New Anarchism: Social and Political Ideas
in Some Recent Feminist Eutopias." In *Women and Utopia,* 3–33.

BUCKINGHAM, JAMES SILK

National Evils and Practical Remedies

Buckingham, James Silk. Preface. *National Evils and Practical Remedies, with the Plan of a Model Town.* By James Silk Buckingham.
Clifton, NJ: Augustus M. Kelley, 1973, xv–xxx.

BURDEKIN, KATHARINE

Swastika Night

Albanski, Nan Bowman. *Women's Utopias in British and American Fiction*, 79, 80, 82, 90–91, 93, 104.

Bonifas, Gilbert. *"Nineteen Eighty-Four* and *Swastika Night." Notes and Queries* 34 (March 1987): 59.

Crossley, Robert. "Dystopian Nights." *Science-Fiction Studies* 14 (March 1987): 93–98.

BURGESS, ANTHONY

General Criticism

Burgess, Anthony. "A Fable for Social Scientists." *Horizon* 15 (Winter 1973): 12–15.

D'Haen, Theo. "Utopia/Dystopie in the Science Fiction of Anthony Burgess and Doris Lessing." In *Just the Other Day,* 315–327.

Evans, Robert O. "The Nouveau Roman, Russian Dystopias, and Anthony Burgess." *Studies in the Literary Imagination* 6 (Fall 1973): 27–37.

Hauge, Hans. "Rationelt og Litteraert Sprog hos Orwell, Burgess og Lasch." *Kredsen* 49, no. 1 (1982): 15–24.

K[arp], W[alter]. "The Clockwork Society." *Horizon* 15 (Winter 1973): 2–3.

Pritchard, William H. "The Novels of Anthony Burgess." *Massachusetts Review* 7 (Summer 1966): 525–539.

Stinson, John J. "Waugh and Anthony Burgess: Some Notes Toward an Assessment of Influence and Affinities." *Evelyn Waugh Newsletter* 10, no. 3 (1976): 11–12.

Sullivan, Walter. "Death without Tears: Anthony Burgess and the Dissolution of the West." *Hollins Critic* 6 (April 1969): 1–11.

Weinkauf, Mary. "The God Figure in Dystopian Fiction." *Riverside Quarterly* 4 (March 1971): 266–271.

A Clockwork Orange

Aggeler, Geoffrey. "The Comic Art of Anthony Burgess." *Arizona Quarterly* 25 (Spring 1969): 234–251.

Barnsley, John H. "Two Lesser Dystopias: *We* and *A Clockwork Orange.*" *World Future Society Bulletin* 18 (January-February 1984): 1–10.

Berger, Harold L. *Science Fiction and the New Dark Age,* 106–107, 165.

Bergonzi, Bernard. *The Situation of the Novel.* Pittsburgh: University of Pittsburgh Press, 1970, pp. 178–187.

Bowie, Robert. "Freedom and Art in *A Clockwork Orange:* Anthony Burgess and the Christian Premises of Dostoevsky." *Thought: A Review of Culture and Idea* 56 (December 1981): 402–416.

Brophy, Elizabeth. "*A Clockwork Orange:* English and Nadsat." *Notes on Contemporary Literature* 2, no. 2 (1972): 4–6.

Carson, J. "Pronominalization in *A Clockwork Orange.*" *Papers on Language and Literature* 12 (Spring 1976): 200–205.

Coleman, Julian. "Burgess' *A Clockwork Orange.*" *Explicator* 42 (Fall 1983): 62–63.

Connelly, Wayne C. "Optimism in Burgess's *A Clockwork Orange.*" *Extrapolation* 14 (December 1972): 25–29.

Cullinan, John. "Anthony Burgess' *A Clockwork Orange:* Two Versions." *English Language Notes* 9 (June 1972): 287–292.

Davis, Robert Gorham. "The Perilous Balance." *Hudson Review* 16 (Summer 1963): 283–285.

De Vitis, A. *Anthony Burgess*. New York: Twayne, 1972, pp. 103–112.

Dimeo, Steven. "The Ticking of the Orange." *Riverside Quarterly* 5 (1973): 318–321.

Dix, Carol M. *Anthony Burgess*. London: Longmans, 1971, pp. 13–16.

Dunn, Thomas P., and Richard D. Erlich. "A Vision of Dystopia: Beehives and Mechanization." *Journal of General Education* 33 (Spring 1981): 45–57.

Evans, Robert O. "Nadsat: The Argot and its Implications in Anthony Burgess' *A Clockwork Orange*." *Journal of Modern Literature* 1 (March 1971): 406–410.

Fiore, Peter Amadeus. "Milton and Kubrick: Eden's Apple or *A Clockwork Orange*." *CEA Critic* 35 (January 1973): 14–17.

Fulkerson, Richard P. "Teaching *A Clockwork Orange*." *CEA Critic* 37 (November 1974): 8–10.

Ingersoll, Earl. "Burgess' *A Clockwork Orange*." *Explicator* 45 (Fall 1986): 60–62.

Kopper, Edward A., Jr. "Joyce's *Ulysses* and Burgess' *A Clockwork Orange*: A Note." *Notes on Modern Irish Literature* 1 (1989): 612–613.

Le Clair, T. "Essential Opposition: The Novels of Anthony Burgess." *Critique* 12 (1977): 77–94.

Mathews, Richard. *The Clockwork Orange Universe of Anthony Burgess*. San Bernardino, CA: Borgo, 1978.

Mentzer, Thomas L. "The Ethics of Behavior Modification: *A Clockwork Orange* Revisited." *Essays in Arts and Sciences* 9 (May 1980): 93–105.

Morris, Robert K. *Consolations of Ambiguity*. Columbia: University of Missouri Press, 1971, pp. 55–74.

Petix, Esther. "Linguistics, Mechanics, and Metaphysics: Anthony Burgess's *A Clockwork Orange*." In *Critical Essays on Anthony Burgess*, 121–131.

Rabinovitz, Rubin. "Ethical Values in Anthony Burgess's *Clockwork Orange.*" *Studies in the Novel* 11 (Spring 1979): 43–50.

———. "Mechanism vs. Organism: Anthony Burgess' *A Clockwork Orange.*" *Modern Fiction Studies* 24 (Winter 1978–1979): 538–541.

Saunders, Trevor J. "Plato's Clockwork Orange." *Durham University Journal* 68 (June 1975–1976): 113–117.

Sheldon, Leslie E. "Newspeak and Nadsat: The Disintegration of Language in *1984* and *A Clockwork Orange.*" *Studies in Contemporary Satire* 6 (1979): 7–13.

Stinson, John J. *Anthony Burgess Revisited,* 52–60.

Stoll, Bettina. "Die Russismen der 'Nasdat'—Sprache in *A Clockwork Orange.*" *Literatur in Wissenschaft und Unterricht* 20, no. 2 (1987): 364–373.

Tilton, John Wightman. *Cosmic Satire in the Contemporary Novel.* Lewisburg, PA: Bucknell University Press, 1977, pp. 21–42.

1985

Parrinder, Patrick. "Updating Orwell? Burgess's Future Fictions." *Encounter* 56 (January 1981): 45–53.

Stinson, John J. *Anthony Burgess Revisited,* 60–63.

Whellens, Arthur. "Anthony Burgess's *1985.*" *Studi dell'Istituto Linguistico* 5 (1982): 223–244.

The Wanting Seed

Berger, Harold L. *Science Fiction and the New Dark Age,* 162–165.

Cullinan, John. "Burgess' *The Wanting Seed.*" *Explicator* 31 (March 1973): Item 51.

Dorenkamp, John H. "Anthony Burgess and the Future of Man: *The Wanting Seed.*" *University of Dayton Review* 15 (Spring 1981): 107–111.

Kateb, George. "Politics and Modernity: The Strategies of Desperation." In *Critical Essays on Anthony Burgess,* 140–151.

Murdoch, B. "The Overpopulated Wasteland: Myth in Anthony Burgess' *The Wanting Seed.*" *Revue des Langues Vivantes* 39 (1973): 203–217.

Stinson, John J. *Anthony Burgess Revisited,* 47–52.

BURROUGHS, EDGAR RICE

General Criticism

Orth, Michael. "Utopia in the Pulps: The Apocalyptic Pastoralism of Edgar Rice Burroughs." *Extrapolation* 27 (Fall 1986): 221–233.

BURROUGHS, WILLIAM S.

General Criticism

Glover, David. "Utopia and Fantasy in the Late 1960's: Burroughs, Moorcock, Tolkien." In *Popular Fiction and Social Change,* 185–211.

Hassan, Ihab. "The Subtracting Machine: The Work of William Burroughs." *Critique* 6 (Summer 1963): 11–21.

Skerl, Jennie. *William S. Burroughs,* 75–94.

The Naked Lunch

Abel, Lionel. "Beyond the Fringe." *Partisan Review* 30 (Spring 1963): 109–112.

Kostelanetz, Richard. "From Nightmare to Serendipity: A Retrospective Look at William Burroughs." *Twentieth Century Literature* 11 (October 1965): 123–130.

McCarthy, Mary. "Burroughs' *Naked Lunch.*" *Encounter* 20 (April 1963): 92–98.

McConnell, Frank D. "William Burroughs and the Literature of Addiction." *Massachusetts Review* 8 (Autumn 1967): 665–680.

Main, Thomas J. "On *Naked Lunch* and Just Desserts." *Chicago Review* 33 (Winter 1983): 81–83.

Mathieson, Kenneth. "The Influence of Science Fiction in the Contemporary American Novel." *Science-Fiction Studies* 12 (March 1985): 22–32.

Selden, E. S. "On *Naked Lunch*." *Evergreen Review* no. 22 (January–February 1962): 110–113.

Skerl, Jennie. *William S. Burroughs,* 36–47.

Nova Express

Bernard, Sidney. "Literati: William Burroughs." *Ramparts* 5 (August 1966): 51–52.

The Ticket that Exploded

Solotaroff, Theodore. "The Algebra Need." *New Republic* 157 (August 5, 1967): 29–34.

BUTLER, SAMUEL

Erewhon

Alcorn, John. *The Nature Novel from Hardy to Lawrence,* 35–41.

Ash, Brian. *Faces of the Future,* 126–127.

Bailey, J. O. *Pilgrims Through Space and Time,* 53–54.

Bekker, Willem G. *An Historical and Critical Review of Samuel Butler's Literary Works.* New York: Haskell House, 1966.

Bisanz, Adam John. "Samuel Butler: A Literary Venture into Atheism and Beyond." *Orbis Litterarum* 29, no. 4 (1974): 316–336.

———. "Samuel Butler's 'Colleges of Unreason.' " *Orbis Litterarum* 28 (1973): 9–22.

———. "Swiftian Patterns of Narrative in Samuel Butler's *Erewhon.*" *Sprachkunst* 3 (1972): 313–326.

Breuer, H. P. "The Source of Morality in Butler's *Erewhon*." *Victorian Studies* 16 (March 1973): 317–328.

Cannan, Gilbert. *Samuel Butler, a Critical Study*. New York: Haskell House, 1970.

Coates, Paul. *The Realist Fantasy: Fiction and Reality since Clarissa*. New York: St. Martin's, 1983, pp. 96–98.

Colmer, J. *Coleridge to 'Catch-22,'* 162–176.

Faulkner, Peter. *Humanism in the English Novel*. London: Elek/Pemberton, 1976, pp. 64–68.

Forster, E. M. *Two Cheers for Democracy*. New York: Harcourt, 1951, pp. 219–223.

Furbank, P. *Samuel Butler, 1835–1902.*

Gounelas, Ruth. "Samuel Butler's Cambridge Background, and *Erewhon*." *English Literature in Transition* 24, no. 1 (1981): 17–33.

Harris, John F. *Samuel Butler, Author of 'Erewhon': The Man and His Work*. New York: Dodd, Mead & Co., 1916.

Henderson, Philip. *Samuel Butler: The Incarnate Bachelor*. London: Cohen & West Ltd., 1953, pp. 94–104.

Holt, Lee E. *Samuel Butler*. Revised edition. Boston: Twayne, 1989, pp. 18–28.

———. "Samuel Butler and His Victorian Critics." *Journal of English Literary History* 8 (June 1941): 146–159.

———. "Samuel Butler's Revisions of *Erewhon*." *Papers of Bibliographical Society of America* 38 (1944): 22–38.

Jeffers, Thomas L. *Samuel Butler Revalued*. University Park: Pennsylvania State University Press, 1981, pp. 48–50.

Jones, Henry F. *Samuel Butler, Author of 'Erewhon' (1835–1902): A Memoir*. New York: Octagon, 1968.

Jones, Joseph. *The Cradle of Erewhon: Samuel Butler in New Zealand.* Austin: University of Texas Press, 1959.

Klein, Jurgen, and Klaus Zollner. "Samuel Butler: 'Erewhon.' " In *Die Utopie in der Angloamerikanischen Literatur,* 80–102.

Knoepflmacher, Ulrich C. *Religious Humanism and the Victorian Novel: Eliot, Pater, and Butler.* Princeton, NJ: Princeton University Press, 1965.

Mazlish, B. "The Fourth Discontinuity." In *Technology and Culture: An Anthology,* edited by Melvin Kranzberg and William Davenport, 216–232. New York: Schocken, 1972.

Muggeridge, Malcolm. *The Earnest Atheist: A Study of Samuel Butler.* New York: Haskell House, 1971.

Norrman, Ralf. *Samuel Butler and the Meaning of Chiasmus.* New York: St. Martin's, 1986, pp. 171–193.

Rattray, Robert F. *Samuel Butler: A Chronicle and an Introduction.* New York: Haskell House, 1974.

Remington, Thomas J. " 'The Mirror up to Nature': Reflections of Victorianism in Samuel Butler's 'Erewhon.' " In *No Place Else,* 33–52.

Rubenstein, Jill. "The Limits of Exploration in Samuel Butler's *Erewhon.*" *Exploration* 1 (1973): 30–35.

Salter, William H. *Essays on Two Moderns: Euripides and Samuel Butler.* Port Washington, NY: Kennikat, 1970.

Sedlak, Werner. "Utopie und Darwinismus." In *Alternative Welten,* 216–238.

Sharma, Govind. "Butler's *Erewhon:* The Machine as Object and Symbol." *Samuel Butler Newsletter* 3, no. 1 (1980): 3–12.

Stillman, Clara G. *Samuel Butler,* 82–93, 95–97, 106–108, 114–119.

Trousson, R. *Voyages aux Pays de Nulle Part,* 199–201.

Vitoux, Pierre. "The Problem of Evolution in *Erewhon.*" *Cahiers d'Études et de Récherches Victoriennes et Edouardiennes* 7 (1978): 21–29.

Warrick, Patricia. "Images of the Man-Machine Intelligence Relationship in Science Fiction." In *Many Futures, Many Worlds*, 196–198.

Westmeyer, R. E. *Modern Economic and Social Systems*, 78–93.

Willey, Basil. *Darwin and Butler: Two Versions of Evolution.* London: Chatto, 1960.

Erewhon Revisited Twenty Years Later

Furbank, P. *Samuel Butler*, 82–94.

Marroni, Francesco. *"Erewhon Revisited: Il Ritorno del Figlio del Sole." In Nel Tempo del Sogno: Le Forme della Narrativa Fantastica dall'Immaginario Vittoriano all'Utopia Contemporanea."* Ravenna: Longo, 1988.

Stillman, Clara G. *Samuel Butler*, 285–295.

CABET, ÉTIENNE

General Criticism

Angrand, Pierre. *Étienne Cabet et la République de 1848.* Paris: Presses Universitaires de France, 1948.

Johnson, Christopher H. *Utopian Communism in France: Cabet and the Icarians, 1839–1851.* Ithaca, NY: Cornell University Press, 1974.

Maxey, C. C. *Political Philosophies.* Revised edition. New York: Macmillan, 1948, pp. 512–530.

Journey to Icaria

Berneri, Marie. Louise. *Journey Through Utopia*, 219–235.

Bloomfield, Paul. *Imaginary Worlds, or the Evolution of Utopia*, 140–158.

Bush, Robert D. "A Generation Gap in Utopia? The Icarian Experience." In *France and North America*, 45–56.

Hertzler, Joyce Oramel. *The History of Utopian Thought,* 204–208.

Kaufmann, M. *Utopias,* 123–142.

Mumford, Lewis. *The Story of Utopias,* 151–159.

Muncy, Raymond Lee. "Women in Utopia." In *France and North America,* 65–69.

Piotrowkski, Sylvester A. *Étienne Cabet and the Voyage en Icarie: A Study in the History of Social Thought.* Washington, DC: Catholic University Press, 1935.

Prudhommeaux, Jules-Jean. *Icarie et son Fondateur Étienne Cabet: Contribution a l'Etude du Socialisme Experimental.* Paris: E. Cornely, 1907.

Ross, Harry. *Utopias Old and New,* 129–139.

Shaw, Albert. *Icaria: A Chapter in the History of Communism.* New York: G. P. Putnam's Sons, 1884.

Westmeyer, R. E. *Modern Economic and Social Systems,* 27–42.

Winter, Michael. "Luxus und Pferdestarken: Die Utopie in der Burgerlichen Revolution: Étienne Cabets 'Icarien.' " In *Literarische Utopien von Morus bis zur Gegenwart,* 125–145.

CALL, HENRY L.

The Coming Revolution

Rooney, Charles J., Jr. *Dreams and Visions,* 30, 48, 50, 112, 114, 144, 149, 183–184,

CALLENBACH, ERNEST WILLIAM

Ecotopia

Boker, Uwe. "Naturbegriff, Okologisches Bewusstsein und Utopisches Denken: Zum Verstandnis von E. Callenbachs *Ecotopia.*" In *Utopian Thought in American Literature,* 69–84.

Brand, David. "A Land Where Ideals and Sensuality Reign: A California Writer's Ecological Classic Wins a New Generation of Admirers." *Time* 132 (October 31, 1988): 10–11.

Crow, Charles L. "Homecoming in the California Visionary Romance." *Western American Literature* 24 (May 1989): 1–19.

Hermand, Jost. "Moghichkeiten Alternativen Zusammenlebens: Ernest Callenbach's *Ecotopia.*" In *Literarische Utopien von Morus bis zur Gegenwart,* 252–264.

Tschachler, Heinz. "Despotic Reason in Arcadia? Ernest Callenbach's Ecological Utopias." *Science-Fiction Studies* 11 (November 1984): 304–317.

————. "Ernest Callenbach: *Ecotopia:* A Novel about Ecology People and Politics in 1999." In *Die Utopie in der Angloamerikanischen Literatur,* 328–348.

CAMPANELLA, TOMMASO

General Criticism

Bonansea, Bernardino M. *Tommaso Campanella: Renaissance Pioneer of Modern Thought.* Washington, DC: Catholic University Press, 1969.

Cro, Roslyn Pesman. "Machiavelli e l'Antiutopia." In *Machiavelli Attuale/Machiavel Actuel,* 27–33.

Danstrup, Aase Lagoni. "Tommaso Campanellas Utopi 'Solstaten': Hans Tanker om Okonimosk Killektivisme og Kvindens Stilling." In *Kvindestudier V,* 72–95.

City of the Sun

Bailey, J. O. *Pilgrims Through Space and Time,* 25.

Berneri, Marie Louise. *Journey Through Utopia,* 88–102.

Blanchet, Leon. *Campanella.* New York: Burt Franklin, 1920, pp. 66–88.

Christensen, Bryce J. *Utopia Against the Family,* 4.

Donno, Daniel J. Introduction. *The City of the Sun: A Poetical Dialogue.* By Tommaso Campanella. Berkeley: University of California Press, 1981, pp. 1–21.

Eurich, Nell. *Science in Utopia,* 108–120.

Gustafsson, Lars. "Tommaso Campanella: Der Sonnenstaat." In *Literarische Utopien von Morus dis Zur Gegenwart,* 44–49.

Hertzler, Joyce Oramel. *The History of Utopian Thought,* 153–165.

Kaufmann, M. *Utopias,* 14–30.

Klein, Ilona. "Tommaso Campanella's *La Citta del Sole:* Topography and Astrology." In *Italiano 1987,* edited by Albert Mancini and Paola Giordano, 197–207. River Forest, IL: Rosary College, 1989.

Laidler, Harry Wellington. *Social-Economic Movements,* 34–37.

Morton, A. L. Introduction. *The City of the Sun.* By Tommaso Campanella. London: Journeyman Press, 1981, pp. 6–13.

Mumford, Lewis. *The Story of Utopias,* 103–106.

Rimmer, Robert H. "Alternate Lifestyles on the Road to Utopia." In *France and North America,* 154.

Ross, Harry. *Utopias Old and New,* 67–74.

Snyder, Jon. "*The City of the Sun* and the Poetics of the Utopian Dialogue." *Stanford Italian Review* 5 (Fall 1985): 175–187.

Spielvogel, Jackson. "Reflections on Renaissance Hermeticism and Seventeenth-Century Utopias." *Utopian Studies* 1 (1987): 188–197.

Stephens, Anthony. "The Sun State and its Shadow: On the Condition of Utopian Writing." In *Utopias,* 1–19.

Walsh, Chad. *From Utopia to Nightmare,* 47–48.

White, Frederic R. *Famous Utopias of the Renaissance.* New York: Hendricks House, 1946, pp. 155–204.

Whitman, John Pratt. *Utopia Dawns,* 53–57.

CAPEK, KAREL

General Criticiism

Bradbrook, B. R. "Chesterton and Karel Capek: A Study in Personal and Literary Relationship." *Chesterton Review* 4 (Fall–Winter 1977–1978): 89–103.

Harkins, William E. Introduction. *The Absolute at Large.* By Karel Capek. Hyperion Press, 1974, iii–vii.

Klima, Ivan. "Capek's Modern Apocalypse." Translated by Robert Streit. *War with the Newts.* By Karl Capek. Evanston, IL: Northwestern University Press, 1985, v–xxi.

Manning, Clarence A. "Karl Capek." *South Atlantic Quarterly* 40 (July 1941): 236–242.

R.U.R.

Bengels, Barbara. " 'Read History': Dehumanization in Karel Capek's *R.U.R.*" In *The Mechanical God,* 13–17.

Chandler, Frank W. *Modern Continental Playwrights.* New York: Harper and Brothers, 1931.

Darlington, W. A. *Literature in the Theatre, and Other Essays.* New York: Holt, 1925, pp. 137–144.

Harkins, William E. *Karel Capek.* New York: Columbia University Press, 1962, pp. 84–95.

————. "The Real Legacy of Karel Capek." In *The Czechoslovak Contribution to World Culture,* edited by Miloslav Recheigl, Jr., 60–62, 64. The Hague: Mouton, 1964.

Matuska, Alexander. *Karel Capek.* London: Allen & Unwin, 1964, pp. 203–206, 216, 217, 326.

Moskowitz, Samuel. *Explorers of the Infinite: Shapers of Science Fiction.* Cleveland, OH: World Publishing, 1963, pp. 208–224.

Pletnev, R. "The Concept of Time and Space in *R.U.R.* by Karel Capek." *Etudes Slaves et Est-Europeennes* 12 (Spring 1967): 17–24.

Wellek, Rene. *Essays on Czech Literature.* The Hague: Mouton, 1963, pp. 50–51.

War with the Newts

Elton, Oliver. *Essays and Addresses.* New York: Longmans, Green and Co., 1939, pp. 179–182.

Maslen, Elizabeth. "Proper Words in Proper Places: The Challenge of Capek's *War with the Newts.*" *Science-Fiction Studies* 14 (March 1987): 82–92.

Wellek, Rene. "Karel Capek." *Slavonic and East European Review* 15 (July 1936): 206.

CARROLL, LEWIS (DODGSON, CHARLES LUTWIDGE)

Alice's Adventures in Wonderland

Auerbach, Nina. "Alice and Wonderland: A Curious Child." *Victorian Studies* 17 (September 1973): 31–47.

Ayres, H. M. *Carroll's Alice.* New York: Columbia University Press, 1936.

Birns, Margaret Boe. "Solving the Mad Hatter's Riddle." *Massachusetts Review* 25 (Autumn 1984): 457–468.

Bivona, Daniel. "Alice the Child-Imperialist and the Games of Wonderland." *Nineteenth-Century Literature* 41 (September 1986): 143–171.

Blake, Kathleen. *Play, Games, and Sport: The Literary Works of Lewis Carroll.* Ithaca, NY: Cornell University Press, 1974, pp. 108–136.

Clark, Beverly Lyon. *Reflections of Fantasy: The Mirror-Worlds of Carroll, Nabokov, and Pynchon.* New York: Peter Lang, 1985.

Crawford, T. D. "Making the World Go Round in *Alice in Wonderland.*" *Notes and Queries* 36 (June 1989): 191–192.

Dreyer, Laurence. "The Mathematical References to the Adoption of the Gregorian Calendar in Lewis Carroll's *Alice's Adventures in Wonderland.*" *Victorian Newsletter* 60 (Fall 1981): 24–26.

Flescher, Jacqueline. "The Language of Nonsense in *Alice.*" *Yale French Studies* 43 (1969): 128–144.

Graham, Neilson. "Sanity, Madness and Alice." *Ariel* 4, no. 2 (1973): 80–89.

Hancher, Michael. "Humpty Dumpty and Verbal Meaning." *Journal of Aesthetics and Art Criticism* 40 (Fall 1981): 49–58.

———. "Pragmatics in Wonderland." *Bucknell Review* 28, no. 2 (1983): 165–182.

Henkle, Roger B. "Carroll's Narratives Underground: 'Modernism' and Form." In *Lewis Carroll,* 89–100.

———. "The Mad Hatter's World.' *Virginia Quarterly Review* 49 (Winter 1973): 100–106, 111–117.

Higbie, Robert. "Lewis Carroll and the Victorian Reaction against Doubt." *Thalia* 3, no. 1 (1980): 21–26.

Holmes, Roger W. "The Philosopher's *Alice in Wonderland.*" *Antioch Review* 19 (Summer 1959): 133–149.

Kibel, Alvin C. "Logic and Satire in *Alice in Wonderland.*" *American Scholar* 43 (Autumn 1974): 605–629.

Kincaid, James R. "Alice's Invasion of Wonderland." *PMLA* 88 (January 1973): 92–99.

Lebovitz, Richard. "Alice and Autism: A Psychological Approach to the Dormouse in 'The Mad Tea-Party.' " *Jabberwocky* 8 (Winter 1978–1979): 8–12.

Leddy, Annette Cecille. "Swift, Carroll, Borges."

Lehmann, John. "*Alice in Wonderland* and Its Sequel." *Revue des Langues Vivantes* 32 (1966): 115–130.

Levin, Harry. "Wonderland Revisited." *Kenyon Review* 27 (Autumn 1965): 591–616.

Little, Judith. "Liberated Alice: Dodgson's Female Hero as Domestic Rebel." *Women's Studies* 3, no. 2 (1976): 195–205.

Madden, William A. "Framing the Alices." *PMLA* 101 (May 1986): 362–373.

Nicholson, Mervyn. "Food and Power: Homer, Carroll, Atwood and Others." *Mosaic* 20 (Summer 1987): 37–55.

Oates, Joyce Carol. "Wonderlands." *Georgia Review* 38 (Fall 1984): 487–506.

Otten, Terry. "After Innocence: Alice in the Garden." In *Lewis Carroll*, 50–61.

Petersen, Calvin R. "Time and Stress: *Alice in Wonderland.*" *Journal of the History of Ideas* 46 (July–September 1985): 427–433.

Petersen, Robert C. "To Sleep, Perchance to Dream: Alice Takes a Little Nap." *Jabberwocky* 8 (Spring 1979): 27–37.

Piggins, David. "The Cheshire Cat and the Stabilised Retinal Image." *Jabberwocky* 9 (Spring 1980): 42–45.

Pycior, Helena M. "At the Intersection of Mathematics and Humor: Lewis Carroll's Alice's and Symbolical Algebra." *Victorian Studies* 28 (Autumn 1984): 149–170.

Rackin, Donald. "Alice's Journey to the End of the Night." *PMLA* 81 (October 1966): 313–326.

———. "Love and Death in Carroll's *Alices.*" *English Language Notes* 20, no. 2 (1982): 26–45.

Rapaport, Herman. "The Disarticulated Image: Gazing in Wonderland." *Enclitic* 6 (Fall 1982): 57–77.

Reichert, Klaus. *Lewis Carroll: Studien zum Literarischen Unsinn.* Munich: Carl Hanser, 1974, pp. 58–118.

Reichertz, Ronald. "Carroll's *Alice in Wonderland.*" *Explicator* 43 (Winter 1985): 21–22.

Rother, Carole. "Lewis Carroll's Lesson: Coping with Fears of Personal Destruction." *Pacific Coast Philology* 19 (November 1984): 89–94.

Schlepper, W[olfgang]. "A Note on the Ways of Carroll's Cheshire Cat." *Anglistik & Englischunterricht* 15 (1981): 123–124.

Stowell, Phyllis. "We're All Mad here." *Children's Literature Association Quarterly* 8 (Summer 1983): 5–8.

Walters, Jennifer R. "The Disquieting Worlds of Lewis Carroll and Boris Vian." *Revue de Litterature Comparee* 46 (1972): 284–294.

Through the Looking-Glass

Auberbach, Nina. "Alice and Wonderland: A Curious Child." *Victorian Studies* 17 (September 1973): 31–47.

Baum, Alwin L. "Carroll's Alice's: The Semiotics of Paradox." *American Imago* 34 (1977): 86–108.

Clark, Beverly Lyon. "Carroll's Well-Versed Narrative: *Through the Looking-Glass.*" *English Language Notes* 20, no. 2 (1982): 65–76.

Harger-Grinling, V., and A. R. Chadwick. "Mirror, Mirror on the Fence? Reflections on and in Alain Robbe-Grillet and Lewis Carroll." *International Fiction Review* 13 (Winter 1986): 20–23.

Henkle, Roger B. "The Mad Hatter's World." *Virginia Quarterly Review* 49 (1973): 107–111.

Leddy, Annette Cecille. "Swift, Carroll, Borges."

Munich, Adrienne Auslander. "Queen Victoria, Empire, and Excess." *Tulsa Studies in Women's Literature* 6 (Fall 1987): 265–281.

Rackin, Donald. "Love and Death in Carroll's *Alice's.*" *English Language Notes* 20 (December 1982): 26–45.

———. "*Through the Looking-Glass:* Alice Becomes an 'I.' " *VIJ: Victorians Institute Journal* 15 (1987): 1–16.

CARYL, CHARLES W.

The New Era

Neustadter, Roger. "Mechanization Takes Command: The Celebration of Technology in the Utopian Novels of Edward Bellamy, Chauncey Thomas, John Jacob Astor, and Charles Caryl." *Extrapolation* 29 (Spring 1988): 21–33.

Parrington, Vernon Louis, Jr. *American Dreams,* 155–158.

Roemer, Kenneth M. *The Obsolete Necessity,* 160–161.

CASTIGLIONE, BALDASSARRE

The Book of the Courtier

Frye, Northrop. "Varieties of Literary Utopias." In *Utopias and Utopian Thought,* 38.

Javitch, Daniel. "Il Cortegiano and the Constraints of Despotism." In *Castiglione: The Ideal and the Real in Renaissance Culture,* edited by Robert Hanning and David Rosand, 17–28. New Haven, CT: Yale University Press, 1983.

Lanham, Richard A. "More, Castiglione, and the Humanist Choice of Utopias." In *Acts of Interpretation,* 327–343.

Puglisse, Olga. "Castiglione's *The Book of the Courtier:* A Matter of Time." *Res Publica Litterarum* 5, no. 2 (1982): 175–187.

Rebhorn, W. A. *Courtly Performances: Masking and Festivity in Castiglione's 'Book of the Courtier.'* Detroit: Wayne State University Press, 1978.

CERVANTES, MIGUEL DE

Don Quixote

Adams, Robert M. *Strains of Discord: Studies in Literary Openness.* Ithaca: Cornell University Press, 1958, pp. 73–85.

Allen, John J. *Don Quixote: Hero or Fool? A Study in Narrative Technique.* Gainesville: University of Florida Press, 1969.

Auerbach, Erich. *Minesis.* New York: Doubleday, 1957, pp. 293–315.

Baena, Julio. "Los Trabajos de Persiles y Sigismunda: La Utopia del Novelista." *Cervantes [Bulletin]* 8 (Fall 1988): 127–140.

Barto, Philip Stephan. "The Subterranean Grail Paradise of Cervantes." *PMLA* 38 (June 1923): 401–411.

Cascardi, Anthony J. "Cervantes and Descartes on the Dream Argument." *Cervantes [Bulletin]* 4 (Fall 1984): 109–122.

Cro, Stelio. "Los Fundamentos Teoricos de la Utopia Hispanoamericano." *Anales de Literatura Hispanoamer.* 11 (1982): 11–37.

———. "Los tres Momentos del Erasmismo en Espana y su Vertiente Utopica: 1526–1616." In *Asdpetti e Problemi delle Letterature Iberiche: Studi Offerti a Franco Meregalli,* edited by Guiseppe Bellini, 123–136. Rome: Bulzoni, 1981.

Maravall, Jose Antonio. *Utopia and Counterutopia in the Quixote.* Translated by Robert Felkel. Detroit, MI: Wayne State University Press, 1991.

Pelorson, Jean-Marc. "Le Theme de la Justice dans le Quichotte: Utopie et Contre-Utopie." In *Le Luste et l'Injuste a la Renaissance et a L'Age Classique,* 211–219. Saint-Etienne: Publications de l'Universités de Saint-Etienne, 1986.

Riley, E. C. "Metamorphosis, Myth and Dream in the Cave of Montesinos." In *Essays on Narrative Fiction in the Iberian Peninsula in Honour of Frank Pierce,* edited by R. Tate, 105–119. Oxford, UK: Dolphin, 1982.

CHAIANOV, ALEKSANDR

Peasant Utopia

Beaujour, Elizabeth Klosty. "Architectural Discourse and Early Soviet Literature." *Journal of the History of Ideas* 44 (July–September 1983): 477–495.

Schwartz, Johathan. Matthew. "Two (Possible) Soviet Antecedents to Orwell's *1984:* Chayanov's *Peasant Utopia* and Zamiatin's *We.*" In *George Orwell and 1984,* 73–81.

Shaw, Nonna D. "The Only Soviet Literary Peasant Utopia." *Slavic and East European Journal* 7 (Fall 1963): 279–283.

Waegemans, Emmanuel. "Le Rêve d'un Bolchevik Atteint de Lassitude, ou le Voyage dans la République Paysanne de Russie en l'an 1984." In *Just the Other Day,* 331–338.

CHAMBLESS, EDGAR

Roadtown

Rooney, Charles J., Jr. *Dreams and Visions,* 32, 66, 76, 130–131, 184.

CHARNAS, SUZY McKEE

General Criticism

Barr, Marleen. "Utopia at the End of a Male Chauvinist Dystopian World: Suzy McKee Charnas's Feminist Science Fiction." In *Women and Utopia,* 43–66.

Motherlines

Albinski, Nan Bowman. *Women's Utopias in British and American Fiction,* 164, 172, 173, 175, 184.

Barr, Marleen. "Permissive, Unspectacular, a Little Baffling: Sex and the Single Feminist Utopian Quasi-Tribesperson." In *Erotic Universe,* 185–196.

————. *Suzy McKee Charnas,* 23–30.

Bartkowski, Frances. "Toward a Feminist Eros."

Kessler, Carol Farley. "The Grand Marital Revolution: Two Feminist Utopias." In *Feminism, Utopia and Narrative,* 78–79.

Miller, Margaret. "The Ideal Woman in Two Feminist Science-Fiction Utopias." *Science-Fiction Studies* 10 (July 1983): 191–198.

Sargent, Lyman Tower. "A New Anarchism: Social and Political Ideas in some Recent Feminist Eutopias." In *Women and Utopia,* 3–33.

Walk to the End of the World

Anderson, Kristine J. "The Great Divorce: Fictions of Feminist Desire." In *Feminism, Utopia and Narrative,* 87–90.

Barr, Marleen. *Suzy McKee Charnas,* 17–22.

Bartkowski, Frances. "Toward a Feminist Eros."

Cranny-Francis, Anne. *Feminist Fiction,* 127–129.

CHATEAUBRIAND, FRANÇOIS-RENÉ, VICOMTE DE

Atala

Beeker, Jon. "Archetype and Myth in Chateaubriand's *Atala.*" *Symposium* 31 (Summer 1977): 93–106.

Facteau, Bernard A. "Notes on Chateaubriand's *Atala.*" *Modern Language Notes* 48 (December 1933): 492–497.

George, Albert J. *Short Fiction in France: 1800–1850.* Syracuse: Syracuse University Press, 1964, pp. 23–28.

Hamilton, James F. "Ritual Passage in Chateaubriand's *Atala.*" *Nineteenth-Century French Studies* 15 (Summer 1987): 385–393.

Lowrie, Joyce O. "Motifs of Kingdom and Exile in *Atala.*" *French Review* 43 (April 1970): 755–764.

Maurois, Andre. *Chateaubriand.* New York: Harper, 1938, pp. 92–101.

O'Neil, Mary Anne. *"Phèdre:* Model for Chateaubriand's *Atala."* *Romance Notes* 28 (Winter 1987): 93–100.

Springer, Dennis J. "The Paradise Setting of Chateaubriand's *Atala." PMLA* 89 (May 1974): 530–536.

Switzer, Richard. *Chateaubriand.* New York: Twayne, 1971, pp. 42–48, 55–56.

CHAVANNES, ALBERT

The Future Commonwealth

Parrington, Vernon Louis, Jr. *American Dreams,* 111–112.

Rooney, Charles J, Jr. *Dreams and Visions,* 35, 116–117, 161, 184.

In Brighter Climes

Parrington, Vernon Louis, Jr. *American Dreams,* 112.

CHERNYSHEVSKII, NIKOLAI GAVRILOVICH

What Is to Be Done?

Barstow, Jane. "Dostoevsky's *Notes from Underground* versus Chernyshevsky's *What Is to Be Done?" College Literature* 5 (Winter 1978): 24–33.

Berman, Marshall. *All that Is Solid Melts into Air,* 212–248.

Edwards, T. *Three Russian Writers and the Irrational,* 1–35.

Frank, Joseph. "N. G. Chernyshevsky: A Russian Utopia." *Southern Review* 3 (January 1967): 68–84.

Freeborn, Richard. *The Russian Revolutionary Novel: Turgenev to Pasternak.* New York: Cambridge University Press, 1982, pp. 4–38.

Katz, Michael R. "Vera Pavlovna's Dream in Chernyshevskii's *What Is to Be Done?*" In *Issues in Russian Literature before 1917,* 150–161.

Katz, Michael R., and William G. Wagner. Introduction. *What Is to Be Done?* By N. G. Chernyshevskii. Translated by Michael R. Katz. Ithaca, NY: Cornell University Press, 1989, pp. 1–36.

Mathewson, Rufus W., Jr. *The Positive Hero in Russian Literature.* Stanford, CA: Stanford University Press, 1975, pp. 74–83.

Moser, Charles A. *Antinihilism in the Russian Novel of the 1860's.* The Hague: Mouton and Co., 1964, pp. 39–43.

Olgin, Moissaye J. *A Guide to Russian Literature, 1820–1917.* New York: Harcourt, Brace and Howe, 1920, pp. 58–60.

Paperno, Irina. *Chernyshevsky and the Age of Realism: A Study in the Semiotics of Behavior.* Stanford, CA: Stanford University Press, 1988, pp. 15–17, 23–38, 172–173, 219–222.

———. "The Novel Myth: N. G. Chernyshevskii's *What Is to Be Done?*" In *Issues in Russian Literature before 1917,* 133–149.

Randall, Francis B. *N. G. Chernyshevskii.* New York: Twayne, 1967, pp. 104–130.

Rawson, Judy. *"Che Fare? Silone and the Russian 'Chto Delat'? Tradition."* *Modern Language Review* 76 (July 1981): 556–565.

Yershov, Peter. *Science Fiction and Utopian Fantasy in Soviet Literature,* 9–10.

Zekulin, G. "Forerunner of Socialist Realism: The Novel *What to Do?* by N. G. Chernyshevsky." *Slavonic and East European Review* 41 (June 1963): 467–483.

CHESTERTON, GILBERT KEITH

General Criticism

Boyd, Ian. *The Novels of G. K. Chesterton: A Study in Art and Propaganda.* New York: Barnes & Noble, 1975.

Bradbrook, B. R. "Chesterton and Karel Capek: A Study in Personal and Literary Relationship." *Chesterton Review* 4 (Fall–Winter 1977–1978): 89–103.

Burkhardt, Louis C. "G. K. Chesterton and *Nineteen Eighty-Four.*" In *George Orwell,* 5–10.

The Flying Inn

Coates, John. "The Philosophy and Religious Background of *The Flying Inn.*" *Chesterton Review* 12 (August 1986): 303–328.

The Napolean of Notting Hill

Amis, Kingsley. "Four Fluent Fellows: An Essay on Chesterton's Fiction." In *G. K. Chesterton: A Centenary Appraisal,* edited by John Sullivan, 28–33. New York: Barnes & Noble, 1974.

Barker, Dudley. *G. K. Chesterton: A Biography.* New York: Stein and Day, 1973, pp. 140–144.

Batchelor, John. "Chesterton as a Edwardian Novelist." *Chesterton Review* 1 (Fall–Winter 1974): 24–27.

Braybrooke, Patrick. *Gilbert Keith Chesterton.* Philadelphia: Lippincott, 1922, pp. 80–82.

Canovan, Margaret. *G. K. Chesterton: Radical Populist.* New York: Harcourt Brace Jovanovich, 1977, pp. 99–107.

Clipper, Lawrence J. *G. K. Chesterton,* 126–129.

Coates, John. *Chesterton and the Edwardian Cultural Crisis,* 102–106, 135–143.

Evans, Maurice. *G. K. Chesterton.* New York: Haskell House, 1972, pp. 76–78.

Haussy, Christiane d'. *La Vision du Monde chex G. K. Chesterton.* Paris: Didier, 1981, pp. 99–102, 124–125.

Hollis, Christopher. *The Mind of Chesterton.* London: Hollis & Carter, 1970, pp. 107–112.

Hunter, Lynette. *G. K. Chesterton: Explorations in Allegory.* New York: St. Martin's, 1979, pp. 55–61.

———. "A Reading of *The Napoleon of Notting Hill.*" *Chesterton Review* 3 (Fall–Winter 1976–1977): 118–128.

Kerridge, Roy. "The Prophets of Notting Hill." *Chesterton Review* 6 (1979–1980): 116–130.

Lea, F. A. *The Wild Knight of Battersea: G. K. Chesterton.* London: James Clarke, 1945, pp. 27–30.

Quinn, Joseph A. "Eden and New Jerusalem: A Study of *The Napoleon of Notting Hill.*" *Chesterton Review* 3 (Spring–Summer 1977): 230–239.

Ward, Masie. *Gilbert Keith Chesterton.* New York: Sheed & Ward, 1943, pp. 173–177.

West, Julius. *G. K. Chesterton: A Critical Study.* New York: Dodd, Mead, 1916, pp. 23–29.

Wills, Garry. *Chesterton: Man and Mask.* New York: Sheed & Ward, 1961, pp. 105–107.

The Return of Don Quixote

Clipper, Lawrence J. *G. K. Chesterton,* 138–140.

Coates, John. *Chesterton and the Edwardian Cultural Crisis,* 115–123.

Conlon, Denis J. " 'La Trahison des Clercs' in Chesterton's Parables for Social Reformers." *Seven* 9 (1988): 29–46.

CHILD, WILLIAM STANLEY

The Legal Revolution of 1902

Rooney, Charles J., Jr. *Dreams and Visions,* 33, 49, 52, 57, 65–66, 150, 184–185.

CIXOUS, HÉLÈNE

General Criticism

Cixous, Hélène. *Prenoms de Personne*. Paris: Seuil, 1974, pp. 183–214.

Richman, Michele. "Sex and Signs: The Language of French Feminist Criticism." *Language and Style* 13 (Fall 1980): 62–80.

"The Laugh of the Medusa"

Lindsay, Cecile. "Body/Language: French Feminist Utopias." *French Review: Journal of the American Association of Teachers of French* 60 (October 1986): 46–55.

Moi, Toril. *Sexual/Textual Politics*. London: Methuen, 1985.

CLARKE, ARTHUR C.

Against the Fall of Night

Hollow, John. *Against the Night, the Stars,* 37–45.

Rabkin, Eric S. "Fairy Tales and Science Fiction." In *Bridges to Science Fiction,* 88–89.

Childhood's End

Abrash, Merritt. "Utopia Subverted: Unstated Messages in *Childhood's End.*" *Extrapolation* 30 (Winter 1989): 372–379.

Galbreath, Robert. "Ambiguous Apocalypse: Transcendental Version of the End." In *The End of the World,* 53–72.

Goldman, Stephen H. "Immortal Man and Mortal Overload: The Case for Intertextuality." In *Death and the Serpent,* 193–207.

———. "Wandering in Mazes Lost; or, the Unhappy life of Arthur C. Clarke's *Childhood's End* in Academia." *Foundation* 41 (Winter 1987): 21–29.

Hollow, John. *Against the Night, the Stars,* 66–87.

Howes, Alan B. "Expectation and Surprise in *Childhood's End.*" In *Arthur C. Clarke,* 149–171.

Hull, Elizabeth Anne. "Fire and Ice: The Ironic Imagery of Arthur C. Clarke's *Childhood's End.*" *Extrapolation* 24 (Spring 1983): 13–30.

McDaniel, Stan. "The Coalescence of Minds." In *Philosophers Look at Science Fiction,* 117–126.

Rabkin, Eric S. *Arthur C. Clarke,* 22–29.

Samuelson, David N. "*Childhood's End:* A Median Stage of Adolescence?" In *Arthur C. Clarke,* 196–210.

Shelton, Robert Frederick. "Forms of Things Unknown."

Tanzy, Eugene. "Contrasting Views of Man and the Evolutionary Process: *Back to Methuselah* and *Childhood's End.*" In *Arthur C. Clarke,* 172–195.

The City and the Stars

Dunn, Thomas P., and Richard D. Erlich. "Environmental Concerns in Arthur C. Clarke's *The City and the Stars.*" In *Aspects of Fantasy: Selected Essays from the Second International Conference on the Fantastic in Literature,* edited by William Coyle, 203–211. Westport, CT: Greenwood Press, 1986.

Hollow, John. *Against the Night, the Stars,* 117–127.

Rabkin, Eric S. *Arthur C. Clarke,* 30–35.

———. "The Unconscious City." In *Hard Science Fiction,* 31–34.

Wolfe, Gary K. *The Known and the Unknown: The Iconography of Science Fiction.* Kent, OH: Kent State University Press, 1979, pp. 110–116.

The Fountains of Paradise

Hollow, John. *Against the Night, the Stars,* 174–178.

Hume, Kathryn. "The Edifice Complex: Motive and Accomplishment in *The Fountains of Paradise.*" *Extrapolation* 24 (Winter 1983): 380–387.

Zaki, Hoda M. *Phoenix Renewed,* 67, 73, 75.

Rendezvous with Rama

Harfst, Betsy. "Of Myths and Polyominoes: Mythological Content in Clarke's Fiction." In *Arthur C. Clarke,* 107–114.

Hollow, John. *Against the Night, the Stars,* 159–165.

Lehman, Steven. "Ruddick on *Rama:* An Amplification." *Science-Fiction Studies* 12 (July 1985): 237.

Rabkin, Eric S. *Arthur C. Clarke,* 45–52.

Ruddick, Nicholas. "The World Turned Inside Out: Decoding Clarke's *Rendezvous with Rama.*" *Science-Fiction Studies* 12 (March 1985): 42–50.

Zaki, Hoda M. *Phoenix Renewed,* 67, 72–73, 75.

CLARKE, JOHN

A Voyage to Cacklogallinia

Bosse, Malcolm J. Introduction. *The Virgin-Seducer, and the Batchelor Keeper, the State of Learning in the Empire of Lilliput, [and] a Voyage to Cacklogallinia.* By John Clarke. New York: Garland, 1972, pp. 7–9.

Welcher, Jeanne K., and George E. Bush, Jr. Introduction. *Gulliveriana IV: Facsimile Reproductions.* Delmar, NY: Scholars' Facsimiles & Reprints, 1973, ix–xiii.

CLEMENS, SAMUEL LANGHORNE. See TWAIN, MARK

CLYDE, IRENE

Beatrice the Sixteenth

Albinski, Nan Bowman. " 'The Laws of Justice, of Nature, and of Right': Victorian Feminist Utopias." In *Feminism, Utopia, and Narrative,* 55.

————. *Women's Utopias in British and American Fiction,* 9, 21, 23, 33, 43, 180.

COLBURN, FRONA EUNICE

Yerma the Dorado

Roemer, Kenneth M. *The Obsolete Necessity,* 71.

COLE, CYRUS

The Auroraphone

Rooney, Charles J., Jr. *Dreams and Visions,* 123, 143, 150, 153, 157–158. 185.

CONDORCET, ANTOINE-NICOLAS DE

General Criticism

Manuel, F. E. *The Prophets of Paris.* Cambridge, MA: Harvard University Press, 1962, pp. 53–102.

Schapiro, J. Salwyn. *Condorcet and the Rise of Liberalism.* New York: Harcourt, Brace, 1934.

Fragment Sur L'Atlantide

Lachterman, David R. "The Conquest of Nature and the Ambivalence of Man in the French Enlightenment: Reflections on Condorcet's *Frag-*

ment Sur l'Atlantide.'' In *Man, God, and Nature in the Enlightenment,* 37–47.

COOPER, JAMES FENIMORE

The Crater

Gates, W. B. ''Cooper's *The Crater* and Two Explorers.'' *American Literature* 23 (May 1951): 243–246.

———. ''A Defense of the Ending of Cooper's *The Crater.*'' *Modern Language Notes* 70 (May 1955): 347–349.

———. ''A Note on Cooper and *Robinson Crusoe.*'' *Modern Language Notes* 67 (June 1952): 421–422.

Grossman, James. *James Fenimore Cooper.* Toronto: William Sloane Associates, 1949, pp. 222–225.

Hamada, Masajiro. ''Two Utopian Types of American Literature— *Typee* and *The Crater.*'' *Studies in English Literature (University of Tokyo)* 40 (March 1964): 199–214.

Ickstadt, Heinz. ''Instructing the American Democrat: Cooper and the Concept of Popular Fiction in Jacksonian America.'' In *James Fenimore Cooper: New Critical Essays,* edited by Robert Clark, 26. Totowa, NJ: Barnes & Noble, 1985.

Long, Robert Emmet. *James Fenimore Cooper.* New York: Continuum, 1990, pp. 157–160.

Lounsbury, Thomas R. *James Fenimore Cooper.* Detroit: Gale Research, 1968, pp. 255–258.

McCloskey, J. C. ''Cooper's Political Views in *The Crater.*'' *Modern Philology* 53 (November 1955): 113–116.

Parrington, Vernon Louis, Jr. *American Dreams,* 22–26, 34.

Phillips, Mary E. *James Fenimore Cooper.* New York: John Lane Co., 1912, pp. 308–309.

Railton, Stephen. *Fenimore Cooper: A Study of his Life and Imagination.* Princeton, NJ: Princeton University Press, 1978, pp. 247–248.

Ringe, Donald A. "Cooper's *The Crater* and the Moral Basis of Society." *Papers of the Michigan Academy of Science, Arts, and Letters* 44 (1959): 371–380.

———. *James Fenimore Cooper.* Updated edition. Boston: Twayne, 1988, pp. 104–107.

Scudder, Harold H. "Cooper's *The Crater.*" *American Literature* 19 (May 1947): 109–126.

CORBETT, ELIZABETH BURGOYNE

New Amazonia

Albinski, Nan Bowman. " 'The Laws of Justice, of Nature, and of Right': Victorian Feminist Utopias." In *Feminism, Utopia and Narrative,* 52–54, 60.

———. *Women's Utopias in British and American Fiction,* 20, 30, 32, 36, 42.

CORTAZAR, JULIO

Los Premios

Duran, Juan Guillermo. "Literatura y Utopia en Hispanoamerica."

CRÈVECOEUR, MICHEL-GUILLAUME ST. JEAN DE

General Criticism

Kolodny, Annette. *The Lay of the Land: Metaphor as Experience and History in American Life and Letters.* Chapel Hill: University of North Carolina Press, 1975, pp. 52–66.

Mannheim, Karl. *Ideology and Utopia.* New York: Harcourt Brace, 1936, pp. 192–263.

Myra, Jehlen. ''J. Hector St. John Crèvecoeur: A Monarcho-Anarchist in Revolutionary America.'' *American Quarterly* 31 (Summer 1979): 204–222.

Philbrick, Thomas. *St. John de Crèvecoeur.* New York: Twayne, 1970, pp. 81–88.

Rapping, Elayne Antler. ''Theory and Experience in Crèvecoeur's America.'' *American Quarterly* 19 (Winter 1967): 707–718.

Slotkin, Richard. *Regeneration Through Violence: The Mythology of the American Frontier, 1600–1860.* Middletown, CT: Wesleyan University Press, 1973, pp. 263–267.

Letters From an American Farmer

Emerson, Everett. ''Hector St. John De Crèvecoeur and the Promise of America.'' In *Forms and Functions of History in American Literature: Essays in Honor of Ursula Brumm,* edited by Winifred Fluck, Jurgen Peper, and Willi Paul Adams, 44–55. Berlin: Schmidt, 1981.

Mohr, James C. ''Calculated Disillusionment: Crèvecoeur's *Letters* Reconsidered.'' *South Atlantic Quarterly* 69 (Summer 1970): 354–363.

Winston, Robert P. '' 'Strange Order of Things': The Journey to Chaos in *Letters from an American Farmer.*'' *Early American Literature* 19, no. 3 (1984–1985): 249–267.

''Sesquehanna''

Hales, John. ''The Landscape of Tragedy: Crèvecoeur's 'Sesquehanna.' '' *Early American Literature* 20, no. 1 (1985): 39.

Sketches of Eighteenth Century America

Robinson, David M. ''Community and Utopia in Crèvecoeur's *Sketches.*'' *American Literature* 62 (March 1990): 17–31.

CROCKER, SAMUEL

That Island

Parrington, Vernon Louis, Jr. *American Dreams,* 98, 102–103.

Rooney, Charles J., Jr. *Dreams and Visions,* 185.

CYRANO DE BERGERAC, SAVINIEN

General Criticism

Hervier, Julien. "Cyrano de Bergerac et le Voyage Spatial: De la Fantaisie à la Science-Fiction." In *Proceedings of the 10th Congress on the International Comparative Literature Association, New York, 1982,* Volume 1, 436–442.

L'Autre Monde

Goux, Jean-Joseph. "Language, Money, Father, Phallus in Cyrano de Bergerac's Utopia." Translated by Katharine Streip. *Representations* 23 (Summer 1988): 105–117.

Harth, Erica. *Cyrano de Bergerac and the Polemics of Modernity.* New York: Columbia University Press, 1970.

Mason, Haydn. *Cyrano de Bergerac: L'Autre Monde.* London: Grant & Cutler, 1984.

Ponnau, Gwenhael. "Sur Quelques Modalités du Voyage Imaginaire." *Littératures* (Autumn 1984): 55–64.

Van Baelen, Jacqueline. "Reality and Illusion in *L'Autre Monde: The Narrative Voyage." Yale French Studies* 49 (1973): 178–184.

Walker, Hallam, and Particia M. Harry. "*L'Autre Monde:* Cyrano de Bergerac's Philosophical Voyages." In *Voyages,* 137–152.

DANTE ALIGHIERI

De Monarchia

Caso, Adolph. ''Power and Technology: Threat to Salvation.'' In *Dante in the Twentieth Century,* 1–8.

Miething, Christoph. ''Platon, Dante et More: Esquisse d'Unne Theorie de l'Utopie Litteraire.'' In *De l'Utopie a l'Uchronie,* 148–153.

————. Politeia und Utopia: Zur Epistemologie der Literarischen Utopie.'' *Germanisch-Romanische Monatsschrift* 37, no. 3 (1987): 247–263.

Paolucci, Anne. ''Dante and Machiavelli: Political Idealism and Political Realism.'' In *Dante in the Twentieth Century,* 9–24.

Silverstein, Theodore. ''On the Genesis of *De Monarchia,* II, v.'' In *Dante in America,* 187–218.

DAVENPORT, BENJAMIN RUSH

Anglo-Saxons, Onward

Roemer, Kenneth M. *The Obsolete Necessity,* 70–71, 72, 143, 204.

DE MILLE, JAMES

General Criticism

Woodcock, George. ''Absence of Utopias.'' *Canadian Literature* no. 42 (Autumn 1969): 3–5.

————. ''De Mille and the Utopian Vision.'' *Journal of Canadian Fiction* 2, no. 3 (1973): 174–179.

A Strange Manuscript Found in a Copper Cylinder

Bailey, J. O. *Pilgrims Through Space and Time,* 64–66, 192.

Gerson, Carole. *Three Writers of Victorian Canada and Their Works.* Downsview, Ontario: ECW Press, 1983, pp. [14]–[17].

Hughes, Kenneth J. *"A Strange Manuscript:* Sources, Satire, a Positive Utopia.'' In *The Canadian Novel: Beginnings,* edited by John Moss, 111–125. Toronto: NC Press Limited, 1980.

Kime, Wayne R. ''The American Antecedents of James De Mille's *A Strange Manuscript Found in a Copper Cylinder.*'' *Dalhousie Review* 55 (Summer 1975): 280–306.

DEFOE, DANIEL

Robinson Crusoe

Bell, Ian A. ''King Crusoe: Locke's Political Theory in *Robinson Crusoe.*'' *English Studies* 69 (February 1988): 27–36.

Benjamin, Edwin R. ''Symbolic Elements in *Robinson Crusoe.*'' *Philological Quarterly* 30 (1951): 206–211.

Benrekassa, Georges. ''Recits de Voyage, Utopie, Robinsonnade: Reflexions sur l'Isle Inconnue.'' *L'Esprit Createur* 25 (Fall 1985): 18–29.

Birkner, Gerd. ''Das Utopische in *Robinson Crusoe.*'' *Literatur in Wissenschaft und Unterricht (Kiel, W. Germany)* 14 (June 1981): 73–90.

Butler, Mary E. ''The Effect of the Narrator's Rhetorical Uncertainty on the Fiction of *Robinson Crusoe.*'' *Studies in the Novel* 15 (Summer 1983): 77–90.

Ducrocq, Jean. ''Rélations de Voyages et Récits Symboliques: Robinson et Gulliver.'' *Studies on Voltaire and the Eighteenth Century* 215 (1982): 1–8.

Flint, Christopher. ''Orphaning the Family: The Role of Kinship in *Robinson Crusoe.*'' *ELH* 55 (Summer 1988): 381–419.

Gerber, Richard. ''The English Island Myth: Remarks on the Englishness of Utopian Fiction.'' *Critical Quarterly* 1 (Spring 1959): 36–43.

Hartog, Curt. ''Authority and Autonomy in *Robinson Crusoe.*'' *Enlightenment Essays* 5, no. 2 (1974): 33–43.

Hearne, John. ''Naked Footprint: An Enquiry into Crusoe's Island.'' *Review of English Literature* 8 (October 1967): 97–107.

Hudson, Nicholas. " 'Why God No Kill the Devil?' The Diabolical Disruption of Order in *Robinson Crusoe*." *Review of English Studies* 39 (November 1988): 494–501.

James, E. Anthony. "Defoe's Narrative Artistry: Naming and Describing in *Robinson Crusoe*." *Costerus* 5 (1972): 52–66.

Johnson, Abby A. "Old Bones Uncovered: A Reconsideration of *Robinson Crusoe*." *College Language Association Journal* 17 (December 1973): 271–278.

Kavanagh, Thomas M. "Unraveling Robinson: The Divided Self in Defoe's *Robinson Crusoe*." *Texas Studies in Literature and Language* 20 (Fall 1978): 416–432.

Kraft, Quentin G. "*Robinson Crusoe* and the Story of the Novel." *College English* 41 (January 1980): 535–548.

MacDonald, Robert H. "The Creation of an Ordered World in *Robinson Crusoe*." *Dalhousie Review* 56 (Spring 1976): 23–34.

Novak, Maximillian E. "Crusoe the King and the Political Evolution of His Island." *Studies in English Literature, 1500–1900* 2 (Summer 1962): 337–350.

———. "Imaginary Islands and Real Beasts: The Imaginative Genesis of *Robinson Crusoe*." *Tennessee Studies in Literature* 19 (1974): 57–78.

———. "Robinson Crusoe's Fear and the Search for Natural Man." *Modern Philology* 58, no. 4 (1961): 238–245.

Parker, George. "The Allegory of *Robinson Crusoe*." *History* 10 (1925): 11–25.

Pearlman, E. "*Robinson Crusoe* and the Cannibals." *Mosaic* 10, no. 1 (1976): 39–55.

Peck, H. Daniel. "*Robinson Crusoe:* The Moral Geography of Limitation." *Journal of Narrative Technique* 3 (January 1973): 20–31.

Seidel, Michael. "Crusoe in Exile." *PMLA* 96 (May 1981): 363–374.

———. *Robinson Crusoe: Island Myths and the Novel.* Boston: Twayne, 1991.

Sill, Geoffrey M. *Defoe and the Idea of Fiction, 1713–1719.* Newark: University of Delaware Press, 1983, pp. 165–169.

Sim, Stuart. "Interrogative an Ideology: Defoe's *Robinson Crusoe.*" *British Journal for Eighteenth Century Studies* 10 (Autumn 1987): 163–173.

Swados, Harvey. "Robinson Crusoe—The Man Alone." *Antioch Review* 18 (Spring 1958): 25–40.

Thornburg, Thomas R. *"Robinson Crusoe." Ball State University Forum* 15, no. 3 (1974): 11–18.

Zimmerman, Everett. "Defoe and Crusoe." *Journal of English Literary History* 38 (1971): 377–396.

———. *Defoe and the Novel.* Berkeley: University of California Press, 1975, pp. 20–47.

DELANY, SAMUEL R.

General Criticism

Alterman, Peter. "The Surreal Translations of Samuel R. Delany." *Science-Fiction Studies* 4 (March 1977): 25–34.

Ebert, Teresa L. "The Convergence of Postmodern Innovative Fiction and Science Fiction: An Encounter with Samuel R. Delany's Technotopia." *Poetics Today (Tel Aviv)* 1, no. 4 (1980): 91–104.

Moylan, Tom. "Beyond Negation: The Critical Utopias of Ursula K. Le Guin and Samuel R. Delany." *Extrapolation* 21 (Fall 1980): 236–253.

Weedman, Jane Branham. "Samuel R. Delany: Present-Day Cultures in Future Literary Worlds." Ph.D. diss., State University of NY at Buffalo, 1979.

Babel-17

Collings, Michael R. "Samuel R. Delany and John Wilkins: Artificial Languages, Science, and Science Fiction." In *Reflections of the Fantastic,* 61–68.

McEvoy, Seth. *Samuel R. Delany,* 45–59.

Scholes, Robert. Introduction. *Babel-17.* By Samuel R. Delany. Boston: Gregg Press, 1976, v–x.

Schuyler, W. M. "Could Anyone Here Speak *Babel-17.*" In *Philosophers Look at Science Fiction,* 87–95.

Stone-Blackburn, Susan. "Adult Telepathy: *Babel-17* and *The Left Hand of Darkness.*" *Extrapolation* 30 (Fall 1989): 243–253.

Weedman, Jane Branham. *Samuel R. Delany,* 41–50.

Zaki, Hoda M. *Phoenix Renewed,* 55–58.

The Einstein Intersection

Gardiner, H. James. "Images of *The Waste Land* in *The Einstein Intersection.*" *Extrapolation* 18 (May 1977): 116–123.

McEvoy, Seth. *Samuel R. Delany,* 60–77.

Pitt, Joseph C. "Will a Rubber Ball Still Bounce?" In *Philosophers Look at Science Fiction,* 57–65.

Scobie, Stephen. "Different Mazes: Mythology in Samuel R. Delany's *The Einstein Intersection.*" *Riverside Quarterly* 5 (July 1971): 12–18.

Weedman, Jane Branham. *Samuel R. Delany,* 51–60.

Zaki, Hoda M. *Phoenix Renewed,* 58–61.

Triton

Fekete, John. "*The Dispossessed* and *Triton:* Act and System in Utopian Science Fiction." *Science-Fiction Studies* 6 (July 1979): 129–143.

Fitting, Peter. "Positioning and Closure: On the 'Reading Effect' of Contemporary Utopian Fiction." *Utopian Studies* 1 (1987): 23–36.

Fox, Robert Elliot. "The Politics of Desire in Delany's *Triton* and *The Tides of Lust.*" *Black American Literature Forum* 18 (Summer 1984): 49–56.

Gawron, Jean Mark. Introduction. *Triton.* By Samuel R. Delany. Boston: Gregg Press, 1977, v–xxiii.

Hardesty, William H. III. "Mapping the Future: Extrapolation in Utopian/Dystopian and Science Fiction." *Utopian Studies* 1 (1987): 160–172.

McEvoy, Seth. *Samuel R. Delany,* 123–125.

Masse, Michelle. " 'All You Have to Do is Know What You Want': Individual Expectations in *Triton.*" In *Coordinates,* 49–64.

Moylan, Tom. *Demand the Impossible,* 156–195.

Sanders, Joe. *"Triton" F & SF Review* 2 (June 1976): 22–23.

Slusser, George. *The Delany Intersection: Samuel R. Delany.* San Bernardino, CA: Borgo Press, 1977, pp. 7–9, 11, 60–62.

Somay, Bulent; and R[obert] P[hilmus], ed.. "Toward an Open-Ended Utopia." *Science-Fiction Studies* 11 (March 1984): 25–38.

DERY, TIBOR

Mr. G. A. in X

Foldes, Anna. "Tibor Dery's *Mr. G. A. in X.*" *New Hungarian Quarterly* 6 (Spring 1965): 164–168.

Hadecke, Wolfgang. "Der Erzahler Tibor Dery." *Neue Rundschau* 77, no. 4 (1966): 638–652.

Reszler, Andre. "Man as Nostalgia: The Image of the Last Man in Twentieth-Century Postutopian Fiction." In *Visions of Apocalypse,* 196–215.

Varnai, Paul. "Tibor Dery and his *Mr. G. A. in X.*" *Canadian Slavonic Papers* 10 (Spring 1968): 100–108.

DEVINNE, PAUL

The Day of Prosperity

Collins, Gail. "Tomorrow Never Knows." *Nation* 252 (January 21, 1991): 58–60.

DIDEROT, DENIS

General Criticism

Rimmer, Robert H. "Alternative Lifestyles on the Road to Utopia." In *France and North America,* 149–163.

Supplement to Bougainville's Voyage

Berneri, Marie Louise. *Journey Through Utopia,* 201–206.

Daniel, Georges. *Le Style de Diderot: Légende et Structure.* Geneve: Librairie Droz, 1986, pp. 252–253.

Fellows, Otis. *Diderot.* Updated edition. Boston: Twayne, 1989, pp. 110–111.

Goodman, Dena. "The Structure of Political Argument in Diderot's *Supplement au Voyage de Bougainville.*" *Diderot Studies* 21 (1983): 123–137.

McDonald, Christie V. "The Reading and Writing of Utopia in Denis Diderot's *Supplement au Voyage de Bougainville.*" *Science-Fiction Studies* 3 (November 1976): 248–253.

Pagden, Anthony. "The Savage Critic: Some European Images of the Primitive." *Yearbook of English Studies* 13 (1983): 32–45.

Papin, Bernard. "L'Utopie Tahitienne du *Supplement au Voyage de Bougainville* ou le 'Modèle Idéal en Politique'." *L'Information Litteraire* 36, no. 3 (1984): 102–105.

Perkins, M. L. "Community Planning in Diderot's *Supplement au Voyage de Bougainville.*" *Kentucky Romance Quarterly* 21, no. 4 (1974): 399–417.

Van Den Abbeele, Georges. "Utopian Sexuality and Its Discontents: Exoticism and Colonialism in the *Supplement au Voyage de Bougainville.*" *L'Esprit Createur* 24 (Spring 1984): 43–52.

Whatley, Janet. "Un Retour Secret vers la Foret: The Problem of Privacy and Order in Diderot's Tahiti." *Kentucky Romance Quarterly* 24, no. 2 (1977): 199–208.

Wilson, Arthur. *Diderot.* New York: Oxford University Press, 1972, pp. 588–593.

DISRAELI, BENJAMIN

General Criticism

Malhomme, Jocelyne. "Disraeli on More's *Utopia.*" *Moreana* 16 (1979): 147–148.

The Voyage of Captain Popanilla

Hertz, Bertha. "Satire and Psychosexual Fantasy in an Expurgated Chapter of Disraeli's *Voyage of Captain Popanilla.*" In *The Scope of the Fantastic: Culture, Biography, Themes, Children's Literature,* edited by Robert Collins and Howard Pearce, 79–83. Westport, CT: Greenwood, 1985.

Literary Gazette (London) no. 594 (June 7, 1828): 360.

DIXIE, FLORENCE

Gloriana

Albinski, Nan Bowman. " 'The Laws of Justice, of Nature, and of Right': Victorian Feminist Utopias." In *Feminism, Utopia, and Narrative,* 57–65.

———. *Women's Utopias in British and American Fiction,* 18, 21, 26, 27, 28, 30–31, 35, 38, 42.

DOBLIN, ALFRED

Mountains, Oceans and Giants

Dollenmayer, David B. *The Berlin Novels of Alfred Doblin.* Berkeley: University of California Press, 1988, pp. 55–57.

Eykman, Christoph. "Man Against Fire: Alfred Doblin's Utopian Novel *Mountains, Oceans and Giants.*" In *Poetics of the Elements in the Human Condition II,* edited by Anna-Teresa Tymieniecka, 191–202. Dordrecht: Kluwer, 1988.

Huguet, Louis. "Parents ou Amants? Alfred Doblin et son Roman d'Anticipation *Berge, Meere und Giganten.*" *Seminar* 23 (February 1987): 42–72.

————. "À la Récherche du 'Point Omega': Les 'Conquerants' dans le Roman d'Anticipation d'Alfred Doblin, *Berge, Meere und Giganten.*" In *Just the Other Day,* 249–266.

Kort, Wolfgang. *Alfred Doblin.* New York: Twayne, 1974, pp. 78–90.

DODD, ANNA BOWMAN

The Republic of the Future

Albinski, Nan Bowman. *Women's Utopias in British and American Fiction,* 49, 60, 63, 72.

Parrington, Vernon Louis, Jr. *American Dreams,* 61–64.

DODGSON, CHARLES LUTWIDGE. See CARROLL, LEWIS

DONNELLY, IGNATIUS

General Criticism

Parrington, Vernon Louis, Jr. *American Dreams,* 104–110.

Atlantis, the Ante-Diluvian World

Parrington, Vernon Louis, Jr. *American Dreams,* 104.

Caesar's Column

Anderson, David D. *Ignatius Donnelly,* 67–79.

Axelrod, A. M. "Ideology and Utopia in the Works of Ignatius Donnelly." *American Studies* 12 (Fall 1971): 47–66.

Gardiner, Helen Jane. "American Utopian Fiction, 1885–1910."

Lang, Hans-Joachim. "Ignatius Donnelly: *Caesar's Column:* A Story of the Twentieth-Century." In *Die Utopie in der Angloamerikanischen Literatur,* 139–160.

Parrington, Vernon Louis, Jr. *American Dreams,* 104–107, 110.

Patterson, J. S. "From Yeoman to Beast: Images of Blackness in *Caesar's Column.*" *American Studies* 12 (Fall 1971): 21–31.

Pfaelzer, Jean. *The Utopian Novel in America, 1886–1896,* 120–140.

Rideout, Walter B. *The Radical Novel in the United States, 1900–1954,* 10, 12.

Saxton, Alexander. *"Caesar's Column,* the Dialogue of Utopia and Catastrophe." *American Quarterly* 19, Supplement (Summer 1967): 224–238.

Schweninger, Lee. "The Building of the City Beautiful: The Motif of the Jeremiad in Three Utopian Novels." *American Literary Realism* 18 (Spring 1985): 107–119.

Ueda, Reed T. "Economic and Technological Evil in the Modern Apocalypse: Donnelly's *Caesar's Column* and *The Golden Bottle.*" *Journal of Popular Culture* 14, no. 1 (1980): 1–9.

The Golden Bottle

Anderson, David D. *Ignatius Donnelly,* 93–103.

Pfaelzer, Jean. *The Utopian Novel in America, 1886–1896,* 115, 126, 129–131.

Ueda, Reed T. "Economic and Technological Evil in the Modern Apocalypse: Donnelly's *Caesar's Column* and *The Golden Bottle.*" *Journal of Popular Culture* 14 (1980): 1–9.

DOSTOEVSKII, FEDOR MIKHAILOVICH

"The Grand Inquisitor"

Arisian, Khoren. " 'The Grand Inquisitor' Revisited: An Inquiry into the Character of Human Freedom." *Crane Review* 9 (1967): 147–158.

Berdyaev, Nicholas. *Dostoevsky,* 188–212.

Carver, Wayne. "The Grand Inquisitor's Long March." *University of Denver Quarterly* 1 (1966): 41–49.

Cox, Roger L. "Dostoevsky's 'Grand Inquisitor.' " *Cross Currents* 17 (Fall 1967): 427–444.

Guardini, Romani. "The Legend of the Grand Inquisitor." *Cross Currents* 3 (Fall 1952): 58–86.

Ivanov, Vyacheslav. *Freedom and the Tragic Life,* 31.

Jackson, Robert L. *The Art of Dostoevsky: Deliriums and Nocturnes.* Princeton, NJ: Princeton University Press, 1979, pp. 335–345.

Jones, Malcolm V. *Dostoevsky,* 180–185.

Kunkel, Francis L. "Dostoevsky's 'Inquisitor': An Emblem of Paradox." *Renascence* 16 (Summer 1964): 208–213.

Lavrin, Janko. *Dostoevsky: A Study.* New York: Macmillan, 1946, pp. 130–138.

Neumann, Harry. "Milton's Adam and Dostoevsky's Inquisitor on the Problem of Freedom before God." *Personalist* 48 (July 1967): 317–327.

Pachmuss, Temira. *F. M. Dostoevsky*, 97–108.

Payne, Robert. *Dostoyevsky: A Human Portrait.* New York: Knopf, 1961, pp. 351–363.

Perring, Ronald E. " 'The Grand Inquisitor.' " *Studies in the Humanities* 7, no. 2 (1979): 52–57.

Rahv, Philip. "The Legend of the Grand Inquisitor." *Partisan Review* 21 (May–June 1954): 249–271.

Richards, D. "Four Utopias." *Slavonic and East European Review* 40 (1962): 220–228.

Riemer, Neal. "Some Reflections on 'The Grand Inquisitor' and Modern Democratic Theory." *Ethics* 67 (1957): 49–57.

Seiden, Melvin. "The Classroom as Underground: Notes on 'The Grand Inquisitor.' " *Journal of General Education* 10, no. 4 (1957): 217–222.

Simons, John D. "The Grand Inquisitor in Schiller, Dostoevsky and Huxley." *New Zealand Slavonic Journal* 8 (Summer 1971): 20–31.

Slonim, Marc. *The Epic of Russian Literature.* New York: Oxford University Press, 1950, pp. 289–291.

Stupple, A. James. "Toward a Definition of Anti-Utopian Literature." *CEA Critic* 37, Supplement (November 1974): 27–28.

Sutherland, Stewart R. "Dostoyevsky and 'The Grand Inquisitor': A Study in Atheism." *Yale Review* 66 (Spring 1977): 364–373.

Trilling, Lionel. *The Experience of Literature.* New York: Holt, Rinehart & Winston, 1967, pp. 482–485.

Notes from Underground

Annas, Julia. "Action and Character in Dostoyevsky's *Notes from Underground.*" *Philosophy and Literature* 1 (Fall 1977): 257–275.

Bakhtin, Mikhail. *Problems of Dostoevsky's Poetics.* Ann Arbor, MI: Ardis, 1973, pp. 190–199.

Barstow, Jane. "Dostoevsky's *Notes from Underground* versus Chernyshevsky's *What is to be Done?*" *College Literature* 5 (Winter 1978): 24–33.

Bercovitch, Sacvan. "Dramatic Irony in *Notes from Underground.*" *Slavic and East European Journal* 8 (Fall 1964): 284–289.

Berdyaev, Nicholas. *Dostoevsky,* 50–54.

Berman, Marshall. *All that Is Solid Melts into Air,* 173–248.

Cardaci, Paul F. "Dostoevsky's Underground as Allusion and Symbol." *Symposium* 28 (Fall 1974): 248–258.

Carrier, Warren. "Artistic Form and Unity in *Notes from Underground.*" *Renascence* 16 (Spring 1964): 142–145.

Cash, Earl A. "The Narrators in *Invisible Man* and *Notes from Underground:* Brothers in the Spirit." *College Language Association Journal* 16 (June 1973): 505–507.

Clive, Geoffrey. "The Sickness into Death in the Underworld: A Study of Nihilism." *Harvard Theological Review* 51 (July 1958): 135–167.

Edwards, T. *Three Russian Writers and the Irrational,* 1–35.

Fagin, N. Bryllion. "Dostoevsky's Underground Man Takes Over." *Antioch Review* 13 (March 1953): 25–32.

Fanger, Donald. *Dostoevsky and Romantic Realism.* Cambridge, MA: Harvard University Press, 1965, pp. 177–183.

Frank, Joseph. "Nihilism and *Notes from Underground.*" *Sewanee Review* 69 (January–March 1961): 1–33.

Freeborn, Richard. *The Rise of the Russian Novel: Studies in the Russian Novel from Eugene Onegin to War and Peace.* London: Cambridge University Press, 1973, pp. 179–183.

Gibson, A. Boyce. *The Religion of Dostoevsky.* London: SCM Press, 1973, pp. 78–87.

Gregg. Richard. "Apollo Underground: His Master's Still, Small Voice." *Russian Review* 32 (January 1973): 64–71.

Hall, J. R. "Abstraction in Dostoyevsky's *Notes from Underground.*" *Modern Language Review* 76 (January 1981): 129–137.

Haltresht, Michael. "Symbolism of Rats and Mice in Dostoevsky's *Notes from Underground.*" *South Atlantic Bulletin* 39 (November 1974): 60–62.

Harper, Ralph. *The Seventh Solitude: Man's Isolation in Kierkegaard, Dostoevsky, and Nietzsche.* Baltimore: Johns Hopkins Press, 1965, pp. 41–46.

Hingley, Ronald. *The Undiscovered Dostoyevsky.* Westport, CT: Greenwood Press, 1975, pp. 69–79.

Holquist, James. "Plot and Counter-Plot in *Notes from Underground.*" *Canadian-American Slavic Studies* 6 (Summer 1972): 225–238.

Holquist, Michael. *Dostoevsky and the Novel.* Princeton, NJ: Princeton University Press, 1977, pp. 54–74.

Ivanov, Vyacheslav. *Freedom and the Tragic Life,* 134–140.

Jackson, Robert Louis. *Dostoevsky's Underground Man in Russian Literature.*

Jones, Malcolm V. *Dostoyevsky,* 55–66.

Kavanagh, Thomas M. "Dostoyevsky's *Notes from Underground: The Form of the Fiction.*" *Texas Studies in Literature and Language* 14 (Fall 1972): 491–507.

La Capra, D. *History, Politics, and the Novel.* Ithaca, NY: Cornell University Press, 1987, pp. 35–55.

Lednicki, W. *Russia, Poland, and the West: Essays in Literary and Cultural History.* New York: Roy Publ., 1954, pp. 180–248.

Lerner, L. *The Literary Imagination: Essays on Literature and Society.* Totowa, NJ: Barnes & Noble Books, 1982, pp. 60–77.

Lethcoe, James. "Self-Deception in Dostoevsky's *Notes from the Underground.*" *Slavic and East European Journal* 10 (Spring 1966): 9–21.

Lord, Robert. *Dostoevsky: Essays and Perspectives.* Berkeley: University of California Press, 1970, pp. 35–47.

McKinney, David M. *"Notes from Underground:* A 'Dostoevskean' Faust." *Canadian-American Slavic Studies* 12 (Summer 1978): 189–229.

Magarshack, David. *Dostoevsky.* New York: Harcourt, Brace and World, 1961, pp. 233–235.

Matlaw, Ralph E. Introduction. *Fyodor Dostoevsky: Notes from Underground and The Grand Inquisitor, with Relevant Works by Chernyshevsky, Shchedrin and Dostoevsky.* By Fyodor Dostoevsky *et al.* Translated and edited by Ralph Matlaw. New York: Dutton, 1960, vii–xxii

―――. "Structure and Integration in *Notes from the Underground.*" *PMLA* 73 (March 1958): 101–109.

Meier-Graefe, Julius. *Dostoevsky: The Man and His Work.* New York: Harcourt, 1928, pp. 98–110.

Merrill, Reed. "The Mistaken Endeavor: Dostoevsky's *Notes from Underground.*" *Modern Fiction Studies* 18 (Winter 1972–1973): 505–516.

Mikhailovsky, Nikolai K. *Dostoevsky: A Cruel Talent.* Ann Arbor, MI: Ardis, 1978, pp. 13–19.

Mochulsky, Konstantin. *Dostoevsky: His Life and Work.* Translated by Michael A. Minihan. Princeton, NJ: Princeton University Press, 1967.

Nisly, Paul W. "A Modernist Impulse: *Notes from Underground* as Model." *College Literature* 4 (1977): 152–158.

Pachmuss, Temira. *F. M. Dostoevsky,* 5–7, 69–72, 99–102, 134–136.

Peace, Richard. *Dostoyevsky: An Examination of the Major Novels.* New York: Cambridge University Press, 1971, pp. 1–18.

Pfleger, Karl. *Wrestlers with Christ.* London: Sheed and Ward, 1936, pp. 191–202.

Phillips, William. "Dostoevsky's Underground Man." *Partisan Review* 12 (1946): 551–561.

Powys, John Cowper. *Dostoievsky.* London: John Lane, 1946, pp. 82–87.

Rahv, Philip. *Essays on Literature and Politics, 1932–1972.* Boston: Houghton, 1978, pp. 174–185.

Riggan, W. *Picaros, Madmen, Naifs, and Clowns: The Unreliable First-Person Narrator.* Norman, OK: University of Oklahoma Press, 1981, pp. 109–143.

Rodoyce, L. "Writers in Hell: Notes on Doestoevsky's Letters." *California Slavic Studies* 9 (1976): 71–122.

Seeley, Frank F. "Dostoyevsky's Women." *Slavonic and East European Review* 39 (1961): 300.

Simmons, Ernest J. *Dostoevsky: The Making of a Novelist.* New York: Vintage Books, 1940, pp. 109–126.

Smalley, Barbara. "The Compulsive Patterns of Dostoyevsky's Underground Man." *Studies in Short Fiction* 10 (Fall 1973): 389–396.

Spilka, Mark. "Playing Crazy in the Underground." *Minnesota Review* 6, no. 3 (1966): 233–243.

Steiner, George. *Tolstoy or Dostoevsky.* New York: Knopf, 1959, pp. 220–230.

Struc, Roman S. "Dostoevsky's 'Confessions' as Critique of Literature." *Research Studies* 46 (June 1978): 84–89.

Traschen, Isadore. "Dostoevsky's *Notes from Underground.*" *Accent* 16 (1956): 255–264.

———. "Existential Ambiguities in *Notes from Underground.*" *South Atlantic Quarterly* 73 (Summer 1974): 363–376.

Troyat, Henry. *Firebrand: A Life of Dostoevsky.* New York: Roy Publ., 1946, pp. 248–290.

Walker, Herbert. "Observations on Fyodor Dostoevsky's *Notes from the Underground.*" *American Imago* 19 (Summer 1962): 195–210.

Warrick, Patricia. "The Sources of Zamyatin's *We* in Dostoevsky's *Notes from Underground.*" *Extrapolation* 17 (December 1975): 63–76.

Wasiolek, Edward. " 'Aut Caesar, Aut Nihil' A Study of Dostoevsky's Moral Dialectic." *PMLA* 78 (March 1963): 94–97.

———. *Dostoevsky: The Major Fiction.* Cambridge: Massachusetts Institute of Technology Press, 1964, pp. 39–59.

Wilson, Colin. *The Outsider.* London: Golancz, 1956, pp. 157–162.

Winfield, William. "Reflection/Negation/Reality: Dostoyevsky and Hegel." *Comparative Literature Studies* 17 (December 1980): 399–408.

Yarmolinsky, Avrahm. *Dostoevsky: A Life.* New York: Harcourt, Brace, 1934, pp. 187–193.

———. *Dostoevsky: His Life and Art.* New York: Criterion Books, 1957, pp. 177–178, 187–192.

———. *Dostoevsky: Works and Days.* New York: Funk and Wagnalls, 1971, pp. 190–197.

Yermilov, V. *Fyodor Dostoyevsky.* Moscow: Foreign Languages Publishing House, [1957?], pp. 143–160.

DU MAURIER, DAPHNE

Rule Britannia

Albinski, Nan Bowman. *Women's Utopias in British and American Fiction,* 139, 158.

Kelly, Richard. *Daphne du Maurier.* Boston: Twayne, 1987, pp. 117–122.

DUVEYRIER, CHARLES

La Ville Nouvelle

Weil, Kari. "Feminocentric Utopia and Male Desire: 'The New Paris of the Saint-Simonians.' '' In *Feminism, Utopia and Narrative,* 159–172.

EAUBONNE, FRANCOISE D'

General Criticism

Arbour, Kathryn Mary. "French Feminist Re-visions."

EDSON, MILAN C.

Solaris Farm

Parrington, Vernon Louis, Jr. *American Dreams,* 158–160.

Rooney, Charles J. Jr. *Dream and Visions,* 65, 107–108, 156, 186.

EFREMOV, IVAN ANTONOVICH

Andromeda

Jehmlich, Reimer. "Cog-Work: The Organization of Labor in Edward Bellamy's *Looking Backward* and in Later Utopian Fiction." In *Clockwork Worlds,* 27–46.

ELGIN, SUZETTE HADEN

General Criticism

Chapman, Edgar L. "Sex, Satire, and Feminism in the Science Fiction of Suzette Haden Elgin." In *The Feminine Eye,* 89–102.

Judas Rose

Anderson, Kristine J. "The Great Divorce: Fictions of Feminist Desire." In *Feminism, Utopia, and Narrative,* 90, 92–93, 95.

Native Tongue

Albinski, Nan Bowman. *Women's Utopias in British and American Fiction,* 170, 184, 185.

Fitting, Peter. "The Turn from Utopia in Recent Feminist Fiction." In *Feminism, Utopia, and Narrative,* 145–150.

ELIOT, JOHN

General Criticism

Tanis, N. E. "Education in John Eliot's Indian Utopias, 1645–1675." *History of Education Quarterly* 10 (1970): 308–323.

The Christian Commonwealth

Holstun, James Ross. "Puritan Utopias of the Interregum." Ph.D. diss., University of California, Irvine, 1983.

Parrington, Vernon Louis, Jr. *American Dreams,* 7–10, 12.

ELLISON, HARLAN JAY

"A Boy and his Dog"

Berger, Harold L. *Science Fiction and the New Dark Age,* 142–145.

Crow, John, and Richard Erlich D. "Mythic Patterns in Ellison's 'A Boy and his Dog.' " *Extrapolation* 18 (May 1977): 162–166.

Slusser, George Edgar. *Harlan Ellison: Unrepentant Harlequin.* San Bernardino, CA: Borgo Press, 1977, pp. 34.

Wendell, Carolyn. "The Alien Species: A Study of Women Characters in the Nebula Award Winners, 1965–1973." *Extrapolation* 20 (Winter 1979): 346.

EMANUEL, VICTOR ROUSSEAU

The Messiah of the Cylinder

Mullen, Richard D. "H. G. Wells and Victor Rousseau Emanuel: *When the Sleeper Wakes* and *The Messiah of the Cyliner.*" *Extrapolation* 8 (May 1967): 31–63.

EVERETT, HENRY L.

The People's Program

Parrington, Vernon Louis, Jr. *American Dreams,* 129–131.

Rooney, Charles J., Jr. *Dreams and Visions,* 108, 186–187.

FAIRBAIRNS, ZOE

Benefits

Albinski, Nan Bowman. *Women's Utopias in British and American Fiction,* 132, 134, 135, 137, 143–145, 158.

Fitting, Peter. "The Turn from Utopia in Recent Feminist Fiction." In *Feminism, Utopia, and Narrative,* 141, 143–144, 148, 154–156.

FAIRMAN, PAUL W.

General Criticism

Berger, Harold L. *Science Fiction and the New Dark Age,* 26–28.

FÉNELON, FRANÇOIS DE SALIGNAC DE LA MOTHE

General Criticism

Carcassonne, Ely. *Fénelon l'Homme et l'Oeuvre.* Paris: Bowin, 1946.

Cherel, Albert. *Fénelon, ou la Religion du Pur Amour.* Paris: Denoel et Steele, 1934.

Granderoute, Robert. *Le Roman Pédagogique de Fénelon à Rousseau.*

Spacemann, Robert. "Fénelon und Jean Paul." *Jahrbuch der Jean-Paul Geseleschaft* 15 (1980): 55–81.

The Adventures of Telemachus

Adler, Alfred. "Fénelon's *Télémaque*: Intention and Effect." *Studies in Philology* 55 (October 1958): 591–602.

Cor, M. Antonia. "The Shield of *Télémaque.*" *Romance Notes* 23 (Fall 1982): 17–21.

Davis, James Herbert, Jr. *Fénelon.* Boston: Twayne, 1979, pp. 90–111.

Desroches, Rosny. "L'Utopie: Évasion ou Anticipation?" In *France and North America,* 83–92.

Gilroy, James P. "Peace and the Pursuit of Happiness in the French Utopian Novel: Fénelon's *Télémaque* and Prévost's *Cleveland.*" *Studies on Voltaire and the Eighteenth Century* 176 (1979): 169–187.

Highet, G. *Classical Tradition: Greek and Roman Influences on Western Literature.* New York: Oxford University Press, 1949.

Kapp, Volker. *Télémaque de Fénelon: La Signification d'une Oeuvre Littéraire à la Fin du Siècle Classique.* Turbingen: Gunter Narr Verlag, 1982.

Malarte, Claire-Lise. "Les Utopies de *Télémaque.*" In *Actes de Baton Rouge,* edited by Selma A. Zebouni, 377–385. Paris: Papers on French Seventeenth Century Literature, 1986.

Mathieu-Kerns, Lyliane D. "*Le Télémaque*: Une Utopie Dynamique." *Nottingham French Studies* 18, no. 2 (1979): 27–38.

Miething, Christoph. "Mythos und Politik: Fénelons Konzept der Politischen Erziehung in *Les Aventures de Télémaque.*" *Romanische Forschungen* 97, nos. 2–3 (1985): 131–145.

Roger, Philippe. "La Trace de Fénelon." In *Sade,* 149–173.

Scaldini, Richard J. "*Les Aventures de Télémaque,* or Alienated in Ogygia." *Yale French Studies* 57 (1979): 164–179.

Tillyard, E. M. W. *English Epic and Its Background.* New York: Oxford University Press, 1954, pp. 482–493.

Whatley, Janet. "Coherent Worlds: Fénelon's *Télémaque* and Marivaux's *Télémaque Travesti.*" *Studies on Voltaire and the Eighteenth Century* 171 (1977): 85–113.

FITZPATRICK, ERNEST HUGH

The Marshal Duke of Denver

Rooney, Charles J., Jr. *Dreams and Visions,* 187.

FLECKER, JAMES ELROY

"The Last Generation"

Munro, John M. *James Elroy Flecker.* Boston: Twayne, 1976, pp. 25, 80–83.

FOIGNY, GABRIEL DE

General Criticism

Minerva, Nadia. "L'Utopiste et le Péché: À Propos de Quelques Utopies de la 'Fruhaufklrung.' " In *Requiem pour l'Utopie?,* 73–91.

La Terre Australe Connue

Benrekassa, Georges. "La Matière du Langage: La Linguistique Utopique de Gabriel de Foigny." In *La Linguistique Fantastique,* 150–165.

Berneri, Marie Louise. *Journey Through Utopia,* 184–201.

Kuon, Peter. "L'Utopie entre 'Mythe' et 'Lumières': *La Terre Australe Connue* de Gabriel de Foigny et *L'Histoire des Sevarambes* de Denis Veiras." *Papers on French Seventeenth Century Literature* 14, no. 26 (1987): 253–272.

Leibacher-Ouvrard, Lise. "L'un et la Double: Hermaphrodisme et Idéologie dans *La Terre Australe Connue* de Gabriel de Foigny."

French Forum 9 (September 1984): 290–304.

Pellandra, Carla. "Transparences Trompeuses: Les Cosmogonies Linguistiques de Foigny et de Veiras." In *Requiem pour l'Utopie?*, 55–71.

Ronzeaud, Pierre. "Du Detournement des Cheminements Culturels: Le Voyage Utopique de G. de Foigny, 1676." In *Voyages*, 353–387.

Sermain, Jean Paul. "La Langue de l'Utopie." In *Croisements Culturels*, 89–114.

Vecchi, Paola. "L'Amour de Soi et la Mort en Utopie: La Perfection Inquiete de Gabriel de Foigny." In *Requiem pour l'Utopie?*, 35–53.

FORBUSH, ZEBINA

The Co-opolitan

Parrington, Vernon Louis, Jr. *American Dreams,* 119–122.

Pfaelzer, Jean. *The Utopian Novel in America, 1886–1896,* 50.

FORD, FORD MADOX

The Simple Life Limited

Batchelor, John. *The Edwardian Novelists.* London: Duckworth, 1982, pp. 115–117.

Cassell, Richard A. *Ford Madox Ford: A Study of His Novels.* Baltimore: Johns Hopkins Press, 1961, pp. 77–78, 82–83.

Hoffmann, Charles G. *Ford Madox Ford.* Updated edition. Boston: Twayne, 1990, pp. 34–36, 37, 40.

Stang, Sondra J. *Ford Madox Ford.* New York: Ungar, 1977, pp. 44–45.

FORREST, KATHERINE

Daughters of a Coral Dawn

Albinski, Nan Bowman. *Women's Utopias in British and American Fiction*, 164, 165, 184.

Zaki, Hoda M. "Utopia and Ideology in *Daughters of a Coral Dawn* and Contemporary Feminist Utopias." *Women's Studies* 14 (December 1987): 119–133.

FORSTER, EDWARD MORGAN

General Criticism

Dunn, Thomas P., and Richard D. Erlich. "A Vision of Dystopia: Beehives and Mechanization." *Journal of General Education* 33 (Spring 1981): 45–57.

Swanson, Roy Arthur. "Love Is the Function of Death: Forster, Lagerkvist, and Zamyatin." *Canadian Review of Comparative Literature* 3 (Spring 1976): 197–211.

Watson, Ian. "From Pan in the Home Countries—To Pain on a Far Planet: E. M. Forster, David Lindsay, and How the *Voyage to Arcturus* Should End." *Foundation* 43 (Summer 1988): 25–36.

"The Machine Stops"

Beauchamp, Gorman. "Technology in the Dystopian Novel." *Modern Fiction Studies* 32 (Spring 1986): 53–63.

Berger, Harold L. *Science Fiction and the New Dark Age*, 25–26, 157.

Berman, Jeffrey. "Forster's Other Cave: The Platonic Structure of 'The Machine Stops.' " *Extrapolation* 17 (May 1976): 172–181.

Cavaliero, Glen. *A Reading of E. M. Forster*. London: Macmillan, 1979, pp. 50–51.

Colmer, J. *E. M. Forster: The Personal Voice*. London: Routledge & Kegan Paul, 1975, pp. 39–40.

Dunn, Thomas P. "The Deep Caves of Thought: Plato, Heinlein and Le Guin." In *Spectrum of the Fantastic: Selected Essays from the Sixth International Conference on the Fantastic in the Arts,* edited by Donald Palumbo, 105–112. Westport, CT: Greenwood Press, 1988.

Elkins, Charles. "E. M. Forster's 'The Machine Stops': Liberal-Humanist Hostility to Technology." In *Clockwork Worlds,* 47–61.

Erlich, Richard D. "Trapped in the Bureaucratic Pinball Machine: A Vision of Dystopia in the Twentieth Century." In *Selected Proceedings of the 1978 Science Fiction Research Association National Conference,* 35.

Garrett, J. C. *Utopias in Literature Since the Romantic Period,* 56.

Herz, Judith Scherer. *The Short Narratives of E. M. Forster*. London: Macmillan Press, 1988, pp. 59–62.

Macaulay, Rose. *The Writings of E. M. Forster*. London: Hogarth, 1938, p. 31.

McDowell, Frederick. *E. M. Forster*. Revised edition. Boston: Twayne, 1982, p. 39.

Shusterman, David. *The Quest for Certitude in E. M. Forster's Fiction*. Bloomington: Indiana University Press, 1965, pp. 51–54.

Stone, Wilfred. *The Cave and the Mountain: A Study of E. M. Forster*. Stanford, CA: Stanford University Press, 1966, pp. 152–155.

Trilling, Lionel. *E. M. Forster*. Norfolk, CT: New Directions, 1943, pp. 47–48.

Walsh, Chad. *From Utopia to Nightmare,* 83–85.

Warner, Rex. *E. M. Forster*. London: Longmans, Green, 1950, p. 23.

Warrick, Patricia. *The Cybernetic Imagination in Science Fiction.* Cambridge, MA: Massachusetts Institute of Technology Press, 1980, pp. 44–46.

FOURIER, FRANÇOIS CHARLES MARIE

General Criticism

Beecher, Jonathan. *Charles Fourier: The Visionary and His World.* Berkeley: University of California Press, 1986, pp. 2, 246–247, 298–302, 318–319.

Beecher, Jonathan, and Richard Bienvenu. *The Utopian Vision of Charles Fourier*. Boston: Beacon Press, 1971, pp. 1–75.

Berneri, Marie Louise. *Journey Through Utopia,* 207, 210–213, 215, 239–242.

Cioranescu, Alexandre. *L'Avenir du Passe, Utopie et Littérature.* Paris: Gallimard, Coll. Les Essais, 1972.

Dahlerup, Drude. ''Fantasien til Magten! Om Charles Fourier.'' In *Kvindestudier V,* 96–119.

Desroche, Henri. *Les Dieux Rêves, Theisme et Atheisme en Utopie.* Paris: Desclee de Brauwer, 1972.

Fein, Albert. ''Fourierism in Nineteenth Century America: A Social and Environmental Perspective.'' In *France and North America,* 133–148.

Francblin, Catherine. ''Le Feminisme Utopique de Ch. Fourier.'' *Tel Quel* 62 (1975): 44–69.

Gide, Charles. Introduction. *Design for Utopia: Selected Writings of Charles Fourier.* By Charles Fourier. New York: Schocken Books, 1971, pp. 9–45.

Hertzler, Joyce Oramel. *The History of Utopian Thought*, pp. 197–204.

Kaufmann, M. *Utopias*, 67–87.

Mumford, Lewis. *The Story of Utopias*, 117–123.

Poster, Mark. Introduction. *Harmonian Man: Selected Writings of Charles Fourier*. By Charles Fourier. Garden City, NY: Anchor Books, 1971, pp. 1–20.

Spencer, M. C. *Charles Fourier*. Boston: Twayne, 1981, pp. 126–142.

FOWLES, JOHN

The Magus

Berets, Ralph. "*The Magus*: A Study in the Creation of a Personal Myth." *Twentieth Century Literature* 19 (April 1973): 89–98.

Binns, Ronald. "John Fowles: Radical Romancer." *Critical Quarterly* 15 (Winter 1973): 326–331.

Chevalier, Jean-Louis. "Ailleurs, Autrefois, Autrement: L'Utopie du 'plan du Conduite' dans *The Magus* de John Fowles." In *De William Shakespeare à William Golding: Mélanges dédiés à la mémoire de Jean-Pierre Vernier*, 27–43. Rouen: University de Rouen, 1984.

Churchill, Thomas. "Waterhouse, Storey, and Fowles: 'Which Way out of the Room?' " *Critique* 10 (Summer 1968): 72–87.

Detweiler, Robert. "The Unity of John Fowles' Fiction." *Notes on Contemporary Literature* 1 (March 1971): 3–4.

Edwards, Lee R. "Changing Our Imaginations." *Massachusetts Review* 11 (Summer 1970): 604–608.

Fleishman, Avrom. "*The Magus* of the Wizard of the West." In *Critical Essays on John Fowles*, 77–93.

Holmes, Frederick M. "Art, Truth and John Fowles's *The Magus*." *Modern Fiction Studies* 31 (Spring 1985): 45–56.

Huffaker, Robert. *John Fowles.* Boston: Twayne, 1980, pp. 44–72.

Laughlin, Rosemary M. "Faces of Power in the Novels of John Fowles." *Critique* 13, no. 3 (1971): 75–84.

McDaniel, Ellen. "*The Magus:* Fowles's Tarot Quest." In *Critical Essays on John Fowles,* 106–117.

Mudrick, Marvin. "Evelyn, Get the Horseradish." *Hudson Review* 19 (Summer 1966): 305–318.

Newquist, Roy. *Counterpoint,* 218–225.

Novak, Frank G., Jr. "The Dialectics of Debasement in *The Magus.*" *Modern Fiction Studies* 31 (Spring 1985): 71–82.

Olshen, Barry N. "John Fowles's *The Magus:* An Allegory of Self-Realization." *Journal of Popular Culture* 9, no. 4 (1976): 916–925.

Onega, Susana. *Form and Meaning in the Novels of John Fowles.* Ann Arbor, MI: UMI Research Press, 1989, pp. 35–67.

Palmer, William J. *The Fiction of John Fowles: Tradition, Art, and the Loneliness of Selfhood.* Columbia: University of Missouri Press, 1974.

Presley, Delma. "The Quest of the Bourgeois Hero: An Approach to Fowles' *The Magus.*" *Journal of Popular Culture* 6 (Fall 1972): 394–398.

Raper, Julius Rowan. "John Fowles: The Psychological Complexity of *The Magus.*" *American Imago* 45 (Spring 1988): 61–83.

Rubenstein, Roberta. "Myth, Mystery, and Irony: John Fowles's *The Magus.*" *Contemporary Literature* 16 (Summer 1975): 328–339.

Tarbox, Katherine. *The Art of John Fowles.* Athens: University of Georgia Press, 1988, pp. 11–37.

Wolfe, Peter. *John Fowles, Magus or Moralist?* Lewisburg, PA: Bucknell University Press, 1976, pp. 81–121.

The Magus: A Revised Version

Binns, Ronald. "A New Version of *The Magus.*" In *Critical Essays on John Fowles,* 100–105.

Fowles, John. "Why I Rewrote *The Magus.*" In *Critical Essays on John Fowles,* 93–99.

Wainwright, J. A. "The Illusion of 'Things as They Are': *The Magus* versus *The Magus: A Revised Version.*" *Dalhousie Review* 63 (Spring 1983): 107–119.

Wight, Douglas A., and Kenneth B. Grant. "Theatrical Deception: Shakespearean Allusion to John Fowles' *The Magus: A Revised Version.*" *University of Dayton Review* 18 (Summer 1987): 85–93.

FRANCE, ANATOLE

Penguin Island

Axelrad, Jacob. *Anatole France: A Life Without Illusions, 1844–1924.* New York: Harper, 1944, pp. 339–341.

Bresky, Dushan. *The Art of Anatole France.* Paris: Mouton, 1969, pp. 189, 192.

Caute, David. *Collisions: Essays and Review.* London: Quartet Books, 1974, pp. 147–158.

Dargan, Edwin Preston. "Penguin Isle." *Sewanee Review* 18 (July 1910): 380–384.

Eccles, F. Y. "The Mantle of Voltaire." *Dublin Review* 144 (April 1909): 357–367.

Guerard, Albert Leon. *Five Masters of French Romance.* New York: Scribner's, 1916, pp. 130–133.

Jefferson, Carter. *Anatole France: The Politics of Skepticism.* New Brunswick, NJ: Rutgers University Press, 1965, pp. 152–156.

Kennett, W. "The Theme of *Penguin Island.*" *Romanic Review* 33 (October, 1942): 275–289.

May, James Lewis. *Anatole France, the Man and his Work: An Essay in Critical Biography.* Port Washington, NY: Kennikat, 1970, pp. 151–153.

Smith, Helen B. *The Skepticism of Anatole France.* Paris: Les Presses Universitaires de France, 1927, pp. 24–25.

Tylden-Wright, David. *Anatole France.* New York: Walker, 1967, pp. 246–251.

Van Doren, Carl. Introduction. *Penguin Island.* By Anatole France. New York: Heritage Press, xi-xvi.

Virtanen, Reino. *Anatole France.* New York: Twayne, 1968, pp. 128–134.

Walton, Loring Baker. *Anatole France and the Greek World.* Durham, NC: Duke University Press, 1950, pp. 206–209.

FRAYN, MICHAEL

A Very Private Life

Fietz, Lothar. "Schreckutopien des Kollektivismus und Individualismus: Aldous Huxleys *Brave New World* und Michael Frayns *A Very Private Life.*" In *Literarische Utopien von Morus bis zur Gegenwart,* 203–217.

FULLER, ALVARADO MORTIMER

A.D. 2000

Lewis, Arthur O. Introduction. *A. D. 2000: A Novel.* By Alvarado M. Fuller. New York: Arno Press, 1971, i-viii.

Parrington, Vernon Louis, Jr. *American Dreams,* 146–147.

Pfaelzer, Jean. *The Utopian Novel in America, 1886–1896,* 101–102.

GALLOWAY, JAMES M.

John Harvey

Rooney, Charles J., Jr. *Dreams and Visions,* 123, 188.

GEARHART, SALLY MILLER

The Wanderground

Albinski, Nan Bowman. *Women's Utopias in British and American Fiction,* 164–165, 171–173, 175–176, 184.

Barr, Marleen. "Permissive, Unspectacular, a Little Baffling: Sex and the Single Feminist Utopian Quasi-Tribesperson." In *Erotic Universe,* 185–196.

Devine, Maureen. "*Woman on the Edge of Time* and *The Wanderground:* Visions in Eco-Feminist Utopias." In *Utopian Thought in American Literature,* 131–145.

Fitting, Peter. "The Turn from Utopia in Recent Feminist Fiction." In *Feminism, Utopia, and Narrative,* 141–142, 146.

Freibert, Lucy M. "World Views in Utopian Novels by Women." In *Women and Utopia,* 67–84.

Howard, June. "Widening the Dialogue on Feminist Science Fiction." In *Feminist Re-Visions,* 64–96.

GEISSLER, LUDWIG A.

Looking Beyond

Egbert, Nelson Norris. "Problems of Form and Content in Six Utopian Responses to Edward Bellamy's *Looking Backward: 2000–1887.*"

GILES, FAYETTE STRATTON

Shadows Before

Rooney, Charles J., Jr. *Dreams and Visions,* 75, 80, 100, 158, 188.

GILLETTE, KING CAMP

The Human Drift

Roemer, Kenneth M. Introduction. *The Human Drift.* By King C. Gillette. Delmar, NY: Scholars' Facsimiles & Reprints, 1976, iii-xxiii.

Rooney, Charles J., Jr. *Dreams and Visions,* 107, 109, 188.

GILMAN, CHARLOTTE PERKINS

General Criticism

Donaldson, L. E. "The Eve of De-struction: Charlotte Perkins Gilman and the Feminist Re-Creation of Paradise." *Women Studies* 16, nos. 3–4 (1989): 373–387.

Smith, Marsha A. "The Disoriented Male Narrator and Societal Conversion: Charlotte Perkins Gilman's Feminist Utopian Vision." *American Transcendental Quarterly* 3 (March 1989): 123–133.

Herland

Bartkowski, Frances. "Toward a Feminist Eros."

Berkson, Dorothy. " 'So We all Became Mothers': Harriet Beecher Stowe, Charlotte Perkins Gilman, and the New World of Women's Culture." In *Feminism, Utopia, and Narrative,* 107–110.

Bleich, David. "Sexism and the Discourse of Perfection." *American Transcendental Quarterly* 3 (March 1989): 11–25.

Boone, J. A. "Centered Lives and Centric Structures in the Novel of Female Community: Counterplotting New Realities in *Millenium Hall, Cranford, The Country of the Pointed Firs* and *Herland.*" In *Tradition*

98   Utopian/Dystopian Literature

Counter Tradition: Love and the Form of Fiction, edited by J. A. Boone, 278–330. Chicago: University of Chicago Press, 1987.

Burton, Deirdre. "Linguistic Innovation in Feminist Utopian Fiction." *Ilha do Desterro* 14, no. 2 (1985): 82–106.

Cranny-Francis, Anne. *Feminist Fiction,* 120–125.

Freibert, Lucy M. "World Views in Utopian Novels by Women." In *Women and Utopia,* 67–84.

Gubar, Susan. "*She* and *Herland:* Feminism as Fantasy." In *Coordinates,* 139–149.

Hill, Mary A. "Charlotte Perkins Gilman: A Feminist's Struggle with Womanhood." In *Charlotte Perkins Gilman: The Woman and Her Work,* edited by Sheryl Meyering, 44–45. Ann Arbor, MI: UMI Research Press, 1989.

Huckle, Patricia. "Women in Utopias." In *The Utopian Vision,* 115–136.

Jones, Libby Falk. "Gilman, Bradley, Piercy, and the Evolving Rhetoric of Feminist Utopias." In *Feminism, Utopia, and Narrative,* 116–119.

Keyser, Elizabeth. "Looking Backward: From *Herland* to *Gulliver's Travels.*" *Studies in Science Fiction* 11 (Spring 1983): 31–46.

Lane, Ann J. Introduction. *Herland.* By Charlotte Perkins Gilman. New York: Pantheon Books, 1979, v-xxiii.

———. *To Herland and Beyond,* 179, 292–294, 304–305.

Martin, J. R. *Reclaiming a Conversation: The Ideal of the Educated Woman.* New Haven, CT: Yale University Press, 1985, pp. 139–170.

Miller, Margaret. "The Ideal Woman in Two Feminist Science-Fiction Utopias." *Science-Fiction Studies* 10 (July 1983): 191–198.

Pearson, Carol. "Coming Home: Four Feminist Utopias and Patriarchal Experience." In *Future Females,* 63–70.

Rawls, Melanie. "*Herland* and *Out of the Silent Planet.*" *Mythlore* 13 (Winter 1986): 51–54.

Scharnhorst, Gary. *Charlotte Perkins Gilman,* 90–95.

Wilson, Christopher P. "Charlotte Perkins Gilman's Steady Burghers: The Terrain of *Herland.*" *Women's Studies* 12, no. 3 (1986): 271–292.

Moving the Mountain

Lane, Ann J. *To Herland and Beyond,* 289, 292–294.

Scharnhorst, Gary. *Charlotte Perkins Gilman,* 87–89.

With Her in Ourland

Albinski, Nan Bowman. *Women's Utopias in British and American Fiction,* 44, 73–74, 122.

Scharnhorst, Gary. *Charlotte Perkins Gilman,* 95–96.

"A Woman's Utopia"

Scharnhorst, Gary. *Charlotte Perkins Gilman,* 80–82.

GILPIN, WILLIAM

The Cosmopolitan Railway

Karnes, Thomas L. *William Gilpin: Western Nationalist.* Austin: University of Texas Press, 1970, pp. 337–339, 341.

GIRAUDEAU, FERNAND

La Cité Nouvelle

Angenot, Marc. "The Emergence of Anti-Utopian Genre in France: Souvestre, Giraudeau, Robida, *et al.*" Translated by R[obert] M. P[hilmus]. *Science-Fiction Studies* 12 (July 1985): 129–135.

GODWIN, FRANCIS

The Man in the Moone

Ash, Brian. *Faces of the Future*, 20–21.

Bachrach, A. G. H. "Luna Mendax: Some Reflections on Moon-Voyages in Early Seventeenth-Century England." In *Between Dream and Nature*, 70–90.

Copeland, Thomas A. "Frances Godwin's *The Man in the Moone:* A Picaresque Satire." *Extrapolation* 16 (May 1975): 156–163.

Hervier, Julien. "Cyrano de Bergerac et le Voyage Spatial: De la Fantaisie à la Science-Fiction." In *Proceedings of the 10th Congress of the International Comparative Literature Association, New York, 1982,* Volume 1, 436–442.

Janssen, Anke. *Francis Godwins 'The Man in the Moone': Die Entdeckung des Romans als Medium der Auseinandersetzung mit Zeitproblemen.* Frankfurt: Peter Lang, 1981.

————. "Wirkung eines Romans als Inspirationsquelle: Francis Godwins *The Man in the Moone.*" *Arcadia* 20, no. 1 (1985): 20–46.

Ponnau, Gwenhael. "Sur Quelques Modalités du Voyage Imaginaire." *Litteratures* 11 (Autumn 1984): 55–64.

Shimada, Takau. "Gonzalez de Mendoza's *Historie* as Possible Source for Godwin's *The Man in The Moone.*" *Notes and Queries* 34 (September 1987): 314–315.

GOLDING, WILLIAM

Lord of the Flies

Babb, Howard. *The Novels of William Golding.* Columbus: Ohio State University Press, 1970, pp. 6–34.

Babbage, Stuart B. *The Mark of Cain: Studies in Literature and Theology.* Grand Rapids, MI: Eerdmans, 1966, pp. 24–28.

Baker, James R. "Why It's No Go: A Study of William Golding's *Lord of the Flies.*" *Arizona Quarterly* 19 (Winter 1963): 293–305.

Berger, Morroe. *Real and Imagined Worlds,* 55–59.

Biles, Jack I. "Piggy: Apologia Pro Vita Sua." *Studies in Literary Imagination* 1 (October 1968): 83–109.

Braybrooke, Neville. "Two William Golding Novels: Two Aspects of His Work." *Queen's Quarterly* 76 (Spring 1969): 92–100.

Broich, Ulrich. "Robinsonade und Science Fiction." *Anglia* 94, nos. 1–2 (1976): 143–146, 152–155.

Bufkin, E. C. "*Lord of the Flies:* An Analysis." *Georgia Review* 19 (Spring 1965): 40–57.

Byczkowska, Ewa. "William Golding's Novels and the Anglo-American Tradition of Allegory in Fiction." *Anglikca Wratislaviensia* 2 (1972): 63–74.

Capey, A. C. " 'Will' and 'Idea' in *Lord of the Flies.*" *Use of English* 24 (1972): 99–107.

Carrington, Ildiko de Papp. "What Is a Face? Imagery and Metaphor in *Lord of the Flies.*" *Modern British Literature* 1 (1976): 66–73.

Cockren, Thomas Marcellus. "Is Golding Calvinistic?" *America* 109 (July 16, 1963): 18–20.

Cohn, Alan M. "The Berengaria Allusion in *Lord of the Flies.*" *Notes and Queries* 13 (November 1966): 419–420.

Cox, C. B. "*Lord of the Flies.*" *Critical Quarterly* 2 (Summer 1960): 112–117.

Davis, W. Eugene. "Mr. Golding's Optical Delusion." *English Language Notes* 3 (December 1965): 125–126.

Delbaere-Garant, Jeanne. "From the Cellar to the Rock: A Recurrent Pattern in William Golding's Novels." *Modern Fiction Studies* 17 (Winter 1971–1972): 503–504.

———. "Rhythm and Expansion in *Lord of the Flies.*" In *William Golding,* 72–86.

Drew, Philip. "Second Reading." *Cambridge Review* 78 (October 27, 1956): 79–84.

Egan, John M. "Golding's View of Man." *America* 108 (January 26, 1963): 140–141.

Elmer, Paul. "Prince of the Devils." *Christianity and Crisis* 23 (February 4, 1963): 7–10.

Fleck, A. D. "The Golding Bough: Aspects of Myth and Ritual in *The Lord of the Flies.*" In *On the Novel,* edited by B. S. Benedikz, 189–204. London: Dent, 1971.

Freese, Peter. "Verweisende Zeichen in William Goldings *Lord of Flies.*" *Die Neueren Sprachen* 71 (1972): 162–172.

Gindin, James. " 'Gimmick' and Metaphor in the Novels of William Golding." *Modern Fiction Studies* 6 (Summer 1960): 145–152.

Golding, William Gerald. *The Hot Gates and Other Occasional Pieces.* New York: Harcourt Brace Jovanovich, 1966, pp. 85–101.

Gordon, Robert C. "Classical Themes in *Lord of the Flies.*" *Modern Fiction Studies* 11 (Winter 1965–1966): 424–427.

Grande, Luke M. "The Appeal of Golding." *Commonweal* 77 (January 25, 1963): 457–459.

Green, Peter. "The World of William Golding." *Review of English Literature* 1 (April 1960): 62–72.

Gulbin, Suzanne. "Parallels and Contrasts in *Lord of the Flies* and *Animal Farm.*" *English Journal* 55 (January 1966): 86–90, 92.

Hadomi, Leah. "Imagery as a Source of Irony in Golding's *Lord of the Flies.*" *Hebrew University Studies in Literature* 9, no. 1 (1981): 126–138.

Hampton, T. "An Error in *Lord of the Flies.*" *Notes and Queries* 12 (July 1965): 275.

Hollahan, Eugene. "Running in Circles: A Major Motif in *Lord of the Flies.*" *Studies in the Novel* 2 (Spring 1970): 22–30.

Kearns, Francis E. "Salinger and Golding: Conflict on the Campus." *America* (January 26, 1963): 136–139.

Kvam, Ragnar. "William Golding." *Vinduet* 13 (Autumn 1959): 292–298.

Lederer, Richard H. "Student Reactions to *Lord of the Flies.*" *English Journal* 53 (November 1964): 575–579.

Leed, Jacob. "Golding's *Lord of the Flies,* Chapter 7." *Explicator* 24 (September 1965): Item 8.

Levitt, Leon. "Trust the Tale: A Second Reading of *Lord of the Flies.*" *English Journal* 58 (April 1969): 521–522.

McCullen, Maurice L. "*Lord of the Flies:* The Critical Quest." In *William Golding,* 203–231.

MacLure, Millar. "Allegories of Innocence." *Dalhousie Review* 40 (Summer 1960): 145–156.

MacShane, Frank. "The Novels of William Golding." *Dalhousie Review* 42 (Summer 1962): 171–183.

Manheim, Leonard Falk, and Eleanor B. Manheim. *Hidden Patterns: Studies in Psychoanalytic Literary Criticism.* New York: Macmillan, 1966, pp. 259–274.

Michel-Michot, Paulette. "The Myth of Innocence." *Revue des Langues Vivantes* 28, no. 6 (1962): 510–520.

Mitchell, Charles. "The *Lord of the Flies* and the Escape from Freedom." *Arizona Quarterly* 22 (Spring 1966): 27–40.

Mitchell, Juliet. "Concepts and Technique in William Golding." *New Left Review* no. 15 (May-June 1962): 63–71.

Morgan, George. "Le Symbolisme du Paysage dans *Lord of the Flies.*" *Annales de la Faculté des Lettres et Sciences Humaines de Nice* 18 (1972): 77–96.

Mueller, William R. "An Old Story Well Told." *Christian Century* 80 (October 2, 1963): 1,203–1,206.

Niemeyer, Carl. "The Coral Island Revisited." *College English* 22 (January 1961): 241–245.

O'Hara, J. D. "Mute Choirboys and Angelic Pigs: The Fable in *Lord of the Flies.*" *Texas Studies in Literature and Language* 7 (Winter 1966): 411–420.

Oldsey, Bern, and Stanley Weintraub. "*Lord of the Flies:* Beezlebub Revisited." *College English* 25 (November 1963): 90–99.

Oliphant, Robert. "Public Voices and Wise Guys." *Virginia Quarterly Review* 37 (Autumn 1961): 522–537.

Oppel, Horst. *Der Moderne Englische Roman: Interpretationen.* Berlin: E. Schmidt, 1965, pp. 328–343.

Page, Norman. "*Lord of the Flies.*" *Use of English* 16 (Autumn 1964): 44–45, 57.

Rosenberg, Bruce A. "Lord of the Fire-Flies." *Centennial Review* 11 (Winter 1967): 128–139.

Rosenfield, Chaire. " 'Men of a Smaller Growth': A Psychological Analysis of William Golding's *Lord of the Flies.*" *Literature and Psychology* 11 (Autumn 1961): 93–101.

Selby, Keith. "Golding's *Lord of the Flies.*" *Explicator* 41 (Spring 1983): 57–59.

Shannon, Jean. "A Comment on *Lord of the Flies.*" *Crux* 4, no. 2 (1970): 30–34.

Smith, Eric. *Some Versions of the Fall: The Myth of the Fall of Man in English Literature.* London: Croom Helm, 1973, pp. 163–202.

Sternlicht, Sanford. "Songs of Innocence and Songs of Experience in *Lord of the Flies* and *The Inheritors.*" *Midwest Quarterly* 9 (July 1968): 383–390.

———. "A Source for Golding's *Lord of the Flies:* Peter Pan?" *English Record* 14 (December 1963): 41–42.

Talon, Henri. "Irony in *Lord of the Flies.*" *Essays in Criticism* 18 (July 1968): 296–309.

Taylor, Harry H. "The Case Against William Golding's Simon-Piggy." *Contemporary Review* 209 (September 1966): 155–160.

Thomas, W. K. "The Lessons of Myth in *Lord of the Flies.*" *Cithara* 16, no. 2 (1977): 33–56.

Thomson, George H. "The Real World of William Golding." *Alphabet* 9 (November 1964): 26–33.

Thumboo, Edwin. "Golding's *Lord of the Flies:* Topography, Character and Theme." *Literary Criterion* 13, no. 3 (1978): 6–17.

Tiger, Virginia. *William Golding.* London: Calder & Boyars, 1974, pp. 38–67.

Townsend, R. C. "*Lord of the Flies:* Fool's Gold?" *Journal of General Education* 16 (July 1964): 153–160.

Trilling. Lionel. "*Lord of the Flies.*" *Mid-Century* no. 45 (October 1962): 10–12.

Veidemanis, Gladys. "*Lord of the Flies* in the Classroom—No Passing Fad." *English Journal* 53 (November 1964): 569–574.

Walters, Margaret. "Two Fabulists: Golding and Camus." *Melbourne Critical Review* 4 (1961): 18–29.

White, Robert J. "Butterfly and Beast in *Lord of the Flies.*" *Modern Fiction Studies* 10 (Summer 1964): 163–170.

Woodward, Kathleen. "On Aggression: William Golding's *Lord of the Flies.*" In *No Place Else,* 199–224.

GOLDSMITH, OLIVER

The Proceedings of Providence Vindicated

Hopkins, Robert H. *The True Genius of Oliver Goldsmith.* Baltimore: Johns Hopkins Press, 1969, pp. 127–128.

Quintana, Ricardo. *Oliver Goldsmith: A Georgian Study.* London: Weidenfeld and Nicolson, 1967, pp. 61–62.

GORDON, REX

Utopia Minus X

Berger, Harold L. *Science Fiction and the New Dark Age,* 72–75, 77.

GOTT, SAMUEL

Nova Solyma, the Ideal City

Berneri, Marie Louise. *Journey Through Utopia,* 104.

Bloomfield, Paul. *Imaginary- Worlds, or the Evolution of Utopia,* 99–109.

Davis, J. C. *Utopia and the Ideal Society,* 139–168.

Eurich, Nell. *Science in Utopia,* 83–86.

Masso, Gildo. *Education in Utopias,* 62, 66, 72–73, 83.

GRAVES, ROBERT

Watch the North Wind Rise

Elliot, Robert C. *The Shape of Utopia,* 106, 117–119, 124–125.

Seymour-Smith, Martin. *Robert Graves.* London: Hutchinson, 1982, pp. 418–419, 421–423.

Snipes, Katherine. *Robert Graves.* New York: Ungar, 1979, pp. 69–79.

GRIFFIN, CRAWFORD S.

Nationalism

Rooney, Charles J., Jr. *Dreams and Visions,* 33, 188–189.

GRIFFITH, MARY

"Three Hundred Years Hence"

Adkins, Nelson F. "An Early American Story of Utopia." *Colophon* n.s. 1 (Summer 1935): 123–132.

Albinski, Nan Bowman. *Women's Utopias in British and American Fiction,* 72.

Nydahl, Joel. Introduction. *An Experiment in Marriage,* xviii-xix.

GRIGSBY, ALCANOAN O.

Nequa

Parrington, Vernon Louis, Jr. *American Dreams,* 98–102, 177–178.

Rooney, Charles J., Jr. *Dreams and Visions,* 70, 157, 189.

GRIMMELSHAUSEN, HANS JAKOB CHRISTOFFEL VON

Der Abenteuerliche Simplicissimus Teutsch

Aylett, R. P. T. *The Nature of Realism in Grimmelshausen's Simplicissimus Cycle of Novels.* Berne: Peter Lang, 1982, pp. 38–84.

Meid, Volker. "Utopie und Satire in Grimmelshausens *Simplicissimus.*" In *Utopieforschung,* Volume 2, 249–265.

GRONLUND, LAURENCE

General Criticism

Gemorah, Solomon. "Laurence Gronlund—Utopian Reformer." *Science and Society* 33 (1969): 446–458.

Spann, E. K. *Brotherly Tomorrows,* 176–190.

The Cooperative Commonwealth in its Outlines

Conkin, Paul K. "Three Authors, Three Books, and Three Colonies: The Cooperative Commonwealth in America." In *France and North America,* 33–44.

Rideout, Walter B. *The Radical Novel in the United States, 1900–1954,* 7.

GUEVARA, ANTONIO DE

Libro Aureo de Marco Aurelio

Jones, Joseph. *Antonio de Guevara.* Boston: Twayne, 1975, pp. 27–52.

HAGGARD, HENRY RIDER

She

Crawford, Claudia. "*She.*" *Sub-Stance* 29 (1981): 83–96.

Etherington, Norman. *Rider Haggard.* Boston: Twayne, 1984, pp. 9–10, 46–47, 77–81, 86–90.

Gilbert, Sandra M. "Rider Haggard's Heart of Darkness." In *Coordinates,* 124–138.

Gubar, Susan. "*She* and *Herland:* Feminism as Fantasy." In *Coordinates,* 139–149.

Hinz, Evelyn. "Rider Haggard's *She:* An Archetypal 'History of Adventure.'" *Studies in the Novel* 4 (Fall 1972): 416–431.

[Oliphant, Margaret]. "The Old Saloon: *She:* A History of Adventure." *Blackwood's Edinburgh Magazine* 141 (February 1887): 101–105.

Shanks, Edward. "Sir Rider Haggard and the Novel of Adventure." *London Mercury* 2, no. 61 (November 1924): 71–79.

HALDEMAN, JOE

The Forever War

Gordon, Joan. *Joe Haldeman.* Mercer Island, WA: Starmont House, 1980, pp. 25–35.

Zaki, Hoda M. *Phoenix Renewed,* 65.

HALE, EDWARD EVERETT

Sybaris and Other Homes

Adams, John R. *Edward Everett Hale,* 48–52.

Holloway, Jean. *Edward Everett Hale: A Biography.* Austin: University of Texas Press, 1956, pp. 170–173.

Parrington, Vernon Louis, Jr. *American Dreams,* 44–46.

10 × 1 Equals 10

Adams, John R. *Edward Everett Hale,* 57, 59–61.

HALL, JOSEPH

Mundus Alter et Idem

Brown, Huntington. Introduction. *The Discovery of a New World.* By Joseph Hall. Cambridge, MA: Harvard University Press, 1937, xv–xxxv.

Eurich, Nell. *Science in Utopia,* 82–84.

McCabe, Richard A. *Joseph Hall: A Study in Satire and Meditation.* Oxford: Clarendon Press, 1982, pp. 73–109, 321–339.

Salyer, Sanford M. "Renaissance Influence in Hall's *Mundus Alter et Idem.*" *Philological Quarterly* 6 (October 1927): 321–334.

Tourney, Leonard D. *Joseph Hall.* Boston: Twayne, 1979, pp. 37–42.

Wands, John M. "Antipodal Imperfection: Hall's *Mundus Alter et Idem* and Its Debt to More's *Utopia.*" *Moreana* 18 (March 1981): 85–100.

HALL, SANDI

The Godmothers

Thomas, Elizabeth. "Inventing Futures: A Notable Trend in Recent New Zealand Women's Fiction." *SPAN: Newsletter of the South Pacific Association for Commonwealth Literature and Language Studies* 24 (April 1987): 122–135.

HARBEN, WILLIAM

The Land of the Changing Sun

Murphy, James K. *Will N. Harben.* Boston: Twayne, 1979, pp. 44–46.

HARRINGTON, JAMES

The Commonwealth of Oceana

Berneri, Marie Louise. *Journey Through Utopia,* 143–145.

Blitzer, Charles. *An Immortal Commonwealth: The Political Thought of James Harrington.* New Haven, CT: Yale University Press, 1960, pp. 205–274.

Borot, Luc. "Hobbes, Harrington, and the Concept of Liberty." *Cahiers Elisabethains* 32 (October 1987): 49–67.

Davis, J. C. *Utopia and the Ideal Society,* 205–276.

Hertzler, Joyce Oramel. *The History of Utopian Thought,* 165–177.

Holstun, James. "Puritan Utopias of the Interregnum." Ph.D. diss., University of California, Irvine, 1983.

Laidler, Harry Wellington. *Social-Economic Movements,* 38–43.

Liljegren, S. B. "Harrington and Leibnitz." In *Studies in English Philology: A Miscellany in Honor of Frederick Klaeber,* edited by K. Malone and M. B. Ruud, 414–426. Minneapolis: University of Minnesota Press, 1929.

Mumford, Lewis. *The Story of Utopias,* 134.

Ross, Harry. *Utopias Old and New,* 82–90.

Steinmetz, Willibald. "Utopie oder Staatsplanung? James Harringtons *Oceana.*" In *Literarische Utopien von Morus bis zur Gegenwart,* 59–72.

HARRIS, FRANK

Pantopia

Pearsall, Robert Brainard. *Frank Harris.* New York: Twayne, 1970, pp. 170–173.

HARRIS, THOMAS LAKE

The New Republic

Parrington, Vernon Louis, Jr. *American Dreams,* 161, 163–165.

HARTLEY, L. P.

Facial Justice

Walsh, Chad. *From Utopia to Nightmare,* 136.

HAUPTMANN, GERHART

Island of the Great Mother

Heuser, Frederick. "The Mystical Hauptmann." *Germanic Review* 7 (January 1932): 33–44.

Maurer, Warren R. *Gerhart Hauptmann.* Boston: Twayne, 1982, p. 132.

Mellen, Philip A. *Gerhart Hauptmann and Utopia.* Stuttgart: Akademischer Verlag Heinz, 1976.

Steinhauer, H. "Hauptmann's Utopian Fantasy, *Die Insel der Grossen Mutter.*" *Modern Language Notes* 53 (November 1938): 516–521.

HAWTHORNE, NATHANIEL

The Blithedale Romance

Abel, Darrel. "Hawthorne's Skepticism about Social Reform with Especial Reference to *The Blithedale Romance.*" *University of Kansas City Review* 19 (1953): 181–193.

Bauer, Dale M. *Feminist Dialogics: A Theory of Failed Community.* Albany: State University of New York Press, 1988, 17–50.

Baym, Nina. "*The Blithedale Romance:* A Radical Reading." *Journal of English and Germanic Philology* 67 (October 1968): 545–569.

Berlant, Lauren. "Fantasies of Utopia in *The Blithedale Romance.*" *American Literary History* 1 (Spring 1989): 30–62.

Brown, John L. "The Life of Paradise Anew." In *France and North America,* 71–81.

Christophersen, Bill. "Behind the White Veil: Self-Awareness in Hawthorne's *The Blithedale Romance.*" *Modern Language Studies* 12 (Spring 1982): 81–92.

Crews, Frederick C. "A New Reading of *The Blithedale Romance.*" *American Literature* 29 (May 1957): 147–170.

———. *The Sins of the Fathers: Hawthorne's Psychological Themes.* New York: Oxford University Press, 1966, pp. 194–212.

———. "Turning the Affair into a Ballad: *The Blithedale Romance.*" In *Nathaniel Hawthorne,* edited by J. Donald Crowley, 87–100. New York: McGraw-Hill, 1975.

Davidson, Frank. "Toward a Re-evaluation of *The Blithedale Romance.*" *New England Quarterly* 25 (September 1952): 374–383.

Draxlbauer, Michael. "Utopia 'Re-remembered': Nathaniel Hawthorne's Brook Farm Romance." In *Utopian Thought in American Literature,* 43–68.

Dryden, Edgar A. *Nathaniel Hawthorne: The Poetics of Enchantment.* Ithaca, NY: Cornell University Press, 1977, pp. 72–75, 93–107.

Elliott, Robert C. *The Shape of Utopia,* 68–83.

Fogle, Richard Harter. *Hawthorne's Imagery.* Norman: University of Oklahoma Press, 1969, pp. 92–124.

Folsom, James K. *Man's Accidents and God's Purposes: Multiplicity in Hawthorne's Fiction.* New Haven, CT: Yale University Press, 1963, pp. 139–141, 147–151.

Gordon, Joseph T. "Nathaniel Hawthorne and Brook Farm." *Emerson Society Quarterly* 33 (1963): 51–61.

Griffith, Kelley, Jr. "Form in *The Blithedale Romance.*" *American Literature* 40 (March 1968): 15–26.

Hedges, William L. "Hawthorne's *Blithedale:* The Function of the Narrator." *Nineteenth-Century Fiction* 14 (March 1960): 303–316.

Hoffman, Daniel G. *Form and Fable in American Fiction.* New York: Oxford University Press, 1961, pp. 202–218.

Howe, Irving. *Politics and the Novel.* New York: Horizon Press, 1957, pp. 163–175.

Jacobs, Naomi. "Substance and Reality in Hawthorne's Meta-Utopia." *Utopian Studies* 1 (1987): 173–187.

Kaul, A. N. *The American Vision: Actual and Ideal Society in Nineteenth-Century Fiction.* New Haven, CT: Yale University Press, 1963, pp. 196–213.

———. "*The Blithedale Romance.*" In *Hawthorne: A Collection of Critical Essays,* edited by A. N. Kaul, 153–163. Englewood Cliffs, NJ: Prentice-Hall, 1966.

Lefcowitz, Allan. "Some Rents in the Veil: New Lights on Priscilla and Zenobia in *The Blithedale Romance.*" *Nineteenth-Century Fiction* 21 (December 1966): 263–275.

Levy, Leo. "*The Blithedale Romance:* Hawthorne's 'Voyage through Chaos.' " *Studies in Romanticism* 8 (Autumn 1968): 1–15.

Male, Roy R. "Hawthorne's Tragic Vision." Austin: University of Texas Press, 1957, pp. 139–156.

————. "Toward the Waste Land: The Theme of *The Blithedale Romance.*" *College English* 16 (February 1955): 277–283.

Murray, Peter B. "Mythopoesis in *The Blithedale Romance.*" *PMLA* 75 (December 1960): 591–596.

O'Hara, Michael Alan. "Utopian Community and Satiric Structure in *The Blithedale Romance:* Hawthorne's Alternatives to Alienation." Ph.D. diss., University of California, San Diego, 1980.

Parrington, Vernon Louis, Jr. *American Dreams.* pp. 38–40.

Poirier, Richard. *A World Elsewhere: The Place of Style in American Literature.* New York: Oxford University Press, 1966, pp. 93–143.

Ragan, James F. "The Irony in Hawthorne's *Blithedale.*" *New England Quarterly* 35 (June 1962): 239–246.

Sanford, Charles L. *The Quest for Paradise,* 182–184.

Schweninger, Lee. " 'In the Middest of that Paradise': Structure and Theme in *The Blithedale Romance.*" *Markham Review* 16 (Fall-Winter 1986): 11–16.

Smith, Julian. "Why does Zenobia Kill Herself." *English Language Notes* 6 (September 1968): 37–39.

Stanton, Robert. "The Trial of Nature: An Analysis of *The Blithedale Romance.*" *PMLA* 76 (December 1961): 528–538.

Stewart, Randall. *Regionalism and Beyond: Essays of Randall Stewart,* edited by George Core. Nashville, Tennessee: Vanderbilt University Press, 1968, pp. 34–44.

Tharpe, Jac. *Nathaniel Hawthorne: Identity and Knowledge.* Carbondale, IL: Southern Illinois University Press, 1967, pp. 40–46, 125–133.

Waggoner, Hyatt Howe. *Hawthorne: A Critical Study.* Cambridge, MA: Harvard University Press, 1963, pp. 175–194.

Wright, Dorena Allen. "Hawthorne's *Blithedale Romance.*" *Explicator* 41 (Summer 1983): 28–29.

HAYWOOD, ELIZA

The Memoirs of a Certain Island Adjacent to the Kingdom of Utopia

Schofield, Mary Anne. *Eliza Haywood.* Boston: Twayne, 1985, pp. 7, 59–60.

————. *Quiet Rebellion: The Fictional Heroines of Eliza Fowler Haywood.* Washington, DC: University Press of America, 1982, pp. 78–81.

HENRY, WALTER O.

Equitania

Rooney, Charles J., Jr. *Dreams and Visions,* 73, 128, 190.

HERTZKA, THEODOR

Freeland

Bailey, J. O. *Pilgrims Through Space and Time,* 57.

Berneri, Marie Louise. *Journey Through Utopia,* 294–296.

Bloomfield, Paul. *Imaginary Worlds, or the Evolution of Utopia,* 179–197.

Hertzler, Joyce Oramel. *The History of Utopian Thought,* 227–236.

Mumford, Lewis. *The Story of Utopias,* 138–147.

Ross, Harry. *Utopias Old and New,* 159–175.

Walsh, Chad. *From Utopia to Nightmare,* 51–52.

Westmeyer, R. E. *Modern Economic and Social Systems,* 78–93.

HERZL, THEODORE

Old-Newland

Adler, Joseph. *The Herzl Paradox: Political, Social, and Economic Theories of a Realist.* New York: Hadrian Press, 1962, pp. 99–117.

Bein, Alex. *Theodore Herzl: A Biography.* Translated by Maurice Samuel. Cleveland, OH: Meridian Books, 1962, pp. 394–410.

Chouraqui, Andre. *A Man Alone: The Life of Theodor Herzl.* Jerusalem: Keter Books, 1970, pp. 175–182.

Cohen, Israel. *Theodore Herzl: Founder of Political Zionism.* New York: Thomas Yoseloff, 1959, pp. 280–284.

Elon, Amon. *Herzl.* New York: Holt, Rinehart and Winston, 1975, pp. 347–351.

Frankl, Oscar Benjamin. *Theodor Herzl: The Jew and the Man.* New York: Storm Publishing, 1949, p. 182.

Hadomi, Leah. "*Altneuland:* Ein Utopischer Roman." In *Juden in der Deutschen Literatur: Ein Deutschisraelisches Symposion,* edited by Stephane Moses and Albrecht Schone, 210–225. Frankfort: Suhrkamp, 1986.

HESSE, HERMANN

The Glass Bead Game

Bandy, Stephen C. "Hermann Hesse's *Das Glasperlenspiel* in Search of Joseph Knecht." *Modern Language Quarterly* 33 (September 1972): 299–311.

Baumer, Franz. *Hermann Hesse.* New York: Ungar, 1970, pp. 84–88, 106–113.

Boa, Elizabeth, and J. H. Reid. *Critical Strategies: German Fiction in the Twentieth Century.* London: Edward Arnold, 1972, pp. 28–34.

Boulby, Mark. " 'Der Vierte Lebenslauf' as a Key to *Das Glasperlenspiel.*" *Modern Language Review* 61 (October 1966): 635–646.

————. *Hermann Hesse: His Mind and Art.* Ithaca, NY: Cornell University Press, 1967, pp. 260–321.

Butler, Colin. "Literary Malpractice in Some Works of Hermann Hesse." *University of Toronto Quarterly* 40 (Winter 1971): 177–180.

Casebeer, Edwin F. *Hermann Hesse.* New York: Crowell, 1972, pp. 141–189.

Cohn, Hilde D. "The Symbolic End of Hermann Hesse's *Glasperlenspiel.*" *Modern Language Quarterly* 11 (September 1950): 347–357.

Colby, Thomas E. "The Impenitent Prodigal: Hermann Hesse's Hero." *German Quartely* 40 (January 1967): 14–23.

Curtius, Ernst Robert. "Hermann Hesse." In *Hesse: A Collection of Critical Essays,* edited by Theodore Ziolkowski, 46–50. Englewood Cliffs, NJ: Prentice-Hall, 1973.

Field, George Wallis. *Hermann Hesse.* New York: Twayne, 1970, pp. 142–172.

————. "Hermann Hesse: Polarities and Symbols of Synthesis." *Queen's Quarterly* 81 (Spring 1974): 96–100.

————. "Music and Morality in Thomas Mann and Hermann Hesse." *University of Toronto Quarterly* 24 (January 1955): 182–189.

————. "On the Genesis of the *Glasperlenspiel.*" *German Quarterly* 41 (November 1968): 673–688.

Freedman, Ralph. *The Lyrical Novel: Studies in Hermann Hesse, André Gide and Virginia Woolf.* Princeton, NJ: Princeton University Press, 1963, pp. 96–114.

————. "Romantic Imagination: Hermann Hesse as a Modern Novelist." *PMLA* 73 (June 1958): 275–284.

Friedrichsmeyer, Erhard. "The Bertram Episode in Hesse's *Glass Bead Game.*" *Germanic Review* 49 (November 1974): 284–297.

Goldgar, Harry. "Hesse's *Glasperlenspiel* and the Game of Go." *German Life and Letters* 20 (January 1967): 132–137.

Gotz, Ignacio L. "Platonic Parallels in [Hesse's] *Das Glasperlenspiel.*" *German Quarterly* 51 (November 1978): 511–519.

Klawitzer, R. J. "The Artist-Intellectual, in or versus Society? A Dilemma." In *Studies in German Literature of the Nineteenth and Twentieth Centuries,* edited by Siegfried Mews, 236–250. Chapel Hill: University of North Carolina Press, 1971.

Koester, Rudolf. "Hesse's Music Master: In Search of a Prototype." *Forum for Modern Language Studies* 3 (April 1967): 135–141.

———. "The Portrayal of Age in Hesse's Narrative Prose." *Germanic Review* 41 (March 1966): 113–116.

Middleton, J. C. "An Enigma Transfigured in Hermann Hesse's *Glasperlenspiel.*" *German Life and Letters* 10 (July 1957): 298–302.

Mileck, Joseph. "*Das Glasperlenspiel.*" In *Hesse Companion,* edited by Anna Otten, 189–221. Frankfurt: Suhrkamp, 1970.

———. *Hermann Hesse: Life and Art.* Berkeley: University of California Press, 1978, pp. 310–313, 333–335.

———. "Hermann Hesse's *Glasperlenspiel.*" *University of California Publications in Modern Philology* 36 (October 1952): 243–270.

Naumann, Walter. "The Individual and Society in the Work of Hermann Hesse." *Monatshefte* 41 (January 1949): 33–42.

Negus, Kenneth. "On the Death of Josef Knecht in Hermann Hesse's *Glasperlenspiel.*" *Monatshefte* 53 (February 1961): 181–189.

Norton, Roger C. "Hermann Hesse's Criticism of Technology." *Germanic Review* 43 (November 1968): 267–273.

———. "Variant Endings of Hesse's *Glasperlenspiel.*" *Monatshefte* 60 (Summer 1968): 141–146.

Pavlyshyn, Marko. "Games with Utopia: Hermann Hesse's *Das Glasperlenspiel.*" In *Just the Other Day,* 339–354.

———. "Music in Hermann Hesse's *Der Steppenwolf* and *Das Glasperlenspiel.*" *Seminar* 15 (February 1979): 39–55.

Peppard, Murray B. "Hermann Hesse: From Eastern Journey to Castalia." *Monatshefte* 50 (October 1958): 247–255.

————. "Hermann Hesse's Ladder of Learning." *Kentucky Foreign Language Quarterly* 3 (1956): 13–20.

Reichert, Herbert W. *The Impact of Nietzche on Hermann Hesse.* Mt. Pleasant, MI: Enigma Press, 1972, pp. 76–86.

Rose, Ernst. *Faith from the Abyss: Hermann Hesse's Way from Romanticism to Modernity.* New York: New York University Press, 1965, pp. 124–141.

Schneider, Christian J. "Hermann Hesse's *Glasperlenspiel.*" In *Hesse Companion,* edited by Anna Otten, 222–259. Frankfurt: Suhrkamp, 1970.

Seidlin, Oskar. "H. Hesse's *Glasperlenspiel.*" *Germanic Review* 23 (1948): 263–273.

Stern, J. P. "A Game of Utopia." *German Life and Letters* 34 (October 1980): 94–107.

Swales, M. *The German Bildungsroman from Wieland to Hesse.* Princeton, NJ: Princeton University Press, 1978, pp. 129–145.

Taylor, Harley U. "The Death Wish and Suicide in the Novels of Hermann Hesse." *West Virginia University Philological Papers* 13 (December 1961): 62–64.

Townsend, Stanley R. "The German Humanist Hermann Hesse." *Modern Language Forum* 32 (March-June 1947): 1–12.

Verma, K. D. "The Quest for the Ideal in Hermann Hesse's *Magister Ludi.*" *South Asian Review* 11–12 (July 1988): 26–40.

Vordtriede, Werner. "Hermann Hesse: *Das Glasperlenspiel.*" *German Quarterly* 19 (1946): 291–294.

Waidson, H. M. "Prose Fiction: Some Outstanding German Novels." In *Twentieth Century German Literature,* edited by August Closs, 118–122. New York: Barnes & Noble, 1969.

Willson, A. Leslie. "Hesse's Veil of Isis." *Monatshefte* 55 (November 1963): 318–321.

Wood, Carl. "Hesse's Literary Glass Bead Game: The Unity of *Das Glasperlenspiel.*" *Far-Western Forum* 1 (February 1974): 95–108.

Zeller, Bernhard. *Portrait of Hesse: An Illustrated Biography.* New York: Herder and Herder, 1971, pp. 134–157.

Ziolkowski, Theodore. "Hermann Hesse: 'Der Vierte Lubenslauf'." *Germanic Review* 42 (March 1967): 124–143.

————. *The Novels of Hermann Hesse: A Study in Theme and Structure.* Princeton, NJ: Princeton University Press, 1965, pp. 283–338.

HEYWOOD, D. HERBERT

The Twentieth Century, A Prophesy of the Coming Age

Rooney, Charles J., Jr. *Dreams and Visions,* 97–98, 190.

HILTON, JAMES

Lost Horizon

Crawford, John W. "The Utopian Dream, Alive and Well." *Cuyahoga Review* 2 (Spring-Summer 1984): 27–33.

Dangerfield, George. "James Hilton's Fantasy." *Saturday Review of Literature* 10 (October 14, 1933): 181.

————. "Utopia in Tibet." *New York Times Book Review* (October 15, 1933): 8–9.

Heck, Francis S. "The Domain as a Symbol of a Paradise Lost: *Lost Horizon* and *Brideshead Revisited.*" *Nassau Review* 4, no. 3 (1982): 24–29.

Parrington, Vernon Louis, Jr. *American Dreams,* 206–208.

Van Eeden, Janet. "The Monastery Months." *Crux: A Journal on the Teaching of English* 21 (February 1987): 22–25.

HOLFORD, COSTELLO N.

Aristopia

Rooney, Charles J., Jr. *Dreams and Visions,* 113, 149, 190.

HOLTBY, WINIFRED

The Astonishing Island

Albinski, Nan Bowman. "Thomas and Peter: Society and Politics in Four British Utopian Novels." *Utopian Studies* 1 (1987): 11–22.

———. *Women's Utopias in British and American Fiction,* 78, 83, 84, 104.

Kennard, Jean. *Vera Brittain & Winifred Holtby: A Working Partnership.* Hanover: University Press of New England, 1989, pp. 122–124.

HOUSE, EDWARD MANDELL

Philip Dru: Administrator

Parrington, Vernon Louis, Jr. *American Dreams,* 187–191.

Smith, Arthur D. *Mr. House of Texas.* New York: Funk & Wagnalls, 1940, pp. 23, 49–50, 369–370.

HOWARD, ALBERT

The Milltillionaire

Parrington, Vernon Louis, Jr. *American Dreams,* 114–115.

Rooney, Charles J., Jr. *Dreams and Visions,* 68, 128, 191.

HOWARD, EBENEZER

Garden Cities of To-Morrow

Fishman, Robert. *Urban Utopias in the Twentieth Century.* New York: Basic Books, 1977, pp. 23–88.

Mumford, Lewis. "The Garden City Idea and Modern Planning." *Garden Cities of To-morrow,* 29–40.

Osborn, F. J. Preface. *Garden Cities of To-morrow,* 9–28.

HOWELLS, WILLIAM DEAN

General Criticism

Hough, Robert L. *The Quiet Rebel: William Dean Howells as Social Commentator.* Lincoln, NE: University of Nebraska Press, 1959.

Kirk, Clara. *W. D. Howells, Traveler from Altruria, 1889–1894.* New Brunswick, NJ: Rutgers University Press, 1962.

Kirk, Clara, and Rudolf Kirk. *William Dean Howells.* New York: Twayne, 1962.

Pratter, Frederick E. "The Mysterious Traveler in the Speculative Fiction of Howells and Twain." In *America as Utopia,* 78–90.

Through the Eye of the Needle

Parrington, Vernon Louis, Jr. *American Dreams,* 173–175.

Pfaelzer, Jean. *The Utopian Novel in America, 1886–1896,* 64–69.

A Traveler From Altruria

Aaron, Daniel. *Men of Good Hope,* 172–207.

Bailey, J. O. *Pilgrims Through Space and Time,* 57–58.

Conkin, Paul K. "Three Authors, Three Books, and Three Colonies: The Cooperative Commonwealth in America." In *France and North America,* 33–44.

Cooke, Delmar Gross. *William Dean Howells: A Critical Study.* New York: Russell & Russell, 1967, pp. 234–236.

Cooperman, Stanley. "Utopian Realism: The Futurist Novels of Bellamy and Howells." *College English* 24 (March 1963): 464–467.

Dowst, Kenneth. " 'Commonplaces' in Utopian Fiction." *Journal of General Eduction* 33 (Spring 1981): 58–68.

Eble, Kenneth E. *William Dean Howells.* Second edition. Boston: Twayne, 1982, pp. 118–122.

Firkins, Oscar W. *William Dean Howells: A Study.* Cambridge, MA: Harvard University Press, 1924, pp. 153–156.

Kirk, Clara. *W. D. Howells: And Art in His Time.* New Brunswick, NJ: Rutgers University Press, 1965, pp. 185–196.

Krauth, Leland. "The Mysterious Stranger of William Dean Howells." *Ball State University Forum* 24 (Winter 1983): 30–37.

Nettels, Elsa. "Howells and Mazzini: The Ideal Commonwealth." *Markham Review* 14 (Fall–Winter 1984–1985): 1–7.

Parrington, Vernon Louis, Jr. *American Dreams,* 170–173.

Pfaelzer, Jean. *The Utopian Novel in America, 1886–1896,* 52–77.

Schweninger, Lee. "The Building of the City Beautiful: The Motif of the Jeremiad in Three Utopian Novels." *American Literary Realism* 18 (Spring 1985): 107–119.

Trimmer, Joseph F. "American Dreams: A Comparative Study of the Utopian Novels of Bellamy and Howells." *Ball State University Forum* 12, no. 3 (1971): 13–21.

Uba, George R. "Howells and the Practicable Utopia: The Allegorical Structure of the Altrurian Romances." *Journal of Narrative Technique* 13 (Fall 1983): 118–130.

Underwood, John C. *Literature and Insurgency.* New York: M. Kennerley, 1914, pp. 87–129.

HOWLAND, MARIE

Papa's Own Girl

Albinski, Nan Bowman. *Women's Utopias in British and American Fiction*, 48, 52, 54, 55, 59, 62, 63, 65, 72.

Kessler, Carol Farley. "The Grand Marital Revolution: Two Feminist Utopias." In *Feminism, Utopia, and Narrative*, 70, 72–76.

HUDSON, WILLIAM HENRY

General Criticism

Nicholson, Mervin. " 'What We See We Feel': The Imaginative World of W. H. Hudson." *University of Toronto Quarterly* 47 (1978): 304–322.

A Crystal Age

Bailey, J. O. *Pilgrims Through Space and Time*, 55–56.

Frederick, John T. *William Henry Hudson*, 40–45.

Garrett, J. C. *Utopias in Literature Since the Romantic Period*, 40.

Jofre Barroso, Haydee M. *Genio y Figura de Guillermo Enrique Hudson*. Buenos Aires: Editorial Universitaria, 1972, pp. 71–74, 186–187.

Jurado, Alicia. *Vida y Obra de W. H. Hudson*. Buenos Aires: Fondo Nacional de las Artes, 1971, pp. 99–104.

Morton, Peter. "Tracing a Theme in W. H. Hudson's *A Crystal Age*." *English Language Notes* 25 (June 1988): 61–65.

———. *The Vital Science: Biology and the Literary Imagination, 1860–1900*. London: Allen & Unwin, 1984, 70–80.

Mumford, Lewis. *The Story of Utopias*, 173–177.

Payne, John R. "W. H. Hudson's *A Crystal Age*." *Papers of the Bibliographical Society of America* 65 (1971): 299–302.

Ross, Harry. *Utopias Old and New,* 94–100.

Green Mansions

Alcorn, John. *The Nature Novel from Hardy to Lawrence,* 68–72.

Baker, Carlos H. "The Source Book for Hudson's *Green Mansions.*" *PMLA* 61 (March 1946): 252–257.

Conrad, Joseph. *Last Essays.* Garden City, NY: Doubleday, Page & Co., 1926, pp. 132–137.

Curle, Richard. "W. H. Hudson." *Fortnightly Review* 118 (October 1922): 602–619.

Fairchild, Hoxie. "Rima's Mother." *PMLA* 68 (June 1953): 365–370.

Fletcher, J. V. "The Creator of Rima, W. H. Hudson: A Belated Romantic." *Sewanee Review* 41 (January 1933): 24–40.

Ford, Ford Madox. "William Henry Hudson: Some Reminiscences." *Little Review* 7 (May-June 1920): 1–12.

Frederick, John T. *William Henry Hudson,* 51–57, 105–106.

Gilkes, Michael. *The West Indian Novel.* Boston: Twayne, 1981, pp. 132–142.

Goddard, Harold. *W. H. Hudson, Bird-Man.* New York: Dutton, 1928.

Hamilton, Robert. "The Spirit of W. H. Hudson: An Evaluation." *Quarterly Review* 275 (October 1940): 239–248.

———. *W. H. Hudson: The Vision of Earth.* Port Washington, NY: Kennikat, 1970.

Harper, George McLean. "Harry, Hudson, Housman." *Scribner's Magazine* 73 (1925): 86–99.

Haymaker, Richard E. *From Pampas to Hedgerows and Down: A Study of W. H. Hudson.* New York: Bookman, 1954.

Landry, Rudolph J. "The Source of the Name 'Rima' in *Green Mansions.*" *Notes and Queries* 3 (December 1956): 545–546.

Rhys, Ernest. "W. H. Hudson, Rare Traveller." *Nineteenth Century* 88 (July 1920): 72–78.

Roberts, Morley. *W. H. Hudson: A Portrait.* London: Dutton, 1924.

Rodker, John. "W. H. Hudson." *Little Review* 7 (May–June 1920): 18–28.

Shrubsall, Dennis. *W. H. Hudson: Writer and Naturalist.* Tisbury, Wiltshire: Compton Press, 1978, pp. 63–64.

Tomalin, Ruth. *W. H. Hudson.* New York: Greenwood Press, 1969.

HUXLEY, ALDOUS

General Criticism

Borinski, Ludwig. "Wells, Huxley und die Utopia." In *Literatur-Kultur-Gesellschaft in England und Amerika: Aspekte und Forschungsbeitrage Friedrich Schubel zum 60. Geburtstag,* edited by G. Muller-Schwefe and K. Tuzinski, 257–277. Frankfurt: Diesterweg, 1966.

Browning, Gordon. "Anti-Utopian Fiction: Definition and Standards of Evaluation." Ph.D. diss., Louisiana State University, 1966.

Dunn, Thomas P., and Richard D. Erlich. "A Vision of Dystopia: Beehives and Mechanization." *Journal of General Education* 33 (Spring 1981): 45–57.

Krause, Gerd. "Die Kulturkrise in der Utopia Aldous Huxleys." In *Die Utopia in der Moderen Englischen Literatur,* by Ludwig Borinski and Gerd Krause. Frankfurt: Diesterweg, 1958.

Lacassagne, Claude. "L'au-dela de l'Utopie." *Récherches Anglaises et Americaines* 6 (1973): 22–31.

Leeper, Geoffrey. "The Happy Utopias of Aldous Huxley and H. G. Wells." *Meanjin* 24, no. 1 (1965): 120–124.

Meckier, Jerome. "Shakespeare and Aldous Huxley." *Shakespeare Quarterly* 22 (Spring 1971): 129–135.

Orwell, George. *The Collected Essays, Journalism and Letters of George Orwell.* Edited by Sonia Orwell and Ian Angus, Volume 2, pp. 30–31; Volume 4, pp. 73–75. New York: Harcourt, 1968.

Thiry, A. "Zamjatins *Wij* als Model voor A. Huxley en G. Orwell." *Dietsche Warande en Belfort* 122 (1977): 508–521.

Wells, Arvin R. "Huxley, Plato and the Just Society." *Centennial Review* 24 (Fall 1980): 475–491.

Woodcock, George. "Five Who Fear the Future." *New Republic* 134 (April 16, 1956): 17–19.

Ape and Essence

Gump, Margaret. "From Ape to Man and from Man to Ape." *Kentucky Foreign Language Quarterly* 4, no. 4 (1957): 177–185.

Higdon, David Leon. " 'Into the Vast Unknown': Directions in the Post-Holocaust Novel." In *War and Peace,* 117–124.

Matter, William W. "The Utopian Tradition and Aldous Huxley." *Science-Fiction Studies* 2 (July 1975): 146–151.

Meckier, Jerome. "Quarles among the Monkeys: Huxley's Zoological Novels." *Modern Language Review* 68 (April 1973): 280–281.

Schmerl, Rudolf B. "The Two Future Worlds of Aldous Huxley." *PMLA* 77 (June 1962): 328–334.

Brave New World

Adorno, T. W. *Prisms.* Translated by Samuel Weber and Shierry Weber. Cambridge, MA: MIT Press, 1982, pp. 95–117.

Aldridge, A. *The Scientific World View in Dystopia,* 45–63.

Bailey, J. O. *Pilgrims Through Space and Time,* 154–156.

Berneri, Marie Louise. *Journey Through Utopia,* 316–317.

Bonicelli, Elena. "Liberta dell'Utopia, Utopia della Liberta in Aldous Huxley." *Revista di Letterature Moderne e Comparate (Firenze)* 26 (1973): 307–314.

Bowering, Peter. *Aldous Huxley,* 98–113.

Brander, Laurence. *Aldous Huxley,* 61–71.

Brown, E. J. *'Brave New World,' '1984,' and 'We.'*

Browning, Gordon. "Toward a Set of Standards for [Evaluating] Anti-Utopian Fiction." *Cithara* 10 (December 1970): 18–32.

Chang, Hui-Chuan. "City of Cats and Anti Utopia: A Generic Investigation." *Tamkang Review* 19 (Autumn-Summer 1988–1989): 573–589.

Chase, Richard V. "The Huxley-Heard Paradise." *Partisan Review* 10 (March–April 1943): 143–158.

Christensen, Bryce J. *Utopia Against the Family,* 10.

Clareson, Thomas D. "The Classic: Aldous Huxley's *Brave New World.*" *Extrapolation* 2 (May 1961): 33–40.

Coleman, D. C. "Bernard Shaw and *Brave New World.*" *Shaw Review* 10 (January 1967): 6–8.

Colmer, J. *Coleridge to Catch-22,* 162–176.

Desroches, Rosny. "L'Utopie: Évasion ou Anticipation?" In *France and North America,* 83–92.

Doxiadis, Constantinos. *Between Dystopia and Utopia,* 16.

Dyson, Anthony E. "Aldous Huxley and the Two Nothings." *Critical Quarterly* 3 (Winter 1961): 300–303.

Enright, D. J. "Mortal Visions." *Times Literary Supplement* (February 17, 1984): 160.

Enroth, Clyde. "Mysticism in Two of Aldous Huxley's Early Novels." *Twentieth Century Literature* 6 (October 1960): 123–132.

Erzgraber, Willi. "Aldous Huxley: *Brave New World.*" In *Die Utopie in der Angloamerikanischen Literatur,* 198–218.

Fietz, Lothar. "Schreckutopien des Kollektivismus und Individualismus: Aldous Huxleys *Brave New World* und Michael Frayns *A Very*

Private Life.'' In *Literarische Utopien von Morus bis zur Gegenwart,* 203–217.

Firchow, Peter E. *Aldous Huxley.*

————. *The End of Utopia: A Study of Aldous Huxley's "Brave New World.''* Lewisburg, PA: Bucknell University Press, 1984.

————. "Science and Conscience in Huxley's *Brave New World.''* *Contemporary Literature* 16 (Summer 1975): 301–316.

Garrett, J. C. *Utopias in Literature since the Romantic Period,* 56–59.

Gill, Kulwant Singh. "Aldous Huxley: The Quest for Identity." *Panjab University Research Bulletin (Arts)* 8 (April–October 1977): 11–26.

Greenblatt, S. J. *Three Modern Satirists: Waugh, Orwell and Huxley.* New Haven, CT: Yale University Press, 1965, pp. 95–101.

Grushow, Ira. *"Brave New World"* and *"The Tempest.''* *College English* 24 (October 1962): 42–45.

Hebert, R. Louis. "Huxley's *Brave New World,* Chapter V." *Explicator* 29 (1971): Item 71.

Hellemans, Karel. "Always the Eyes Watching You." In *Essays from Oceania and Eurasia,* 27–33.

Henderson, Alexander. *Aldous Huxley.* New York: Harper, 1936, pp. 87–111.

Hoffecker, W. Andrew. "A Reading in *Brave New World:* Dystopian-ism in Historical Perspective." *Christianity and Literature* 29, no. 2 (1980): 45–62.

Hoffman, Charles G. "The Changes in Huxley's Approach to the Novel of Ideas." *Personalist* 42 (Winter 1961): 85–90.

Holmes, Charles M. *Aldous Huxley and the Way to Reality,* 82–89.

Huxley, Julian. "My Brother Aldous." *Humanist* 25 (January 1965): 25.

Jones, Joseph. "Utopias as Dirge." *American Quarterly* 2 (Fall 1950): 214–226.

Jones, William M. "The Iago of *Brave New World.*" *Western Humanites Review* 15 (Summer 1961): 275–278.

Karl, Frederick R., and M. Magalaner. *A Reader's Guide to Great Twentieth-Century English Novels.* New York: Noonday, 1959, pp. 257–284.

Kessler, Martin. "Power and the Perfect State: A Study in Disillusionment as Reflected in Orwell's *Nineteen Eighty-Four* and Huxley's *Brave New World.*" *Political Science Quarterly* 72 (December 1957): 565–577.

Kumar, Krishan. *Utopia and Anti-Utopia in Modern Times,* 224–287.

Larsen, Peter M. "Synthetic Myths in Aldous Huxley's *Brave New World:* A Note." *English Studies* 62 (December 1981): 506–508.

Le Roy, Gaylord C. "A. F. 632 to 1984." *College English* 12 (December 1950): 135–138.

Leyburn, Ellen Douglass. *Satiric Allegory: Mirror of Man.* New Haven, CT: Yale University Press, 1956, pp. 114–125.

Lobb, Edward. "The Subversion of Drama in Huxley's *Brave New World.*" *International Fiction Review* 11 (Summer 1984): 94–101.

Macey, Samuel L. "The Role of Clocks and Time in Dystopias: Zamyatin's *We* and Huxley's *Brave New World.*" In *Explorations,* 24–43.

Malak, Amin. "Margaret Atwood's *The Handmaid's Tale* and the Dystopian Tradition." *Canadian Literature* 112 (Spring 1987): 9–16.

Matter, William W. "On *Brave New World.*" In *No Place Else,* 94–109.

Mav, Keith. *Aldous Huxley.* London: Elek, 1972, pp. 98–117.

Meckier, Jerome. *Aldous Huxley: Satire and Structure.* New York: Barnes & Noble, 1969, pp. 17–19, 175–183.

———. "Boffin and Podsnap in Utopia." *Dickensian* 77 (Autumn 1981): 154–161.

———. "Dickens and the Dystopian Novel." In *The Novel and its Changing Form,* edited by R. G. Collins, 51–58. Winnipeg: University of Manitoba Press, 1972.

———. "A Neglected Huxley 'Preface': His Earliest Synopsis of *Brave New World.*" *Twentieth Century Literature* 25 (1979): 1–20.

———. "Poetry in the Future, the Future of Poetry: Huxley and Orwell on Zamyatin." *Renaissance and Modern Studies* 28 (1984): 18–39.

Millichap, Joseph A. "Huxley's *Brave New World,* Chapter V." *Explicator* 32 (1973): Item 1.

Muhlheim, Ulrike. "Utopie, Anti-Utopie and Science Fiction." In *Alternative Welten,* 315–328.

Mulvihill, James D. "A Source for Huxley's 'Savage Reservation.' " *Notes and Queries* 31 (March 1984): 83–84.

Pendexter, Hugh III. "Huxley's *Brave New World.*" *Explicator* 20 (March 1962): 58.

Petre, M. D. "Bolshevist Ideals and the *Brave New World.*" *Hibbert Journal* 31 (October 1932): 61–71.

Plank, William. "Orwell and Huxley: Social Control through Standardized Eroticism." *Recovering Literature* 12 (1984): 29–39.

Postman, Neil. "Amusing Ourselves to Death." *ETC* 42 (Spring 1985): 13–18.

Reszler, Andre. "Man as Nostalgia: The Image of the Last Man in Twentieth-century Post-Utopian Fiction." In *Visions of Apocalypse,* 196–215.

Richards, D. "Four Utopias." *Slavonic and East European Review* 40 (1962): 220–228.

Rose, Steven. "The Fear of Utopia." *Essays in Criticism (Oxford)* 24 (1974): 55–70.

Rosenfeld, Isaac. "Second Thoughts on Huxley's *Brave New World.*" *Nation* 163 (October 19, 1945): 445–447.

Ross, Harry. *Utopias Old and New,* 195–200.

Schmerl, Rudolf B. "Fantasy as Technique." *Virginia Quarterly Review* 43 (Autumn 1967): 644–656.

———. "The Two Future Worlds of Aldous Huxley." *PMLA* 77 (June 1962): 328–334.

Simons, John D. "The Grand Inquisitor in Schiller, Dostoevsky, and Huxley." *New Zealand Slavonic Journal* 8 (Summer 1971): 20–31.

Snow, Malinda. "The Gray Parody in *Brave New World.*" *Papers on Language and Literature* 13 (1977): 85–88.

Sullivan, E. D. S. "Place in No Place: Examples of the Ordered Society in Literature." In *The Utopian Vision,* 24–49.

Thomas, W. K. "*Brave New World* and the Houyhnhnms." *Revue de l'Universite Ottawa* 37 (October-December 1967): 686–696.

Vitoux, Pierre. "Le Conflit Idéologique dans *Brave New World.*" In *Autour de l'Idée de Nature,* 211–214.

Walsh, Chad. *From Utopia to Nightmare,* 25–26, 112–113.

Watt, Donald. "The Problem of Existence in Anti-Utopian Fiction." *Review of Existential Psychology and Psychiatry* 14 (1975–1976): 42–44.

———. "Vision and Symbol in Aldous Huxley's *Island.*" *Twentieth Century Literature* 14 (October 1968): 149–160.

Watts, Harold H. *Aldous Huxley,* 72–84.

Wilson, Robert. "*Brave New World* as Shakespeare Criticism." *Shakespeare Association Bulletin* 21 (July 1946): 99–107.

Wing, George. "The Shakespearean Voice of Conscience in *Brave New World.*" *Dalhousie Review* 51 (Summer 1971): 153–164.

Woodcock, George. *Dawn and the Darkest Hour: A Study of Aldous Huxley.* New York: Viking, 1972, pp. 173–181.

————. "Utopias in Negative." *Sewanee Review* 64 (Winter 1956): 81–97.

Brave New World Revisited

Schmerl, Rudolf B. "Aldous Huxley's Social Criticism." *Chicago Review* 13 (Winter-Spring 1959): 37–58.

Walsh, Chad. *From Utopia to Nightmare,* 97–98.

Island

Bowering, Peter. *Aldous Huxley,* 181–212.

Brander, Laurence. *Aldous Huxley,* 101–110.

Cloudhary, Nora S. "*Island:* Huxley's Attempt as Practical Philosophy." *Literature East & West* 16 (1972): 1,155–1,167.

Crawford, John W. "The Utopian Dream, Alive and Well." *Cuyahoga Review* 2 (Spring-Summer 1984): 27–33.

Elliott, Robert C. *The Shape of Utopia,* 129, 137–153.

Firchow, Peter E. *Aldous Huxley,* 177–189.

Holmes, Charles M. *Aldous Huxley and the Way to Reality,* 180–199.

Jehmlich, Reimer. "Cog-Work: The Organization of Labor in Edward Bellamy's *Looking Backward* and in Later Utopian Fiction." In *Clockwork Worlds,* 27–46.

Kennedy, Richard S. "Aldous Huxley: The Final Wisdom." *Southwest Review* 50 (Winter 1965): 37–47.

Leeper, Geoffrey. "The Happy Utopias of Aldous Huxley and H. G. Wells." *Meanjin* 24 (1963): 120–124.

May, Keith. *Aldous Huxley.* London: Elek, 1972, pp. 206–223.

Meckier, Jerome. *Aldous Huxley: Satire and Structure.* New York: Barnes & Noble, 1969, pp. 196–205.

————. "Cancer in Utopia: Positive and Negative Elements in Huxley's *Island.*" *Dalhousie Review* 54 (Winter 1974–1975): 619–633.

Parsons, David. "Dartington: A Principal Source of Inspiration behind Aldous Huxley's *Island.*" *Journal of General Education* 39, no. 1 (1987): 10–25.

Sponberg, Florence I. "Huxley's Perennial Preoccupation." *Mankato State College Studies* 3 (December 1968): 1–18.

Stewart, D. H. "Aldous Huxley's *Island.*" *Queen's Quarterly* 70 (Autumn 1963): 326–335.

Watt, Donald J. "Vision and Symbol in Aldous Huxley's *Island.*" *Twentieth Century Literature* 14 (October 1968): 149–160.

Watts, Harold H. *Aldous Huxley,* 139–145.

JAMESON, STORM

In the Second Year

Albinski, Nan Bowman. "Thomas and Peter: Society and Politics in Four British Utopian Novels." *Utopian Studies* 1 (1987): 11–22.

————. *Women's Utopias in British and American Fiction,* 90, 91–92, 104.

A Moment of Truth

Behrend, Hanna. "Storm Jameson: Decline of a Fellow-Traveller." *Zeitschrift fur Anglistik und Amerikanistik* 26 (1978): 237–238.

JEAN PAUL (RICHTER, JOHANN PAUL FRIEDRICH)

General Criticism

Alt, Johannes. *Jean Paul.* Munich: Beck, 1925.

Hedinger-Frohner, Dorothee. *Jean Paul: Der Utopische Gehalt des Hesperus.* Bonn: Bouvier, 1977.

Titan

Berger, Dorothea. *Jean Paul Friedrich Richter*. New York: Twayne, 1972, pp. 55–82.

Geissendoerfer, Theodore. "Jacobi's *Allwill* and Jean Paul's *Titan*." *Journal of English and Germanic Philology* 27 (July 1928): 365–370.

Lee, Eliza Buckminster. *Life of Jean Paul Frederic Richter*. Volume 2. Translated by Eliza Buckminster Lee. New York: Appleton, 1850, pp. 64–71.

Rose, Ernst. *History of German Literature*. New York: New York University Press, 1960, p. 208.

Rose, William. *From Goethe to Byron*. London: Routledge & Sons, 1924, pp. 173–180.

Schweikert, Uwe. *Jean Paul*. Stuttgart: J. B. Metzlersche Verlagsbuchhandlung, 1970, pp. 38–51.

Spacemann, Robert. "Fenelon und Jean Paul." *Jahrbuch der Jean-Paul—Gesellschaft* 15 (1980): 55–81.

Swediuk-Cheyne, Helen. " 'Einkraftigkeit,' Jean Paul's Term for Self-Destruction." *German Life and Letters* 26 (January 1973): 136–142.

JEROME, JEROME K.

General Criticism

Beauchamp, Gorman. "Proto-Dystopia of Jerome K. Jerome." *Extrapolation* 24 (Summer 1983): 170–181.

"The New Utopia"

Faurot, Ruth Marie. *Jerome K. Jerome*. New York: Twayne, 1974, p. 49.

JEURY, MICHEL

Le Temps Incertain

Khouri, Nadia. "The Dialectic of Power: Utopia in the Science Fiction of Le Guin, Jeury, and Piercy." *Science-Fiction Studies* 7 (March 1980): 49–59.

JOHNSON, SAMUEL

Rasselas

Bate, W. Jackson. "Johnson and Satire Manque." In *Eighteenth-Century Studies in Honor of Donald F. Hyde,* edited by W. H. Bond, 156–159. New York: Grolier, 1970.

————. *Samuel Johnson.* New York: Harcourt Brace Jovanovich, 1977, pp. 298–316, 337–340.

Belloc, Hilaire. *Short Talks with the Dead, and Others.* New York: Harper, 1926, pp. 173–183.

Bentley, G. E., Jr. "*Rasselas* and *Gaudentio di Lucca* in the Mountains of the Moon." *Revista Canaria de Estudios Ingleses* 9 (November 1984): 1–11.

Brinton, George. "Rasselas and the Problem of Evil." *Papers on Language and Literature* 8 (1972): 92–96.

Bronson, B. H. "Johnson, Traveling Companion, in Fancy and Fact." In *Johnson and His Age,* edited by J. Engell, 163–187. Cambridge, MA: Harvard University Press, 1984.

Brunkhorst, Martin. "Vermittlungsebenen im Philosophischen Roman: *Candide, Rasselas* und *Don Sylvio.*" *Arcadia* 14 (1979): 133–139.

Byrd, Max. *Visits to Bedlam: Madness and Literature in the Eighteenth Century.* Columbia: University of South Carolina Press, 1974, pp. 94–102.

Chesterton, G. K. *G. K. C. as M. C.: Being a Collection of Thirty-Seven Introductions.* London: Methuen, 1929, pp. 196–201.

Curley, Thomas M. *Samuel Johnson and the Age of Travel.* Athens: University of Georgia Press, 1976.

———. "The Spiritual Journey Moralized in *Rasselas.*" *Anglia* 91, no. 1 (1973): 35–55.

Damrosch, L. "Johnson's *Rasselas:* Limits of Wisdom, Limits of Art." In *Augustan Studies: Essays in Honor of Irvin Ehrenpreis,* edited by D. L. Patey and T. Keegan, 205–214. Newark: University of Delaware Press, 1985.

Ehrenpreis, Irvin. "Rasselas and Some Meanings of 'Structure' in Literary Criticism." *Novel* 14 (Winter 1981): 101–117.

Feingold, R. *Moralized Song: The Character of Augustan Lyricism.* New Brunswick, NJ: Rutgers University Press, 1989, pp. 94–138.

Greene, Donald J. *Samuel Johnson.* New York: Twayne, 1970, pp. 133–139.

Gross, G. S. "Dr. Johnson's Practice: The Medical Context for *Rasselas.*" In *Studies in Eighteenth-Century Culture,* Volume 15, 275–288.

Hardy, J. P. *Samuel Johnson: A Critical Study.* London: Routledge & Kegan Paul, 1979, pp. 127–148.

Hewitt, Regina. "Time in *Rasselas:* Johnson's Use of Locke's Concept." *Studies in Eighteenth-Century Culture* 19 (1989): 267–276.

Jones, E. "Artistic Form of *Rasselas.*" *Review of English Studies* 18 (November 1967): 387–401.

Joost, Nicholas. "Whispers of Fancy; or, the Meaning of *Rasselas.*" *Modern Age* 1 (1957): 166–173.

Keener, Frederick. *The Chain of Becoming: The Philosophical Tale, the Novel, and a Neglected Realism of the Enlightenment—Swift, Montesquieu, Voltaire, Johnson, and Austen.* New York: Columbia University Press, 1983, pp. 217–240.

Kolb, Gwin. "The 'Paradise' in Abyssinia and the 'Happy Valley' in *Rasselas.*" *Modern Philology* 56, no. 1 (1958): 10–16.

————. "Rousseau and the Background of the 'Life led According to Nature' in Chapter 22 of *Rasselas.*" *Modern Philology* 73 (1976): 566–573.

Lascelles, Mary. *Notions and Facts: Collected Criticism and Research.* Oxford: Clarendon, 1972, pp. 102–129.

Leyburn, Ellen Douglass. "No Romantic Absurdities or Incredible Fictions: The Relation of Johnson's *Rasselas* to Lobo's *Voyage to Abyssinia.*" *PMLA* 70 (December 1955): 1,059–1,067.

Margolis, John. "Pekuah and the Theme of Imprisonment in Johnson's *Rasselas.*" *English Studies* 53 (August 1972): 339–343.

Mezciems, Jenny. "Utopia and 'the Thing Which Is Not': More, Swift, and other Lying Idealists." *University of Toronto Quarterly* 52 (1982): 58–59.

Orr, Leonard. "The Structural and Thematic Importance of the Astronomer in *Rasselas.*" *Recovering Literature* 9 (1981): 15–21.

Pagliaro, H. E. "Structural Patterns of Control in *Rasselas.*" In *English Writers of the Eighteenth Century,* edited by John Middendorf, 208–229. New York: Columbia University Press, 1971.

Preston, T. R. "Biblical Context of Johnson's *Rasselas.*" *PMLA* 84 (March 1969): 274–281.

Richter, D. H. *Fable's End,* 22–60.

Rose, Steven. "The Fear of Utopia." *Essays in Criticism* 24 (1974): 56–58.

Sherburn, George. "*Rasselas* Returns—to What?" *Philological Quarterly* 38 (July 1959): 383–384.

Soupel, Serge. "Les Mouvements de Rasselas." *Etudes Anglaises* 38 (1985): 13–23.

Suderman, Elmer F. "*Candide, Rasselas* and Optimism." *Iowa English Yearbook* 11 (1966): 37–43.

Sutherland, W. *The Art of the Satirist: Essays on the Satire of Augustan England.* Arlington: University of Texas Press, 1965, pp. 92–104.

Tomarken, E. L. "Travels into the Unknown: *Rasselas* and *A Journey to the Western Islands of Scotland.*" In *The Unknown Samuel Johnson,* edited by J. J. Burke and D. Kay, 150–167. Madison: University of Wisconsin Press, 1983.

Uphaus, R. W. *The Impossible Observer: Reason and the Reader in 18th-Century Prose.* Lexington: University Press of Kentucky, 1979, pp. 89–107.

Wharton, T. F. *Samuel Johnson and the Theme of Hope.* New York: St. Martin's, 1984, pp. 89–118.

White, Ian. "On *Rasselas.*" *Cambridge Quarterly* 6, no. 1 (1972): 6–31.

Wiltshire, John. "Dr. Johnson's Seriousness." *Critical Review* 10 (1967): 63–73.

Woodruff, J. F. "Rasselas and the Traditions of 'Menippean Satire.' In *Samuel Johnson: New Criticial Essays,* edited by I. Grundy, 158–185. Totowa, NJ: Barnes & Noble, 1984.

JONES, DENNIS FELTHAM

Colossus

Beauchamp, Gordon. "Technology in the Dystopian Novel." *Modern Fiction Studies* 32 (Spring 1986): 53–63.

JUDD, SYLVESTER

Margaret

Dedmond, Francis B. *Sylvester Judd,* 60–86.

Nydahl, Joel. Introduction. *An Experiment in Marriage,* xix-xx.

Parrington, Vernon Louis, Jr. *American Dreams,* 10, 27–34.

Margaret (Revised Edition)

Dedmond, Francis B. *Sylvester Judd,* 81–85.

KARP, DAVID

One

Berger, Harold L. *Science Fiction and the New Dark Age,* 95–96, 105.

KASACK, HERMANN

Die Stadt Hinter dem Strom

Vos, Jaak de. "Hermann Kasacks *Die Stadt Hinter dem Strom:* Die Utopische Synthese Elecktrischer Weisheit." In *Just the Other Day,* 355–382.

KEARNEY, CHALMERS

Erone

Bailey, J. O. *Pilgrims Through Space and Time,* 305.

KELLER, GOTTFRIED

Der Grune Heinrich

Hart, Gail K. "The Functions of Fictions: Imaginations and Socialization in Both Versions of Keller's *Der Grune Heinrich.*" *German Quarterly* 59 (Fall 1986): 595–610.

Horisch, Jochen. *Gott, Geld und Gluck: Zur Logik der Liebe in den Bildungsromanen Goethes, Kellers und Thomas Manns.* Frankfurt: Suhrkamp, 1983, pp. 116–168.

Kaiser, Gerhard. "Der Gefrorene Grune Heinrich: Ein bild Gottfried Kellers." *Merkur* 37 (January 1983): 66–72.

Laufhutte, Hartmut. *Wirklichkeit und Kunst in Gottfried Kellers Roman 'Der Grune Heinrich.'* " Bonn: Bouvier, 1969.

Morgenthaler, Walter. *Bedrangte Positivitat: Zu Romanen von Immermann, Keller, Fontane.* Bonn: Bouvier, 1979, pp. 149–278.

Schubert, Bernard. "Die Idealitat des Alt-Burgerlichen in Gottfried Kellers *Der Grune Heinrich.*" *Jahrbuch der Jean-Paul-Gesellschaft* 19 (1984): 85–119.

KEYES, DANIEL

Flowers for Algernon

Zaki, Hoda M. *Phoenix Renewed,* 61.

KIPLING, RUDYARD

"As Easy as A. B. C."

Armytage, W. H. G. *Yesterday's Tomorrows,* 114–115.

Thornton-Duesbery, J. P. "The Electric Hedge." *Notes and Queries* 6 (September 1959): 338.

"With the Night Mail"

Dobree, Bonamy. *Rudyard Kipling.* London: Longmans, Green 1951, pp. 150–151.

Walsh, Chad. *From Utopia to Nightmare,* 61.

KNIGHT, DAMON

General Criticism

Robillard, Douglas. "Uncertain Futures: Damon Knight's Science Fiction." In *Voices for the Future III,* edited by Thomas Wymer, 30–51. Bowling Green, OH: BG University Popular Press, 1984.

"A Country of the Kind"

Berger, Harold L. *Science Fiction and the New Dark Age,* 187.

Hell's Pavement

Berger, Harold L. *Science Fiction and the New Dark Age,* 121–122.

KOESTLER, ARTHUR

General Criticism

Elkins, Charles. "George Orwell, 1903–1950." In *Science Fiction Writers,* 233–241.

Fink, Howard. "Orwell versus Koestler: *Nineteen Eighty-Four* as Optimistic Satire." In *George Orwell,* 101–109.

Laborda, J. Javier. "1984, con Orwell y sin Koestler." *Quimera* 35 (January 1984): 43–45.

Woodcock, George. "Five Who Fear the Future." *New Republic* 134 (April 16, 1956): 17–19.

Darkness at Noon

Axthelm, Peter M. *The Modern Confessional Novel.* New Haven, CT: Yale University Press, 1967, pp. 97–127.

Beadle, Gordon. "Anti-Totalitarian Fiction." *English Record* 25 (Summer 1974): 30–33.

Beum, Robert. "Epigraphs for Rubashov: Koestler's *Darkness at Noon.*" *Dalhousie Review* 42 (Spring 1962): 86–91.

Garaudy, Roger. *Literature of the Graveyard.* New York: International Publ., 1948, pp. 50–55.

Geering, R. G. "*Darkness at Noon* and *1984*—A Comparative Study." *Australian Quarterly* 30 (September 1958): 90–96.

Hartt, Julian. *Lost Image of Man.* Baton Rouge: Louisiana State University Press, 1963, pp. 76–79.

Huerta, Alberto. "Politica Apocaliptica: Zamyatin, Koestler, Orwell y Milosz." *Religion y Cultura* 30 (July-October 1984): 141–142.

Levene, Mark. *Arthur Koestler,* 55–77.

Lewis, Wyndham. *The Writer and the Absolute.* London: Methuen, 1952, pp. 180–184.

Pearson, Sidney A., Jr. *Arthur Koestler.* Boston: Twayne, 1978, pp. 51–67, 138–146.

Steele, Peter. *"Darkness at Noon." Critical Review* 12 (1969): 73–82.

Walsh, Chad. *From Utopia to Nightmare,* 129, 133, 157.

Thieves in the Night

Calder, Jenni. *Chronicles of Conscience,* 200–202, 212–220.

Levene, Mark. *Arthur Koestler,* 96–112.

LAFFERTY, R. A.

Past Master

Berger, Harold L. *Science Fiction and the New Dark Age,* 74–76.

Hardesty, William H., III. "The Programmed Utopia of R. A. Lafferty's *Past Master.*" In *Clockwork Worlds,* 105–113.

LAGERKVIST, PAR

The Last Man

Ahlenius, Holger. "The Dramatic Works of Par Lagerkvist." *American Scandinavian Review* 28 (1940): 301–308.

Mjoberg, Joran. "Par Lagerkvist and the Ancient Greek Drama." *Scandinavian Studies* 25 (1953): 46–51.

Sjoberg, Leif. *Par Lagerkvist.* New York: Columbia University Press, 1976, pp. 12–13.

Swanson, Roy Arthur. "Love is the Function of Death: Forster, Lagerkvist, and Zamyatin." *Canadian Review of Comparative Literature*
3 (Spring 1976): 197–211.

LANE, MARY BRADLEY

Mizora

Albinski, Nan Bowman. *Women's Utopias in British and American
Fiction,* 48, 49, 50, 59, 72, 170, 171.

Anderson, Kristine J. "The Great Divorce: Fictions of Feminist Desire." In *Feminism, Utopia, and Narrative,* 85–89, 95.

Pearson, Carol. "Coming Home: Four Feminist Utopias and Patriarchal
Experience." In *Future Females,* 63–70.

LE GUIN, URSULA K.

General Criticism

Benford, Gregory. "Reactionary Utopias." In *Storm Warnings,* 73–83.

Bittner, James W. *Approaches to the Fiction of Ursula K. Le Guin.* Ann
Arbor, MI: UMI Research Press, 1984.

Farrelly, James P. "The Promised Land: Moses, Nearing, Skinner, Le
Guin." *Journal of General Education* 33 (Spring 1981): 15–23.

Jameson, F. "World-Reduction in Le Guin: The Emergence of Utopian
Narrative." *Science-Fiction Studies* 2 (November 1975): 221–230.

Moylan, Tom. "Beyond Negation: The Critical Utopias of Ursula K. Le
Guin and Samuel R. Delany." *Extrapolation* 21 (Fall 1980): 236–253.

Nudelman, Rafail. "An Approach to the Structure of Le Guin's SF."
Translated by Alan G. Meyers. *Science-Fiction Studies* 2 (November
1975): 210–220.

Pagetti, Carlo. "Tra Universo Tecnologico e Tempo del Sogno: La
Narrativa di Ursula K. Le Guin." In *Nel Tempo del Sogno: Le Forme
della Narrativa Fantistica dall'Immaginario Vittoriano All'Utopia*

Contemporanea, edited by Carlo Pagetti, 109–141. Ravenna: Longo, 1988.

Russ, Joanna. "Recent Feminist Utopias." In *Future Females,* 71–75.

Sargent, Lyman. "A New Anarchism: Social and Political Ideas in Some Recent Feminist Eutopias." In *Women and Utopia,* 3–33.

Shippey, T. A. "Variations on Newspeak: The Open Question of *Nineteen Eighty-Four.*" In *Storm Warnings,* 172–193.

Zaki, Hoda M. *Phoenix Renewed,* 80–111.

Always Coming Home

Crow, Charles L. "Homecoming in the California Visionary Romance." *Western American Literature* 24 (May 1989): 1–19.

Fitting, Peter. "The Turn from Utopia in Recent Feminist Fiction." In *Feminism, Utopia, and Narrative,* 151–152.

Franko, Carol. "Self-Conscious Narration as the Complex Representation of Hope in Le Guin's *Always Coming Home.*" *Mythlore* 15 (Spring 1989): 57–60.

Heldreth, L. M. "To Defend or to Correct: Patterns of Culture in *Always Coming Home.*" *Mythlore* 16 (Autumn 1989): 58–63, 66.

Jacobs, Naomi. "Beyond Stasis and Symmetry: Lessing, Le Guin, and the Remodeling of Utopia." *Extrapolation* 29 (Spring 1988): 34–45.

Khanna, Lee Cullen. "Women's Utopias: New Worlds, New Texts." In *Feminism, Utopia, and Narrative,* 130–140.

Wytenbroek, J. R. "*Always Coming Home:* Pacificism and Anarchy in Le Guin's Latest Utopia." *Extrapolation* 28 (Winter 1987): 330–339.

The Dispossessed

Bierman, Judah. "Ambiguity in Utopia: *The Dispossessed.*" *Science-Fiction Studies* 2 (November 1975): 249–255.

Bittner, James W. "Chronosophy, Aesthetics, and Ethics in Le Guin's *The Dispossessed:* An Ambiguous Utopia." In *No Place Else,* 244–270.

Brennan, John P., and Michael C. Downs. "Anarchism and Utopian Tradition in *The Dispossessed.*" In *Ursula K. Le Guin,* 116–152.

Burton, Deirdre. "Linguistic Innovation in Feminist Utopian Fiction." *Ilha do Desterrro* 14, no. 2 (1985): 82–106.

Cogell, Elizabeth Cummins. "Taoist Configurations: *The Dispossessed.*" In *Ursula K. Le Guin: Voyager to Inner Lands and to Outer Space,* 153–179.

Delany, Samuel R. *The Jewel-Hinged Jaw: Notes on the Language of Science Fiction.* Elizabethtown, NY: Dragon Press, 1977, pp. 239–308.

Dunn, Thomas P. "Theme and Narrative Structure in Ursula K. Le Guin's *The Dispossessed.*" In *Reflections on the Fantastic,* 87–95.

Fekete, John. "*The Dispossessed* and *Triton:* Act and System in Utopian Science Fiction." *Science-Fiction Studies* 6 (July 1979): 129–143.

Ferns, Chris. "Dreams of Freedom: Ideology and Narrative Structure in the Utopian Fictions of Marge Piercy and Ursula Le Guin." *English Studies in Canada* 14 (December 1988): 453–466.

Finney, Kathe Davis. "The Days of Future Past; or, Utopians Lessing and Le Guin Fight Future Nostalgia." In *Patterns of the Fantastic,* 31–40.

Fitting, Peter. "Positioning and Closure: On the 'Reading Effect' of Contemporary Utopian Fiction." *Utopian Studies* 1 (1987): 23–36.

Fleck, Leonard M. "Science Fiction as a Tool of Speculative Philosophy: A Philosophic Analysis of Selected Anarchistic and Utopian Themes in Le Guin's *The Dispossessed.*" In *Selected Proceedings of the 1978 Science Fiction Research Association National Conference,* 133–145.

Freibert, Lucy M. "World Views in Utopian Novels by Women." In *Women and Utopia,* 67–84.

Hardesty, William H., III. "Mapping the Future: Extrapolation in Utopian/Dystopian and Science Fiction." *Utopian Studies* 1 (1987): 160–172.

Khouri, Nadia. "The Dialectics of Power: Utopia in the Science Fiction of Le Guin, Jeury, and Piercy." *Science-Fiction Studies* 7 (March 1980): 49–59.

Masse, Michelle. " 'All You Have to Do is Know What You Want': Individual Expectations in *Triton.*" In *Coordinates,* 49–64.

Moylan, Tom. *Demand the Impossible,* 91–120.

Seeber, Hans Ulrich. "Tradition and Innovation in Ursula Le Guin's *The Dispossessed.*" In *Utopian Thought In American Literature,* 147–169.

Smith, Philip E., II. "Unbuilding Walls: Human Nature and the Nature of Evolutionary and Political Theory in *The Dispossessed.*" In *Ursula K. Le Guin,* 77–96.

Somay, Bulend; R[obert] P[hilimus], ed. "Toward an Open-Ended Utopia." *Science-Fiction Studies* 11 (March 1984): 25–38.

Spivack, Charlotte. *Ursula K. Le Guin,* 74–93.

Tifft, Larry L., and Dennis C. Sullivan. "Possessed Sociology and Le Guin's *Dispossessed:* From Exile to Anarchism." In *Ursula K. Le Guin: Voyages to Inner Lands and to Outer Space,* 180–197.

Urbanowicz, Victor. "Personal and Political in *The Dispossessed.*" *Science-Fiction Studies* 5 (July 1978): 110–117.

Widmer, Kingsley. "The Dialectics of Utopianism: Le Guin's *The Dispossessed.*" *Liberal and Fine Arts Review* 3 (January-July 1983): 1–11.

———. "Utopian, Dystopian, Diatopian Libertarianism: Le Guin's *The Dispossessed.*" *Sphinx* 4, no. 1 (1981): 55–65.

The Left Hand of Darkness

Bickman, Martin. "Le Guin's *The Left Hand of Darkness:* Form and Context." In *Ursula K. Le Guin's 'The Left Hand of Darkness,'* 53–62.

Brown, Barbara. "*The Left Hand of Darkness:* Androgyny, Future, Present, and Past." In *Ursula K. Le Guin's 'The Left Hand of Darkness,'* 91–99.

Bucknall, Barbara J. "Androgynes in Outer Space." In *Critical Encounters: Writers and Themes in Science Fiction,* edited by Dick Riley, 56–69. New York: Ungar, 1978.

Finney, Kathe Davis. "The Days of Future Past; or, Utopians, Lessing and Le Guin Fight Future Nostalgia." In *Patterns of the Fantastic,* 31–40.

Getz, John. "A Peace-Studies Approach to *The Left Hand of Darkness.*" *Mosaic* 21 (Spring 1988): 203–214.

Hayles, N. B. "Androgyny, Ambivalence, and Assimilation in *The Left Hand of Darkness.*" In *Ursula K. Le Guin,* 97–115.

Holland, Norman N. "You, U. K. Le Guin." In *Future Females,* 125–137.

Ketterer, David. "*The Left Hand of Darkness:* Ursula K. Le Guin." In *Ursula K. Le Guin's 'The Left Hand of Darkness,'* 11–21.

Lake, David J. "Le Guin's Twofold Vision: Contrary Image-Sets in *The Left Hand of Darkness.*" *Science-Fiction Studies* 8 (July 1981): 156–164.

McGuirk, Carol. "Optimism and the Limits of Subversion in *The Dispossessed* and *The Left Hand of Darkness.*" In *Ursula K. Le Guin's 'The Left Hand of Darkness,'* 117–134.

Myers, Victoria. "Conversational Techniques in Ursula Le Guin: A Speech-Act Analysis." In *Ursula K. Le Guin's 'The Left Hand of Darkness,'* 101–115.

Peel, Ellen Susan. "Both Ends of the Candle."

Rabkin, Eric S. "Determinism, Free Will, and Point of View in Le Guin's *The Left Hand of Darkness.*" In *Ursula K. Le Guin's 'The Left Hand of Darkness,'* 75–90.

Rhodes, Jewell Parker. "Ursula Le Guin's *The Left Hand of Darkness:* Androgyny and the Feminist Utopia." In *Women and Utopia,* 108–120.

Spector, Judith. "The Functions of Sexuality in the Science Fiction of Russ, Piercy, and Le Guin." In *Erotic Universe,* 197–207.

Spivack, Charlotte. *Ursula K. Le Guin,* 44–59.

Stone-Blackburn, Susan. "Adult Telepathy: *Babel-17* and *The Left Hand of Darkness.*" *Extrapolation* 30 (Fall 1989): 243–253.

Theall, Donald F. "The Art of Social-Science Fiction: The Ambitious Utopian Dialectics of Ursula K. Le Guin." In *Ursula K. Le Guin's 'The Left Hand of Darkness,'* 39–52.

Walker, Jeanne Murray. "Myth, Exchange and History in *The Left Hand of Darkness.*" In *Ursula K. Le Guin's 'The Left Hand of Darkness,'* 63–73.

"The New Atlantis"

Albinski, Nan Bowman. *Women's Utopias in British and American Fiction,* 169, 179, 184.

Bucknall, Barbara J. *Ursula K. Le Guin.* New York: Ungar, 1981, pp. 124–126.

The Word for World Is Forest

Baggesen, Soren. "Utopian and Dystopian Pessimism: Le Guin's *The Word for World Is Forest* and Tiptree's 'We Who Stole the Dream.'" *Science-Fiction Studies* 14 (March 1987): 34–43.

Collings, Michael. "Sentences and Structured Meaning: Ursula K. Le Guin's *The Word for World Is Forest.*" *Cuyahoga Review* 2 (Spring-Summer 1984): 45–59.

Hovanec, Carol P. "Visions of Nature in *The Word for World Is Forest:* A Mirror of the American Consciousness." *Extrapolation* 30 (Spring 1989): 84–92.

Spivack, Charlotte. *Ursula K. Le Guin,* 67–71.

L'EPY, HÉLIOGÈNE DE

A Voyage into Tartary

Bleiler, E. F. "L'Epy's *A Voyage into Tartary:* An Enlightenment Ideal Society." *Extrapolation* (Summer 1988): 95–111.

LESSING, DORIS

General Criticism

D'Haen, Theo. "Utopia/Dystopie in the Science Fiction of Anthony Burgess and Doris Lessing." In *Just the Other Day,* 315–327.

Duplessis, Rachel. "The Feminist Apologues of Lessing, Piercy, and Russ." *Frontiers* 4 (Spring 1979): 1–8.

Fishburn, Katherine. "Anti-American Regionalism in the Fiction of Doris Lessing." *Regionalism and the Female Imagination* 4 (Fall 1978): 19–25.

Fullbrook, Kate. *Free Women,* 141–169.

Hardin, Nancy Shields. "Doris Lessing and the Sufi Way." *Contemporary Literature* 14 (Autumn 1973): 565–582.

Howe, Florence. "A Conversation with Doris Lessing." *Contemporary Literature* 14 (Autumn 1973): 418–436.

Kaplan, Sydney Janet. *Feminine Consciousness in the Modern British Novel.* Urbana: University of Illinois Press, 1975, pp. 136–173.

Karl, Frederick R. "Doris Lessing in the Sixties: The New Anatomy of Melancholy." *Contemporary Literature* 13 (Winter 1972): 15–33.

Newquist, Roy. *Counterpoint,* 413–424.

Smith, David. *Socialist Propaganda in the Twentieth-Century British Novel.* London: Macmillan, 1978, pp. 148–151.

Spacks, Patricia Meyer. *The Female Imagination.* New York: Alfred A. Knopf, 1975.

White, T. I. "Opposing Necessity and Truth: The Argument against Politics in Doris Lessing's Utopian Vision." In *Women and Utopia,* 134–147.

Canopus in Argos

Albinski, Nan Bowman. *Women's Utopias in British and American Fiction,* 131, 148–152.

Jouve, Nicole Ward. "Doris Lessing: A 'Female Voice'—Past, Present, or Future." In *Doris Lessing,* 127–133.

Kaplan, Carey. "Britain's Imperialist Past in Doris Lessing's Futuristic Fiction." In *Doris Lessing,* 149–158.

Kums, Guido. "The Satirical Cosmos: *Canopus in Argos.*" In *Just the Other Day,* 267–280.

Pickering, Jean. *Understanding Doris Lessing,* 142–143.

The Four-Gated City

Gohlman, Susan A. "Martha Hesse of *The Four-Gated City:* A *Bildungsroman* Already Behind Her." *South Atlantic Bulletin* 43 (November 1978): 95–107.

Kaplan, Sydney Janet. "The Limits of Consciousness in the Novels of Doris Lessing." *Contemporary Literature* 14 (Autumn 1973): 536- 550.

Karl, Frederick R. "The Four-Gaited Beast of the Apocalypse: Doris Lessing's *The Four-Gated City.*" In *Old Lines, New Forces,* 181–200.

Lewis, M. Susan. "Conscious Evolution in *The Four-Gated City.*" *Anonymous: A Journal for the Woman Writer* 1 (Spring 1974): 56–71.

Pickering, Jean. *Understanding Doris Lessing,* 72–89.

Rigney, Barbara Hill. " 'A Rehearsal for Madness': Hysteria as Sanity in *The Four-Gated City.*" In *Doris Lessing,* edited by Harold Bloom, 133–149. New York: Chelsea House, 1986.

Rubenstein, Roberta. *The Novelistic Vision of Doris Lessing,* 125–171.

———. "Outer Space, Inner Space: Doris Lessing's Metaphor of Science Fiction." *World Literature Written in English* 14 (April 1975): 187–198.

Seligman, Dee. "The Sufi Quest." *World Literature Written in English* 12 (November 1973): 190–206.

Sprague, Claire. " 'Without Contraries Is No Progression': Lessing's *The Four-Gated City.*" *Modern Fiction Studies* 26 (Spring 1980): 99–116.

Thorpe, Michael. "Martha's Utopian Quest." In *Commonwealth,* edited by Anna Rutherford, 101–113. Aarhus, Denmark: Aarhus University, 1971.

Walker, Melissa G. "Doris Lessing's *The Four-Gated City*: Consciousness and Community—a Different History." *Southern Review* 17 (January 1981): 97–120.

The Golden Notebook

Barnouw, Dagmar. "Disorderly Company: From *The Golden Notebook* to *The Four-Gated City.*" *Contemporary Literature* 14 (Autumn 1973): 491–514.

Bourgeois, Susan. "Golden Notebooks: Patterns in *The Golden Notebook.*" *Doris Lessing Newsletter* 3 (Winter 1979): 5, 12.

Brewster, Dorothy. *Doris Lessing.* New York: Twayne, 1965, pp. 136–157.

Brooks, Ellen W. "The Image of Woman in Lessing's *The Golden Notebook.*" *Critique* 15, no. 1 (1973): 101–109.

Brown, Lloyd W. "The Shape of Things: Sexual Image and the Sense of Form in Doris Lessing's Fiction." *World Literature Written in English* 14 (April 1975): 176–186.

Burkom, Selma R. " 'Only Connect': Form and Content in the Works of Doris Lessing." *Critique* 11, no. 1 (1968): 51–68.

Carey, John L. "Art and Reality in *The Golden Notebook.*" *Contemporary Literature* 14 (Autumn 1973): 437–456.

Carnes, Valerie. " 'Chaos, That's the Point': Art as Metaphor in Doris Lessing's *The Golden Notebook.*" *World Literature Written in English* 15 (April 1976): 17–28.

Cohen, M. " 'Out of the Chaos, and a New Kind of Strength': Doris Lessing's *The Golden Notebook*" In *The Authority of Experience: Essays in Feminist Criticism,* edited by Arlyn Diamond and Lee Edwards, 178–193. Amherst: University of Massachusetts Press, 1977.

Craig, Joanne. "*The Golden Notebook*: The Novelist as Heroine." *University of Windsor Review* 10 (Fall-Winter 1974): 55–66.

Greene, Gayle. "Women and Men in Doris Lessing's *Golden Notebook*: Divided Selves." In *The (M)other Tongue: Essays in Feminist Psychoanalytic Interpretation,* edited by Shirley Garner, Claire Kahane, and Madelon Sprengnether, 280–305. Ithaca, NY: Cornell University Press, 1985.

Hinz, Evelyn, and John J. Teunissen. "The Pieta as Icon in *The Golden Notebook*." *Contemporary Literature* 14 (Autumn 1973): 457–470.

Hite, Molly. "Doris Lessing's *The Golden Notebook* and *The Four-Gated City*: Ideology, Coherence, and Possibility." *Twentieth Century Literature* 34 (Spring 1988): 16–29.

———. "En Gendering Metafiction: Doris Lessing's Rehearsals for *The Golden Notebook*." *Modern Fiction Studies* 34 (Autumn 1988): 481–500.

———. "Subverting the Ideology of Coherence: *The Golden Notebook* and *The Four-Gated City*." In *Doris Lessing,* 61–69.

Howe, Florence. "A Talk with Doris Lessing." *Nation* 204 (March 7, 1967): 311–313.

Hynes, Joseph. "The Construction of *The Golden Notebook*." *Iowa Review* 4 (Summer 1973): 100–113.

Kaplan, Sydney Janet. "The Limits of Consciousness in the Novels of Doris Lessing." *Contemporary Literature* 14 (Autumn 1973): 536–549.

Lebowitz, Naomi. *Humanism and the Absurd in the Modern Novel.* Evanston, IL: Northwestern University Press, 1971, pp. 130–136.

Libby, Marion V. "Sex and the New Woman in *The Golden Notebook*." *Iowa Review* 5 (Fall 1974): 106–120.

Lifson, Martha. "Structural Patterns in *The Golden Notebook*." *Michigan Papers in Women's Studies* 2, no. 4 (1978): 95–108.

Lightfoot, Marjorie J. "Breakthrough in *The Golden Notebook*." *Studies in the Novel* 7 (Summer 1975): 277–285.

———. " 'Fiction' vs. 'Reality': Clues and Conclusions in *The Golden Notebook*." *Modern British Literature* 2 (Fall 1977): 182–188.

McCrindle, Jean. "Reading *The Golden Notebook* in 1962." In *Notebooks/Memoirs/Archives: Reading and Rereading Doris Lessing,* edited by Jenny Taylor, 43–56. Boston: Routledge, 1982.

McDowell, Frederick. " 'The Devious Involutions of Human Character and Emotions': Reflections of Some Recent British Novels." *Wisconsin Studies in Contemporary Literature* 4 (Autumn 1963): 746–750.

————. "The Fiction of Doris Lessing: An Interim View." *Arizona Quarterly* 21 (Winter 1965): 328–330.

Magie, Michael L. "Doris Lessing and Romanticism." *College English* 38 (February 1977): 531–552.

Marchino, Lois A. "The Search for Self in the Novels of Doris Lessing." *Studies in the Novel* 4 (Summer 1972): 252–262.

Maslen, Elizabeth. "One Man's Tomorrow is Another's Today: The Reader's World and its Impact on *Nineteen Eighty-Four.*" In *Storm Warnings,* 146–158.

Morgan, Ellen. "Alienation of the Woman Writer in *The Golden Notebook.*" *Contemporary Literature* 14 (Autumn 1973): 471–480.

Mulkeen, Anne M. "Twentieth Century Realism: The 'Grid' Structure of *The Golden Notebook.*" *Studies in the Novel* 4 (Summer 1972): 262–274.

Mutti, Giuliana. "Female Roles and the Function of Art in *The Golden Notebook.*" *Massachusetts Studies in English* 3 (Spring 1972): 78–83.

Pickering, Jean. *Understanding Doris Lessing,* 90–123.

Porter, Dennis. "Realism and Failure in *The Golden Notebook.*" *Modern Language Quarterly* 35 (March 1974): 56–65.

Rubens, Robert. "Footnote to *The Golden Notebook.*" *Queen* 21 (August 1962): 31–32.

Rubenstein, Roberta. "Doris Lessing's *The Golden Notebook*: The Meaning of its Shape." *American Imago* 32 (Spring 1975): 40–58.

————. *The Novelistic Vision of Doris Lessing*, 71–112.

Schlueter, Paul. *The Novels of Doris Lessing*. Carbondale, IL: Southern Illinois University Press, 1973, pp. 77–116.

Showalter, Elaine. *A Literature of Their Own: British Women Novelists from Brontë to Lessing*. Princeton, NJ: Princeton University Press, 1977, pp. 307–312.

Singleton, Mary Ann. *The City and the Veld*, 83–130.

Sprague, Claire. "Doubletalk and Doubles Talk in *The Golden Notebook*." *Papers on Language and Literature* 18 (Spring 1982): 181–197.

Thorpe, Michael. *Doris Lessing*. Harlow, England: Longman, 1973, pp. 25–29.

Watson, Barbara Bellow. "Leaving the Safety of Myth: Doris Lessing's *The Golden Notebook*." In *Old Lines, New Forces*, 12–37.

The Marriages Between Zones Three, Four and Five

Burton, Deirdre. "Linguistic Innovation in Feminist Utopian Fiction." *Ilha do Desterro* 14, no. 2 (1985): 82–106.

Cleary, Rochelle. "What's in a Name? Lessing's Message in *The Marriages Between Zones Three, Four and Five*." *Doris Lessing Newsletter* 6 (Winter 1982): 8–9.

Jacobs, Naomi. "Beyond Stasis and Symmetry: Lessing, Le Guin and the Remodeling of Utopia." *Extrapolation* 29 (Spring 1988): 34–45.

Khanna, Lee Cullen. "Truth and Art in Women's Worlds: Doris Lessing's *The Marriages Between Zones Three, Four and Five*." In *Women and Utopia*, 121–133.

Peel, Ellen Susan. "Both Ends of the Candle."

————. "Leaving the Self Behind in *Marriages*." *Doris Lessing Newsletter* 11 (Fall 1987): 3, 10.

————. "Utopian Feminism, Skeptical Feminism, and Narrative Energy." In *Feminism, Utopia, and Narrative*, 34–38, 43.

Pickering, Jean. *Understanding Doris Lessing,* 150–158.

Sheiner, Marcy. "Thematic Consistency in the Work of Doris Lessing: The Marriage Between Martha Quest and Zones Three, Four and Five." *Doris Lessing Newsletter* 11 (Fall 1987): 4, 14.

The Memoirs of a Survivor

Carter, Nancy Corson. "Journey Toward Wholeness: A Meditation on Doris Lessing's *The Memoirs of a Survivor.*" *Journal of Evolutionary Psychology* 2 (August 1981): 33–47.

Daymond, M. J. "Areas of the Mind: *The Memoirs of a Survivor* and Doris Lessing's African Stories." *Ariel* 17 (July 1986): 65–82.

Draine, Betsy. "Changing Frames: Doris Lessing's *Memoirs of a Survivor.*" *Studies in the Novel* 11 (Spring 1979): 51–62.

Gardiner, Judith Kegan. "Evil, Apocalypse, and Feminist Fiction." *Frontiers* 7, no. 2 (1983): 74–80.

Green, Martin. "The Doom of Empire: *Memoirs of a Survivor.*" *Doris Lessing Newsletter* 6 (Winter 1982): 6–7, 10.

Hardin, Nancy Shield. "The Sufi Teaching Story and Doris Lessing." *Twentieth Century Literature* 23 (October 1977): 314–325.

Hoffeld, Laura, and Roni Natov. " 'The Summer before the Dark' and *The Memoirs of a Survivor:* Lessing's New Female Bondings." *Doris Lessing Newsletter* 3 (Winter 1979): 11–12.

Lebeau, Cecilia H. "The World Behind the Wall." *Doris Lessing Newsletter* 1 (Fall 1977): 7, 10.

Lott, Sandra. "The Evolving Consciousness of Feminine Identity in Doris Lessing's *The Memoirs of a Survivor* and Lewis Carroll's *Alice in Wonderland* and *Through the Looking-Glass.*" In *Women Worldwalkers,* 165–179.

Matheson, Sue. "Lessing on Stage: An Examination of Theatrical Metaphor and Architectural Motif in *The Memoirs of a Survivor.*" *Doris Lessing Newsletter* 10 (Fall 1986): 8–9.

Newman, Robert D. "Doris Lessing's Mythological Egg in *The Memoirs of a Survivor.*" *Notes on Contemporary Literature* 14 (May 1984): 3–4.

Rubenstein, Roberta. *The Novelistic Vision of Doris Lessing.*

Schutz-Guth, Gudrun. "Doris Lessing: *The Memoirs of a Survivor.*" In *Die Utopie in der Angloamerikanischen Literatur,* 310–327.

Singleton, Mary Ann. *The City and the Veld.*

Walker, Jeanne Murray. "Memory and Culture Within the Individual: The Breakdown of Social Exchange in *Memoirs of a Survivor.*" In *Doris Lessing,* 93–114.

Shikasta

Finney, Kathe Davis. "The Days of Future Past; or, Utopians Lessing and Le Guin Fight Future Nostalgia." In *Patterns of the Fantastic,* 31–40.

Frost, Cheryl. "Breakdown and Regeneration: Some Major Themes in Doris Lessing's Latest Fiction." *LINQ (Literature in North Queensland)* 8, no. 3 (1980): 128–133.

Gray, Stephen. "Circular Imperial History and Zimbabwe in *Shikasta.*" *Doris Lessing Newsletter* 9 (Fall 1985): 11, 16.

Mooney, Jane. "*Shikasta*: Vision or Reality." *Doris Lessing Newsletter* 8 (Spring 1984): 12–14.

Pickering, Jean. *Understanding Doris Lessing,* 143–150.

Wilson, Raymond, III. "Doris Lessing's Symbolic Motifs: The Canopus Novels." *Doris Lessing Newsletter* 6 (Summer 1982): 1, 9–11.

LEWIN, LEONARD C.

Triage

Berger, Harold L. *Science Fiction and the New Dark Age,* 78–82.

LEWIS, C. S.

General Criticism

Sellin, Bernard. "Le Voyage Cosmique: H. G. Wells, David Lindsey, C. S. Lewis." In *Just the Other Day,* 235–248.

Perelandra

Brown, Robert F. "Temptation and Freedom in *Perelandra.*" *Renascence* 37 (Autumn 1984): 52–68.

Burgess, Andrew J. "The Concept of Eden." In *Transcendent Adventure,* 73–81.

Carnell, Corbin Scott. "Ransom in C. S. Lewis' *Perelandra* as Hero in Transformation: Notes Toward a Jungian Reading of the Novel." *Studies in the Literary Imagination* 14 (Fall 1981): 67–71.

Clare, Tullis. "Paradise Unlost." *Time and Tide* 24 (May 1, 1943): 362–363.

Hannay, Margaret P. "The Mythology of *Perelandra.*" *Mythlore* 2, no. 1 (1970): 14–16.

———. "A Preface to *Perelandra.*" In *The Longing for a Form: Essays on the Fiction of C. S. Lewis,* edited by Peter Schakel, 73–90. Kent, OH: Kent State University Press, 1977.

Hobson, Harold. "A Novel of Adam and Eve on the Planet Venus: A London Letter." *Christian Science Monitor* (June 5, 1943): 11 (Weekly Magazine Section).

Hodgens, Richard M. "On the Nature of the Prohibition in *Perelandra.*" *Bulletin of the New York C. S. Lewis Society* 16 (July 1985): 1–6.

Holbrook, David. *The Skeleton in the Wardrobe—C. S. Lewis's Fantasies: A Phenomenological Study.* Lewisburg, PA: Bucknell University Press, 1991, pp. 244–250.

Knight, Bettie Jo. "Paradise Retained: *Perelandra* as Epic." Ph.D. diss., Oklahoma State University, 1983.

Logan, Darlene. "Battle Strategy in *Perelandra*: *Beowulf* Revisited." *Mythlore* 9 (Autumn 1982): 19, 21.

Manlove, C. N. *C. S. Lewis: His Literary Achievement.* London: Macmillan, 1987, pp. 45–74.

Rogers, Katherin A. "Augustinian Evil in C. S. Lewis's *Perelandra.*" In *The Transcendent Adventure,* 83–91.

Wilson, A. N. *C. S. Lewis: A Biography.* London: Collins, 1990, pp. 175, 183–184.

The Ransom Trilogy

Samaan, Angele Botros. "C. S. Lewis, the Utopist, and His Critics." *Cairo Studies in English* (1963–1966): 137–166.

LEWIS, OSCAR

La Vida

Camigliano, Albert J., and Roland A. Champagne. "The Semiotics of Documentary Prose: In Between the Words of *La Vida.*" *Sphinx* 4 (1982): 126–137.

LEWIS, SINCLAIR

It Can't Happen Here

Blotner, Joseph. *Modern American Political Novel.* Austin: University of Texas Press, 1966.

Dooley, D. J. *Art of Sinclair Lewis.* Lincoln: University of Nebraska Press, 1967, pp. 191–195.

Geismar, M. *Last of the Provincials: The American Novel, 1915–1925.* Boston: Houghton Mifflin, 1947, pp. 117–122.

Grebstein, Sheldon N. *Sinclair Lewis.* New York: Twayne, 1962, pp. 139–147.

Jones, James T. "A Middle-Class Utopia: Lewis's *It Can't Happen Here.*" In *Sinclair Lewis at 100: Papers Presented at a Centennial Conference,* edited by Michael Connaughton, 213–225. St. Cloud, MN: St. Cloud State University, 1985.

Milne, G. *The American Political Novel.* Norman, OK: University of Oklahoma Press, 1966, pp. 128–132.

Schorer, M. *Sinclair Lewis: An American Life.* New York: McGraw, 1961, pp. 608–612.

LINDSAY, DAVID

A Voyage to Arcturus

Bloom, Harold. "Clinamen: Towards a Theory of Fantasy." In *Bridges to Fantasy,* edited by George Slusser, Eric Rabkin, and Robert Scholes, 1–20. Carbondale: Southern Illinois University Press, 1982.

Bold, Alan. *Modern Scottish Literature.* London: Longman, 1983, pp. 193–198.

Hume, Kathryn. "Visionary Allegory in David Lindsay's *A Voyage to Arcturus.*" *Journal of English and Germanic Philology* 77 (January 1978): 72–91.

McClure, J. D. "Language and Logic in *A Voyage to Arcturus.*" *Scottish Literary Journal* 1 (1974): 29–38.

MacKey, Douglas A. "Science Fiction and Gnosticism." *Missouri Review* 7, no. 2 (1984): 112–120.

Pohl, Jay. "Dualities in David Lindsay's *A Voyage to Arcturus.*" *Extrapolation* 22 (Summer 1981): 164–169.

Raff, Melvin. "The Structure of *A Voyage to Arcturus.*" *Studies in Scottish Literature* 15 (1980): 262–268.

Sellin, Bernard. *The Life and Works of David Lindsay.* Translated by Kenneth Gunnell. London: Cambridge University Press, 1981, pp. 22–25, 41–52, 56–59.

————. "Le Voyage Cosmique: H. G. Wells, David Lindsay, C. S. Lewis." In *Just the Other Day,* 235–248.

Watson, Ian. "From Pan in the Home Countries—To Pain on a Far Planet: E. M. Forster, David Lindsay, and How the Voyage to Arcturus Should End." *Foundation* 43 (Summer 1988): 25–36.

Wilson, Colin. *The Haunted Man: The Strange Genius of David Lindsay.* San Bernardino, CA: Borgo Press, 1979, pp. 14–33.

Wolfe, Gary K. *David Lindsay.* Mercer Island, WA: Starmont House, 1982, pp. 8–11, 14–39.

LOBATO, JOSE MONTEIRO

Farm of the Yellow Woodpecker

Alex, Nola Kortner. *A Brazilian Oz?* Louisville, KY: Popular Culture Association, 1985. ERIC (ED 291098).

LONDON, JACK

General Criticism

Khouri, Nadia. "The Other Side of Otherness."

"The Dream of Debs"

McClintock, James. *White Logic: Jack London's Short Stories.* Grand Rapids, MI: Wolf House Books, 1975, pp. 127–128.

"Goliah"

Walker, Dale L. *The Alien Worlds of Jack London.* Grand Rapids, Michigan, MI: Wolf House, 1973.

The Iron Heel

Ainsa, Fernando. "Antes de *1984.*" *Plural* 15 (May 1986): 37–41.

Baskett, Sam S. "A Source of *The Iron Heel.*" *American Literature* 27 (May 1955): 268–270.

Beauchamp, Gorman. *"The Iron Heel* and *Looking Backward*: Two Paths to Utopia." *American Literary Realism, 1870–1910* 9 (Autumn 1976): 307–314.

——. "Jack London's Utopian Dystopia and Dystopian Utopia." In *America as Utopia,* 91–107.

Karrer, Wolfgang. "Jack London: *The Iron Heel.*" In *Die Utopie in der Angloamerikanischen Literatur,* 176–195.

Ketterer, David. *New Worlds for Old,* 123–156.

Portelli, Alessandro. "Jack London's Missing Revolution: Notes on *The Iron Heel.*" *Science-Fiction Studies* 9 (July 1982): 180–194.

Rideout, Walter B. *The Radical Novel in the United States, 1900–1954,* 42, 44, 46, 47, 53, 60.

Siegel, Paul N. "Jack London's *Iron Heel*: Its Significance for Today." *International Socialist Review* (July-August 1974): 18–29.

Tambling, Victor. "Jack London and George Orwell: A Literary Kinship." In *George Orwell,* 171–175.

Ward, Susan. "Ideology for the Masses: Jack London's *The Iron Heel.*" In *Critical Essays on Jack London,* edited by Jacqueline Tavernier-Courbin, 166–179. Boston: Hall, 1983.

The Valley of the Moon

Crow, Charles L. "Homecoming in the California Visionary Romance." *Western American Literature* 24 (May 1989): 1–19.

LONGLEY, ALCANDER

What Is Communism?

Rooney, Charles J., Jr. *Dreams and Visions,* 105, 192.

LONGUEVILLE, PETER

The Hermit

Harkins, Patricia. "From Robinson Crusoe to Philip Quarll: The Transformation of a Robinsonade." *Publications of the Mississippi Philological Association* (1988): 64–73.

LUCIAN

General Criticism

Branham, R. Bracht. "Utopian Laughter: Lucian and Thomas More."
Moreana 22 (July 1985): 23–43.

Mezciems, Jenny. "Swift's Praise of Gulliver: Some Renaissance
Background to the *Travels.*" In *The Character of Swift's Satire,*
245–281.

Icaromennipus

Bailey, J. O. *Pilgrims Through Space and Time,* 167, 221.

Branham, R. Bracht. *Unruly Eloquence: Lucian and the Comedy of
Traditions.* Cambridge, MA: Harvard Univesity Press, 1989, pp. 14–16.

Nablow, Ralph Arthur. "Was Voltaire Influenced by Lucian in *Micromegas?*" *Romance Notes* 22 (Winter 1981): 186–191.

LYTTON, EDWARD GEORGE EARLE

The Coming Race

Aldridge, A. *The Scientific World View in Dystopia,* 9–11.

Bailey, J. O. *Pilgrims Through Space and Time,* 51–54.

Berneri, Marie Louise. *Journey Through Utopia,* 235–243.

Campbell, James L., Sr. *Edward Bulwer-Lytton.* Boston: Twayne, 1986,
pp. 125–127.

————. "Edward Bulwer-Lytton's *The Coming Race* as a Condemnation of Advanced Ideas." *Essays in Arts and Sciences* 16 (May 1987): 55–63.

Christensen, Allan Conrad. *Edward Bulwer-Lytton: The Fiction of New Regions.* Athens: University of Georgia Press, 1976, pp. 177–181, 218–220.

Furbank, P. *Samuel Butler, 82–94.*

Garrett, J. C. *Utopias in Literature Since the Romantic Period,* 29–34.

Knepper, B. G. "*The Coming Race*: Hell? or Paradise Foretasted?" In *No Place Else,* 11–32.

Lamarca Margalef, Jordi. *Ciencia y Literatura: El Cientifico en la Literaturea Inglesa de Los Siglos XIX y XX.* Barcelona: Ediciones de la Universidad de Barcelona, 1983, pp. 61–62, 92, 160.

Ross, Harry. *Utopias Old and New,* 101–117.

Sedlak, Werner. "Utopie und Darwinismus." In *Alternative Welten,* 216–238.

Seeber, Hans Ulrich. "Gegenutopie und Roman: Bulwer-Lyttons *The Coming Race.*" *Deutsche Vierteljahresschrift* 45 (1971): 150–180.

————. *Wandlungen der Form in der Literarischen Utopie: Studien zur Entfaltung des Utopischen Romans in England.* Goppingen: Kummerle, 1970, pp. 207–214.

Suvin, Darko. "The Extraordinary Voyage, the Future War, and Bulwer's *The Coming Race*: Three Sub-Genres of British Science Fiction, 1871–1885." *Literature and History* 10 (Autumn 1984): 231–248.

Trousson, Raymond. *Voyages aux Pays de Nulle Part,* 222–223.

Wagner, Geoffrey. "A Forgotten Satire: Bulwer-Lytton's *The Coming Race.*" *Nineteenth-Century Fiction* 19 (March 1965): 379–385.

Wolff, Robert Lee. *Strange Stories and Other Explorations in Victorian Fiction.* Boston: Gambit, 1971, pp. 323–333.

MACAULAY, ROSE

What Not

Albinski, Nan Bowman. "Thomas and Peter: Society and Poetics in Four British Utopian Novels." *Utopian Studies* 1 (1987): 11–22.

———. *Women's Utopias in British and American Fiction,* 79, 80, 82, 83, 103.

Bensen, Alice. *Rose Macaulay.* New York: Twayne, 1969, pp. 50, 64–68.

Passty, Jeanette N. *Eros and Androgyny: The Legacy of Rose Macaulay.* London: Associated University Presses, 1988, pp. 45–46, 116–117.

McCOY, JOHN

A Prophetic Romance

Rooney, Charles J., Jr. *Dreams and Visions,* 118, 192–193.

MACHIAVELLI, NICCOLO

General Criticism

Ianziti, Gary. "Rabelais and Machiavelli." *Romance Notes* 16 (Winter 1975): 460–473.

The Prince

Cro, Roslyn Pesman. "Machiavelli e l'Antiutopia." In *Machiavelli Attuale/Machiavel Actuel,* 27–33.

Di Scipio, Giuseppe C. "*De re Militari* in Machiavelli's *Prince* and More's *Utopia.*" *Moreana* 20 (February 1983): 11–22.

Ruffo-Fiore, Silvia. *Niccola Machiavelli.* Boston: Twayne, 1982, pp. 29–60.

Tinkler, John. "Praise and Advice: Rhetorical Approaches in More's *Utopia* and Machiavelli's *The Prince.*" *Sixteenth Century Journal* 19 (Summer 1988): 187–207.

McINTYRE, VONDA

Dream Snake

Albinski, Nan Bowman. *Women's Utopias in British and American Fiction,* 98, 172, 176, 184.

Zaki, Hoda M. *Phoenix Renewed,* 65–66, 67, 73.

MACNIE, J.

The Diothas

Cranny-Francis, Anne. *Feminist Fiction,* 116.

Frye, Northrop. "Varieties of Literary Utopias." In *Utopias and Utopian Thought,* 30–31.

Parrington, Vernon Louis, Jr. *American Dreams,* 57–61.

MADARIAGA Y ROJO, SALVADOR DE

General Criticism

Sacks, Norman P. "Salvador de Madariaga and George Orwell: Parallels and Contrasts." In *Estudios en Honor de Rodolfo Oroz,* 285–297.

MAITLAND, EDWARD

By and By

Seavey, Ormond. Introduction. *By and By: An Historical Romance of the Future.* By Edward Maitland. Boston: Gregg Press, 1977, v-xii.

MALLOCK, WILLIAM H.

The New Republic

Jaudel, Philippe. "*The New Republic* de William Hurrell Mallock: Dialogue de Mandarms dans la Bonne Société Victorienne." In *Essais sur de Dialogue*, 139–155. Grenoble, France: Publications del'Universités des Langues & Lettres, 1980.

Ross, Harry. *Utopias Old and New*, 91–94.

MARQUIS DE SADE. See SADE, DONATIEN ALPHONSE FRANÇOIS, COMTE DE

MARQUIS, DON

The Almost Perfect State

Frye, Northrop. "Varieties of Literary Utopias." In *Utopias and Utopian Thought*, 44.

MASON, DOUGLAS R.

Eight Against Utopia

Berger, Harold L. *Science Fiction and the New Dark Age*, 97–98.

MEARS, AMELIA GARLAND

Mercia, The Astronomer Royal

Albinski, Nan Bowman. " 'The Laws of Justice, of Nature, and of Right': Victorian Feminist Utopias." In *Feminism, Utopia, and Narrative*, 52, 54, 58.

MEHRING, FRANZ

Herrn Eugen Richters Bilder aus der Gegenwart

Asholt, Wolfgang. "Sozialistische Irrlehren und Liberale Zerrbilder: Die Anfrange der Anti-Utopie." *Germanisch-Romanische Monatsschrift Grundzuge* 35, no. 4 (1985): 369–381.

MELVILLE, HERMAN

General Criticism

Greiner, Jean. "L'Utopie du Mal." *Nouvelle Revue Francaise* 14 (October 1966): 678–688.

Mardi

Arvin, Newton. "Melville's *Mardi.*" *American Quarterly* 2 (Spring 1950): 71–81.

Bernard, Kenneth. "Melville's *Mardi* and the Second Loss of Paradise." *Lock Haven Review* 7 (1965): 23–30.

Collins, Carvel. "Melville's *Mardi.*" *Explicator* 12 (May 1954): Item 42.

Freeman, John. *Herman Melville.* New York: Macmillan, 1926, pp. 95–108.

Graham, Philip. "The Riddle of Melville's *Mardi*: A Re-Interpretation." *Texas Studies in English* 36 (1957): 93–99.

Jaffe, David. "Some Sources of Melville's *Mardi.*" *American Literature* 9 (March 1937): 56–69.

Larrabee, Stephen A. "Melville Against the World." *South Atlantic Quarterly* 34 (October 1935): 410–418.

Mason, Ronald. *The Spirit Above the Dust,* 38–65.

Miller, James E., Jr. "The Many Masks of *Mardi.*" *Journal of English and Germanic Philology* 58 (July 1959): 400–413.

Mumford, Lewis. *Herman Melville.* New York: Harcourt, Brace, 1929, pp. 93–107.

Sedgwick, William Ellery. *Herman Melville,* 37–61.

Stern, Milton R. *The Fine Hammered Steel of Herman Melville,* 66–149.

Stone, Geoffrey. *Melville.* New York: Sheed and Ward, 1949, pp. 86–108.

Thompson, Lawrance. *Melville's Quarrel with God.* Princeton, NJ: Princeton University Press, 1952, pp. 59–69.

Wright, Nathalia. "The Head and the Heart in Melville's *Mardi.*" *PMLA* 66 (June 1951): 351–362.

Typee

Beauchamp, Gorman. "Melville and the Tradition of Primitive Utopia." *Journal of General Education* 33 (Spring 1981): 6–14.

———. "Montaigne, Melville, and the Cannibals." *Arizona Quarterly* 37 (Winter 1981): 293–309.

Berthold, Michael C. " 'Portentous Somethings': Melville's *Typee* and the Language of Captivity." *New England Quarterly* 60 (December 1987): 549–567.

Firebaugh, J. J. "Humanist as Rebel: The Melville of *Typee.*" *Nineteenth-Century Fiction* 9 (September 1954): 108–120.

Frederix, Pierre. *Herman Melville.* Paris: Gallimard, 1950, pp. 132–147.

Hamada, Masajiro. "Two Utopian Types of American Literature— *Typee* and *The Crater.*" *Studies in English Literature (U. of Tokyo)* 40 (March 1964): 119–214.

Lawrence, D. H. *Studies in Classic American Literature.* New York: Doubleday, 1955, pp. 142–156.

Mason, Ronald. *The Spirit Above the Dust,* 21–30.

Ruland, Richard. "Melville and the Fortunate Fall: *Typee* as Eden." *Nineteenth-Century Fiction* 23 (December 1968): 312–323.

Sedgwick, William Ellery. *Herman Melville,* 19–35.

Short, Byron. " 'The Author at the Time': Tommo and Melville's Self-Discovery in *Typee.*" *Texas Studies in Literature and Language* 31 (Fall 1989): 386–405.

Stanton, Robert. *"Typee* and Milton: Paradise Well Lost." *Modern Language Notes* 74 (May 1959): 407–411.

Stern, Milton R. *The Fine Hammered Steel of Herman Melville,* 29–65.

MENDES, HENRY PEREIRA

Looking Ahead

Rooney, Charles J., Jr. *Dreams and Visions,* 127–128, 193.

MERCIER, LOUIS-SÉBASTIEN

L'an Deux Mille Quatre Cent Quarante

Bailey, J. O. *Pilgrims Through Space and Time,* 26–27.

Bloomfield, Paul. *Imaginary Worlds, or the Evolution of Utopia,* 125–139.

Denoit, Nicole. "La Rencontre de l'Utopie et de Certaines Valeurs-Clés des Lumières: Louis-Sébastien Mercier Utopiste, *L'An 2440.*" *Studies on Voltaire and the Eighteenth Century* 265 (1989): 1625–1628.

Doring, Ulrich. "Images d'Un Monde Meilleur? Louis-Sébastien Mercier: *L'An 2440*: Rêve S'il en fut Jamais." In *Ouverture et Dialogue,* edited by Ulrich Doring, Antiopy Lyroudias, and Rainer Zaiser, 653–668. Tubingen: Narr, 1988.

Fohrmann, Jurgen. "Utopie und Untergang: L. S. Merciers *L'An 2440.*" In *Literarische Utopien von Morus dis zur Gegenwart,* 105–124.

Hadarits, Jozsef. "Mercier's Utopia in Hungarian Miniature." *Studies on Voltaire and the Eighteenth Century* 265 (1989): 1,719–1,722.

Walsh, Chad. *From Utopia to Nightmare,* 59.

MERRILL, ALBERT ADAMS

The Great Awakening

Parrington, Vernon Louis, Jr. *American Dreams,* 149–151.

Rooney, Charles J., Jr. *Dreams and Visions,* 74, 117, 150, 193–194.

MICHAELIS, RICHARD

Looking Further Forward

Bailey, J. O. *Pilgrims Through Space and Time,* 57.

Egbert, Nelson Norris. "Problems of Form and Content in Six Utopian Responses to Edward Bellamy's *Looking Backward: 2000–1887.*"

Parrington, Vernon Louis, Jr. *American Dreams,* 84–86.

Walsh, Chad. *From Utopia to Nightmare,* 75.

MILLER, JOAQUIN

The Building of the City Beautiful

Parrington, Vernon Louis, Jr. *American Dreams,* 161–163.

Roemer, Kenneth M. *The Obsolete Necessity,* 68, 73.

MILLER, WALTER MICHAEL, JR.

A Canticle for Leibowitz

Hanzo, Thomas A. "The Past of Science Fiction." In *Bridges to Science Fiction,* 131–146.

Kievitt, Frank David. "Walter M. Miller's *A Canticle for Leibowitz* as a Third Testament." In *The Transcendent Adventures,* 169–175.

Manganiello, Dominic. "History as Judgment and Promise in *A Canticle for Leibowitz*." *Science-Fiction Studies* 13 (July 1986): 159–169.

Scheick, William J. "Continuative and Ethical Predictions: The Post-Nuclear Holocaust Novel of the 1980s" *North Dakota Quarterly* 56 (Spring 1988): 61–82.

Spector, Judith. "Walter Miller's *A Canticle for Leibowitz*: A Parable for our Time?" *Midwest Quarterly* 22 (Summer 1981): 337–345.

Wagar, W. Warren. "Round Trip to Doomsday." In *The End of the World*, 73–96.

Young, R. V. "Catholic Science Fiction and the Comic Apocalypse: Walker Percy and Walter Miller." *Renascence* 40 (Winter 1988): 95–110.

Zaki, Hoda M. *Phoenix Renewed*, 29.

MINNETT, CORA

The Day After Tomorrow

Albinski, Nan Bowman. *Women's Utopias in British and American Fiction*, 26, 30, 43.

———. " 'The Laws of Justice, of Nature, and of Right': Victorian Feminist Utopias." in *Feminism, Utopia, and Narrative*, 52, 54.

MITCHISON, NAOMI MARGARET

We Have Been Warned

Albinski, Nan Bowman. *Women's Utopias in British and American Fiction*, 76, 78, 79, 90, 104.

Mitchison, Naomi Margaret. *You May Well Ask: A Memoir, 1920–1940*. London: Victor Gollancz, 1979, pp. 172–179.

MONTAIGNE, MICHEL EYQUEM DE

"Des Cannibales"

Beauchamp, Gorman. "Montaigne, Melville, and the Cannibals." *Arizona Quarterly* 37 (Winter 1981): 293–309.

Certeau, Michel de. "Le lieu de L'Autre Montaigne: 'Des Cannibales.' " *Oeuvres and Critiques* 8, nos. 1–2 (1983): 59–62.

DeFaux, Gerard. "Un Cannibale en haut de Chausses: Montaigne, la Différence et la Logique de l'Identité." *Modern Language Notes* 97 (May 1982): 918–957.

Duval, Edwin M. "Lessons of the New World: Design and Meaning in Montaigne's 'Des Cannibales' and 'Des Coches.' " In *Montaigne: Essays in Reading,* edited by Gerard DeFaux, 95–112. New Haven, CT: Yale French Studies, 1983.

Francon, Marcel. "Cannibales, Rabelais et Montaigne." *Bulletin de la Societé des Amis de Montaigne* 13–14 (1983): 106–108.

Giordano, Michael J. "Re-Reading 'Des Cannibales': 'Véritable Tesmoignage' and the Chain of Supplements." *Neophilologus (Groningen, Netherlands)* 69 (January 1985): 25–33.

Scaglione, A. D. "A Note on Montaigne's 'Des Cannibales' and the Humanist Tradition." In *First Images of America: The Impact of the New World on the Old,* edited by Fredi Chiappelli, 63–70. Berkeley: University of California Press, 1976.

White, Frederic R. *Famous Utopias of the Renaissance,* 139–150.

MOORCOCK, MICHAEL

General Criticism

Nicholls, Peter. "Moorcock, Michael, 1939– ." In *Science Fiction Writers: Critical Studies of the Major Authors from the Early Nineteenth Century to the Present Day,* edited by Everett Franklin Bleiler, 449–457. New York: Scribner's, 1982.

The Final Programme

Glover, David. "Utopia and Fantasy in the Late 1960's: Burroughs, Moorcock, Tolkien." In *Popular Fiction and Social Change,* 201–203.

Greenland, Colin. *The Entropy Exhibition: Michael Moorcock and the British 'New Wave' in Science Fiction.* London: Routledge & Kegan Paul, 1983, pp. 140–145.

MOORE, M. LOUISE

Al-Modad

Albinski, Nan Bowman. *Women's Utopias in British and American Fiction,* 73.

Rooney, Charles J., Jr. *Dreams and Visions,* 101, 194.

MORE, [SIR] THOMAS

Utopia

Abrash, Merritt. "Missing the Point in More's *Utopia.*" *Extrapolation* 19 (December 1977): 27–38.

Adams, Robert P. "The Philosophic Unity of More's *Utopia.*" *Studies in Philology* 38 (January 1941): 45–65.

Ainsa, Fernando. "America como Proyecto Ideal de Europa: Mito y Utopia del Descubrimiento y la Conquista." *Pailinure* (1985–1986): 12–21.

Allen, Peter R. "*Utopia* and European Humanism: The Function of the Prefatory Letters and Verses." *Studies in the Renaissance* 10 (1963): 91–107.

Allen, Ward. "More and the Bible." *Moreana* 8 (May 1971): 45–46.

———. "More, Shakespeare, and the Bible." *Moreana* 7 (December 1970): 24.

Ames, Russell. *Citizen Thomas More and His Utopia.* Princeton, NJ: Princeton University Press, 1949.

Astell, Ann W. "Rhetorical Strategy and the Fiction of Audience in More's *Utopia.*" *Centennial Review* 29 (Summer 1985): 302–319.

Bailey, J. O. *Pilgrims Through Space and Time,* 11, 24, 237, 262, 297.

Baker-Smith, Dominic. "The Escape from the Cave: Thomas More and the Vision of Utopia." In *Between Dream and Nature,* 5–19.

Berger, Harry. *Second World and Green World: Studies in Renaissance Fiction Making.* Berkeley: University of California Press, 1988, pp. 3–40, 229–248.

Berneri, Marie Louise. *Journey Through Utopia,* 58–88.

Bevington, David M. "The Dialogue in *Utopia*: Two Sides to the Question." *Studies in Philology* 58 (July 1961): 496–509.

Blaim, Artur. "More's *Utopia*: Persuasion or Polyphony?" *Moreana* 19 (March 1982): 5–20.

Bleich, David. "More's *Utopia*: Confessional Modes." *American Imago* 28 (1971): 24–52.

Boewe, Charles. "Human Nature in More's Utopia." *Personalist* 41 (Summer 1960): 303–309.

Borardus, E. S. *Development of Social Thought.* 3rd edition. New York: Longmans, 1955, pp. 179–195.

Bourles, Charles. "La Place de l'Utopie dans la Littérature de Science Fiction." *Moreana* 21 (December 1984): 197–203.

Bradshaw, David. "Thomas White on Plato and *Utopia.*" *Moreana* 21 (December 1984): 51–53.

Branham, R. Bracht. "Utopian Laughter: Lucian and Thomas More." *Moreana* 22 (July 1985): 23–43.

Brewer, J. S. *The Reign of Henry VIII from His Accession to the Death of Wolsey.* Volume 1. Edited by James Gairdner. London: John Murray, 1884, pp. 285–297.

Bridgett, Thomas E. *Life and Writings of Sir Thomas More.* New York: Scholarly Press, 1976.

Bude, Guillaume. Letter to Thomas Lupset on July 31, 1517. In *More's Utopia and Its Critics,* 81–86.

Busleyden, Jerome. Letter to Thomas More. In *More's Utopia and Its Critics,* 87–89.

Campbell, W. E. *More's Utopia and His Social Teaching.* London: Eyre & Spottiswoode, 1930.

Cavanaugh, John R. "*Utopia*: Sound from Nowhere." *Moreana* 9 (1972): 27–38.

Chambers, R. W. *The Place of Saint Thomas More in English Literature and History.* Brooklyn, NY: Haskell, 1969.

———. *Thomas More.* London: Cape, 1935.

Chesterton, G. K. "Thomas More." In *The English Way: Studies in English Sanctity from St. Bede to Newman,* edited by Maisie Ward, 211–212. London: Sheed and Ward, 1933.

Christensen, Bryce J. *Utopia Against the Family,* 2–3.

Clarke, I. F. "The Future Is Another Place (From Space to Time)." *Futures* 22 (September 1990): 752–760.

Cranny-Francis, Anne. *Feminist Fiction,* 109–111.

Cro, Stelio. "Machiavelli e l'Antiutopia." In *Machiavelli Attuale/ Machiavel Actuel,* 27–33.

———. *Realidad y Utopia en el Descubrimiento y Conquista de la America Hispana.* Troy, MI: International Book Publishers, 1983.

Davis, J. C. *Utopia and the Ideal Society,* 41–61.

Derrett, J. "The Utopians' Stoic Chamber-Pots." *Moreana* 19 (March 1982): 75–76.

Desroche, Henri. "De Thomas More à Etienne Cabet." *Moreana* 8 1971): 215–219.

Desroches, Rosny. "L'Utopie: Évasion ou Anticipation?" In *France and North America,* 83–92.

Di Scipio, Giuseppe C. "*De re Militari* in Machiavelli's *Prince* and More's *Utopia.*" *Moreana* 20 (February 1983): 11–22.

Donner, Henry W. Introduction. *Utopia.* By Sir Thomas More. Freeport, NY: Books for Libraries Press, 1969.

Dooley, Patrick. "More's *Utopia* and the New World Utopias: Is the Good Life an Easy Life?" *Thought* 60 (March 1985): 31–48.

———. "Theory in *Utopia* vs. Practice in Utopias." *Moreana* 22 (November 1985): 57–60.

Downs, R. B. *Molders of the Modern Mind,* 13–17.

Doyle, Charles C. "*Utopia* and the Proper Place of Gold: Classical Sources and Renaissance Analogues." *Moreana* 8 (1971): 47–49.

Duhamel, P. Albert. "Medievalism of More's *Utopia.*" *Studies in Philology* 52 (April 1955): 99–126.

Erzgraber, Willi. "Thomas Morun: *Utopia.*" In *Literarische Utopien von Morus bis zur Gengenwart,* 25–43.

Evans, John X. "Utopia on Prospero's Island." *Moreana* 18 (March 1981): 81–83.

Fleisher, Martin. *Radical Reform and Political Persuasion in the Life and Writings of Thomas More.* Geneva: Droz, 1973.

Fox, Alistair. "In Search of the Real Thomas More: An Approach to *Utopia.*" In *Thomas More: The Rhetoric of Character,* edited by Alistair Fox and Peter Leech, 17–34. Dunedin, New Zealand: Department of University Extension, University of Otago, 1979.

Gallagher, Ligeia, ed. *More's Utopia and Its Critics.*

Garavaglia, Gian-Paolo. "I Livellatori e *L'Utopia.*" *Moreana* 8 (1971): 191–196.

Gordon, Walter M. "Dialogue, Myth, and More's Utopian Drama." *Cithara* 25 (November 1985): 19–34.

Grace, William. "The Conception of Society in More's *Utopia.*" *Thought* 22 (June 1947): 283–296.

Graziani, Rene. "Non-Utopian Euthanasia: An Italian Report, c. 1554." *Renaissance Quarterly* 22 (Winter 1969): 329–333.

Greenblatt, S. J. *Renaissance Self-Fashioning: From More to Shakespeare.* Chicago: University of Chicago Press, 1980, pp. 11–73.

Gueguen, John A. "Reading More's *Utopia* as a Criticism of Plato." In *Quincentennial Essays on St. Thomas More,* edited by Michael Moore, 43–54. Boone, NC: Albion, 1978.

Gury, Jacques. "Nouvelles Lectures de l'*Utopie.*" *Moreana* 24 (December 1987): 125–130.

Hammond, Eugene R. "Nature—Reason—Justice in *Utopia* and *Gulliver's Travels.*" *SEL: Studies in English Literature, 1500–1900* 22 (Summer 1982): 446–468.

Harbison, E. H. "Machiavelli's *Prince* and More's *Utopia.*" In *Facets of the Renaissance,* edited by W. H. Werkmeister, 41–71. Los Angeles: University of Southern California Press, 1959.

Hardesty, William H., III. "The Programmed Utopia of R. A. Lafferty's *Past Master.*" In *Clockwork Worlds,* 105–113.

Heiserman, A. R. "Satire in the *Utopia.*" *PMLA* 78 (June 1963): 163–174.

Helgerson, Richard. "Inventing Noplace, or the Power of Negative Thinking." *Genre* 15 (Spring-Summer 1982): 101–121.

Hertzler, Joyce Oramel. *The History of Utopian Thought,* 127–146.

Hewitt, Janice L. "More to Orwell: An Early Leap from *Utopia* to *Nineteen Eighty-Four.*" In *George Orwell,* 127–133.

Hexter, J. H. *More's Utopia: The Biography of an Idea.* Princeton, NJ: Princeton University Press, 1952.

———. "Utopia and Geneva." In *Action and Conviction in Early Modern Europe: Essays in Memory of E. H. Harbison,* 77–89.

————. *Vision of Politics on the Eve of the Reformation: More, Machiavelli, Seyssel.* New York: Basic Books, 1973, pp. 19–137.

Ho, Koon-Ki T. "Utopianism: A Unique Theme in Western Literature? A Short Survey on Chinese Utopianism." *Tamkang Review* 13 (Fall 1982): 87–108.

Johnson, Robbin S. *More's 'Utopia': Ideal and Illusion.* New Haven, CT: Yale University Press, 1969.

Jones, E. "Commoners and Kings: Book One of More's *Utopia.*" In *Medieval Studies for J. A. W. Bennett,* edited by P. L. Heyworth, 255–272. Oxford: Clarendon, 1981.

Jones, Judith Paterson. "Recent Studies in More." *English Literary Renaissance* 9 (Autumn 1979): 442–458.

Kaufmann, M. *Utopias,* 1–13.

Kautsky, Karl. *Thomas More and His Utopia.* Translated by H. J. Stenning. New York: Russell, 1959.

Kennedy, W. J. *Rhetorical Norms in Renaissance Literature.* New Haven, CT: Yale University Press, 1978, pp. 79–127.

Khanna, Lee Cullen. "More's *Utopia*: A Literary Perspective on Social Reform." Ph.D. diss., Columbia University, 1969.

Kinney, A. F. *Humanist Poetics: Thought, Rhetoric, and Fiction in Sixteenth-Century England.* Amherst: University of Massachusetts Press, 1986.

————. "Rhetoric as Poetic: Humanist Fiction in the Renaissance." *ELH* 43 (Winter 1976): 413–443.

Koppenfels, Werner von. "Thomas Morus und die Humanistische Utopie der Renaissance." In *Alternative Welten,* 96–113.

Laidler, Harry Wellington. *Social-Economic Movements,* 22–29.

Lange, Bernd-Peter. "Thomas More: *Utopia.*" In *Die Utopie in der Angloamerikanischen Literatur,* 11–31.

Lanham, Richard A. "More, Castiglione, and the Humanist Choice of Utopias." In *Acts of Interpretation,* 327–343.

Lederer, Dietrich. "Thomas Morus' *Utopia*: Weltbild, Menschenbild und Literatur." *Weimarer Beitrage* 31, no. 7 (1985): 1,150–1,160.

Logan, George M. *The Meaning of More's 'Utopia.'* Princeton, NJ: Princeton University Press, 1983.

Ludwig, Hans-Werner. "Thomas More's *Utopia*: Historical Setting and Literary Effectiveness." In *Intellectuals and Writers in Fourteenth-Century Europe,* edited by Peiro Boitani, 244–264. Tubingen, Germany: Narr, 1986.

McCutcheon, Elizabeth. "The Language of Utopia Negation: Book II of More's *Utopia.*" In *Acts Conventus Neo-Latini Bononiensis,* edited by R. Schoeck, 510–519. Binghamton, NY: Medieval and Renaissance Texts & Studies, 1985.

————. "Time in More's *Utopia.*" In *Acta Conventus Neo-Latini Turonensis: Troisieme Congres International d'Etudes Neo-Latins, Tours,* edited by Jean-Claude Margolin, 697–707. Paris: Librairie Philosophique J Vrin, 1980.

Major, J. R. "The Renaissance Monarchy as Seen by Erasmus, More, Seyssel, and Machiavelli." In *Action and Conviction in Early Modern Europe,* 17–31.

Marin, Louis. "Voyages en Utopie." *L'Ésprit Créateur* 25 (Fall 1985): 42–51.

Marius, Richard. *Thomas More: A Biography.* New York: Knopf, 1984.

Mason, H. A. *Humanism and Poetry in the Early Tudor Period.* New York: Barnes & Noble, 1959.

Metscher, Thomas. "The Irony of Thomas More: Reflections on the Literary and Ideological Status of Utopia." *Shakespeare Jahrbuch* 118 (1982): 120–130.

Mezciems, Jenny. "Utopia and 'The Thing Which Is Not': More, Swift, and other Lying Idealists." *University of Toronto Quarterly* 52 (Fall 1982): 40–62.

Miething, Christoph. "Platon, Dante et More: Esquisse d'Une Théorie de l'Utopie Littéraire." In *De l'Utopie à l'Unchronie,* 153–155.

————. "Politeia und Utopia: Zur Epistemologie der Literarischen Utopie." *Germanisch-Romanische Monatsschrift* 37, no. 3 (1987): 247–263.

Miles, Leland. "Literary Artistry of Thomas More." *Studies in English Literature* 6 (1966): 7–33.

Morgan, Alice B. "Philosophic Reality and Human Construction in the *Utopia.*" *Moreana* 10 (September 1973): 15–23.

Mortimer, Anthony. "Hythlodaeus and Persona More: The Narrative Voices of *Utopia.*" *Cahiers Elisabethains* 28 (October 1985): 23- 35.

Mumford, Lewis. *The Story of Utopias,* 59–78.

Nagel, Alan F. "Lies and the Limitable Inane: Contradiction in More's *Utopia.*" *Renaissance Quarterly* 26 (Summer 1973): 173–180.

Papazu, Monica. "La Tentation Utopique." *Moreana* 22 (November 1985): 157–166.

Perlette, John M. "Of Sites and Parasites: The Centrality of the Marginal Anecdote in Book 1 of More's *Utopia.*" *ELH* 54 (Summer 1987): 231–252.

Raitiere, Martin N. "More's *Utopia* and *The City of God.*" *Studies in the Renaissance* 20 (1973): 144–168.

Rebhorn, W. A. "Thomas More's Enclosed Garden: Utopia and Renaissance Humanism." *English Literary Renaissance* 6 (Spring 1976): 140–155.

Reynolds, E. E. "A Present-Day Communist View of More's *Utopia.*" *Moreana* 9 (1972): 31–32.

————. "Three Views of *Utopia.*" *Moreana* 8 (November 1971): 209–214.

Rimmer, Robert H. "Alternative Lifestyles on the Road to Utopia." In *France and North America,* 149–163.

Ross, Harry. *Utopias Old and New,* 54–63.

Samaan, Angele Botros. "Death and the Death-Penalty in More's *Utopia* and Some Utopian Novels." *Moreana* 23 (June 1986): 5–15.

————. "More's *Utopia* and the Utopian Novel: The Popularity of the Genre." *Moreana* 15, no. 58 (1978): 33–39.

Sanderlin, George. "The Meaning of Thomas More's *Utopia.*" *College English* 12 (1950): 74–77.

Sawada, Paul A. "Toward a Definition of *Utopia.*" *Moreana* 8 (November 1971): 135–146.

Schoeck, Richard J. "More, Plutarch, and King Agis: Spartan History and the Meaning of *Utopia.*" *Philological Quarterly* 35 (1956): 366–375.

Seeber, Hans Ulrich. "Thomas Morus' *Utopia* und Edward Bellamys *Looking Backward*: Ein Funktionsgeschichtlicher Vergleich." In *Utopieforschung,* Volume 3, 357–377.

Skinner, Quentin. "More's *Utopia.*" *Past and Present* 38 (1967): 153–168.

————. "Sir Thomas More's *Utopia* and the Language of Renaissance Humanism." In *The Languages of Political Theory in Early-Modern Europe,* edited by A. Pagden, 123–157. New York: Cambridge University Press, 1987.

Slavin, A. J. "The American Principle from More to Locke." In *First Images of America: The Impact of the New World on the Old,* edited by Fred Chiappell, 139–164. Berkeley: University of California Press, 1976.

Smith, C. N. "Andre Raulin's *l'Utopiste.*" *Moreana* 21 (December 1984): 44.

Sowards, J. K. "Some Factors in the Re-Evaluation of Thomas More's *Utopia.*" *Northwest Missouri State College Studies* 16 (June 1, 1952): 31–58.

Sullivan, E. D. S. "Place in No Place: Examples of the Ordered Society in Literature." In *The Utopian Vision,* 29–49.

Surtz, Edward. "Logic in Utopia." *Philological Quarterly* 29 (October 1950): 389–401.

———. *The Praise of Pleasure: Philosophy, Education, and Communism in More's Utopia.* Cambridge, MA: Harvard University Press, 1957.

———. "Thomas More and Communism." *PMLA* 64 (June 1949): 549–564.

Suvin, Darko. *Metamorphoses of Science Fiction: On the Poetics and History of a Literary Genre.* New Haven, CT: Yale University Press, 1979.

———. "*The Time Machine* versus *Utopia* as a Structural Model for Science Fiction." *Comparative Literature Studies* 10 (December 1973): 334–357.

Suzuki, Yorhinori. "*Utopia* Reinterpreted." *Moreana* 17 (1980): 31–34.

Sylvester, Richard S., ed. *Sir Thomas More—Action and Contemplation.* New Haven, CT: Yale University Press, 1972.

"Thomas More and Hythloday: Some Speculations on *Utopia.*" *Bibliotheque d'Humanisme et Renaissance* 43, no. 1 (1981): 123–127.

Tinkler, John. "Praise and Advice: Rhetorical Approaches in More's *Utopia* and Machiavelli's *The Prince.*" *Sixteenth Century Journal* 19 (Summer 1988): 187–207.

Traugott, J. A. "A Voyage to Nowhere with Thomas More and Jonathan Swift: *Utopia* and the Voyage to the Houyhnhnms." In *Swift: A Collection of Critical Essays,* edited by E. L. Tuveson, 143–169. Englewood Cliffs, NJ: Prentice-Hall, 1964.

Trevor-Roper, H. R. *Renaissance Essays.* Chicago: University of Chicago Press, 1985.

Truchet, Sybil. "The Eutopians." *Cahiers Elisabethains* 28 (October 1985): 17–22.

Vickers, Brian. "The Satiric Structure of *Gulliver's Travels* and More's *Utopia.* In *The World of Jonathan Swift,* 240–257.

Wands, John M. "Antipodal Imperfection: Hall's *Mundus Alter et Idem* and Its Debt to More's *Utopia*." *Moreana* 18 (March 1981): 85–100.

Wegemer, Gerald B. "The Literary and Philosophic Design of Thomas More's *Utopia*." Ph.D. diss., University of Notre Dame, 1986.

Weiner, Andrew D. "Raphael's Eutopia and More's *Utopia*: Christian Humanism and the Limits of Reason." *Huntington Library Quarterly* 39 (1975): 1–27.

White, Frederic R. *Famous Utopias of the Renaissance,* 3–117.

White, H. C. *Social Criticism in Popular Religious Literature of Sixteenth Century.* New York: Macmillan, 1944, pp. 41–81.

White, Thomas. "Pride and the Public Good: Thomas More's Use of Plato in *Utopia*." *Journal of the History of Philosophy* 20 (October 1982): 329–354.

Whiteman, John Pratt. *Utopia Dawns,* 37–42.

Winkler, Gerhard B. "Conobium, Religion und Toleranz, Oder: Wie Christlich sind Thomas Mores *Utopier*?" In *A Yearbook of Studies in English Language and Literature 1985/86,* 277–286.

Wooden, Warren W. "Utopia and Arcadia: An Approach to More's *Utopia*." *College Literature* 6 (1979): 30–40.

———. "Utopia and Dystopia: The Paradigm of Thomas More's *Utopia*." *Southern Humanities Review* 14 (Spring 1980): 97–110.

———. "The Wit of Thomas More's *Utopia*." *Studies in the Humanities* 7, no. 2 (1979): 43–51.

Zavala, Silvio. "Noticias de Literatura Utopica en España e Hispanoamerica." *Thesaurus* 42 (May-August 1987): 362–369.

MORELLY, ABBÉ

General Criticism

Berneri, Marie Louise. *Journey Through Utopia,* 182–184.

Rimmer, Robert H. "Alternative Lifestyles on the Road to Utopia." In *France and North America,* 149–163.

Basiliade

Kaufmann, M. *Utopias,* 31–48.

Minerva, Nadia. "De l'Utopie Littéraire a l'Utopisme Reformateur: *La Basiliade* et le *Code de la Nature* de Morelly." *Studies on Voltaire and the Eighteenth Century* 265 (1989): 1,228–1,232.

MORRIS, WILLIAM

General Criticism

Frye, Northrop. "The Meeting of Past and Future in William Morris." *Studies in Romanticism* 21 (Fall 1982): 303–318.

Marshall, Roderick. *William Morris and His Earthly Paradises.* Tisbury, England: Compton Press, 1979.

A Dream of John Ball

Boos, Florence, and William Boos. "Orwell's Morris and 'Old Major's' Dream." *English Studies* 71 (August 1990): 361–371.

Goode, John. "William Morris and the Dream of Revolution." In *Literature and Politics in the Nineteenth Century,* edited by John Lucas, 247–261. London: Methuen, 1971.

Kirchhoff, Frederick. *William Morris.* Boston: Twayne, 1979, pp. 118–121.

Mann, Nancy D. "Eros and Community in the Fiction of William Morris." *Nineteenth-Century Fiction* 34 (December 1979): 317–318.

Meier, Paul. *La Pensée Utopique de William Morris.* Paris: Editions Sociales, 1972, pp. 381–388.

Silver, Carole. "Eden and Apocalypse: William Morris' Marxist Vision in the 1880s." *University of Hartford Studies in Literature* 13 (1981): 70–71.

"The Earthly Paradise"

Latham, David. "Paradise Lost: Morris's Re-Writing of *'The Earthly Paradise.'* " *Journal of Pre-Raphaelite and Aesthetic Studies* 1 (Fall 1987): 67–75.

News from Nowhere

Bailey, J. O. *Pilgrims Through Space and Time,* 57, 236.

Berneri, Marie Louise. *Journey Through Utopia,* 255–281.

Christensen, Bryce J. *Utopia Against the Family,* 5–6.

Coleman, Stephen. "The Economics of Utopia: Morris and Bellamy Contrasted." *Journal of the William Morris Society* 8 (Spring 1989): 2–6.

Frye, Northrop. "Varieties of Literary Utopias." In *Utopias and Utopian Thought,* 44–46.

Furbank, P. *Samuel Butler,* 83–88.

Hillgartner, Rudiger. "William Morris: *News from Nowhere,* or An Epoch of Rest; Being Some Chapters from a Utopian Romance." In *Die Utopie in der Angloamerikanischen Literatur,* 120–138.

Holzman, Michael. "Anarchism and Utopia: William Morris's *News from Nowhere.*" *ELH* 51 (Fall 1984): 589–603.

——. "The Pleasures of William Morris's Twenty-Second Century." *Journal of Pre-Raphaelite Studies* 4 (November 1983): 26–37.

Jehmlich, Reimer. "Cog-Work: The Organization of Labor in Edward Bellamy's *Looking Backward* and in Later Utopian Fiction." In *Clockwork Worlds,* 27–46.

Khouri, Nadia. "The Clockwork and Eros: Models of Utopia in Edward Bellamy and William Morris." *College Language Association Journal* 24 (March 1981): 376–399.

Kluge, Walter. "Sozialismus und Utopie im Spaten Neunzehnten Jahrhundert." In *Alternative Welten,* 197–215.

Lewis, Roger. *"News from Nowhere*: Utopia, Arcadia, or Elysium?" *Journal of Pre-Raphaelite Studies* 5 (November 1984): 55–67.

Liberman, Michael. "Major Textual Changes in William Morris's *News from Nowhere*." *Nineteenth-Century Literature* 41 (December 1986): 349–356.

Menichelli, Alfredo. "Utopia e Desiderio in *News from Nowhere*." In *Studi Inglesi: Raccolta di Saggi e Ricerche,* edited by Agostino Lombardo, 165–188. Bari: Adriatica, 1978.

Philmus, Robert M. " 'A Story of the Days to Come' and *News from Nowhere*: H. G. Wells as a Writer of Anti-Utopian Fiction." *English Literature in Transition (1880–1920)* 30, no. 4 (1987): 450–455.

Ross, Harry. *Utopias Old and New,* 219–232.

Sander, Hans-Jochen. *"News from Nowhere*: William Morris' Kommunistische Zukunftsvision als Utopischer Diskurs neuen Typs." *Wissenschaftliche Zeitschrift der Friedrich-Schiller-Universitat Jena* 38, no. 1 (1989): 98–103.

Sussman, Herbert. "The Language of the Future in Victorian Science Fiction." In *Hard Science Fiction,* 121–130.

Suvin, Darko. "Anticipating the Sunburst—Dream and Vision: The Exemplary Case of Bellamy and Morris." In *America as Utopia,* 57–77.

Whitman, John Pratt. *Utopia Dawns,* 95–101.

NABOKOV, VLADIMIR

Bend Sinister

Boyd, Brian. *Vladimir Nabokov: The Russian Years.* London: Chatto & Windus, 1990, pp. 314–317.

Clancy, Laurie. *The Novels of Vladimir Nabokov.* London: Macmillan, 1984, pp. 92–100.

Feuer, Lois. "The Unnatural Mirror: *Bend Sinister* and *Hamlet*." *Critique* 30 (Fall 1988): 3–12.

Field, Andrew. *Nabokov: His Life in Art.* Boston: Little, Brown, 1967, pp. 198–203.

————. *VN: The Life and Art of Vladimir Nabokov.* New York: Crown, 1986, pp. 106, 233, 237, 249–252.

Hyde, G. M. *Vladimir Nabokov: America's Russian Novelist.* London: Marion Boyers, 1977, pp. 97–99, 129–133, 140–148.

Johnson, D. Barton. " 'Don't Touch my Circles': The Two Worlds of Nabokov's *Bend Sinister.*" *Delta: Revue du Centre d'Estudes et de Recherche sur les Ecrivains du Sud aux États-Unis* 17 (October 1983): 33–52.

————. "The 'Yablochko' Chastushka in *Bend Sinister.*" *Vladimir Nabokov Research Newsletter* 9 (Fall 1982): 40–42.

Kermode, Frank. "Aesthetic Bliss." *Encounter* 14 (June 1960): 81–86.

Lee, L. L. "*Bend Sinister*: Nabokov's Political Dream." *Wisconsin Studies in Contemporary Literature* 8 (Spring 1967): 193–203.

————. *Vladimir Nabokov.* Boston: Twayne, 1976, pp. 104–114.

Rowe, W. W. *Nabokov's Spectral Dimension.* Ann Arbor, MI: Ardis, 1981, pp. 57–61.

Stegner, Page. *Escape into Aesthetics: The Art of Vladimir Nabokov.* New York: Dial, 1966, pp. 76–89.

Toker, Leona. *Nabokov: The Mystery of Literary Structures.* Ithaca, NY: Cornell University Press, 1989, pp. 177–197, 228–229.

Walker, David. "The Person from Porlock: *Bend Sinister* and the Problem of Art." In *Vladimir Nabokov,* edited by Harold Bloom, 259–282. New York: Chelsea, 1987.

Walsh, Chad. *From Utopia to Nightmare,* 105–106.

NIVEN, LAURENCE VAN COTT (LARRY)

Ringworld

Remington, Thomas J. "The Niven of Oz: *Ringworld* as Science Fictional Reinterpretation." In *Science Fiction Dialogues,* 99–111.

Zaki, Hoda M. *Phoenix Renewed,* 67, 73, 75.

NORWAY, NEVIL SHUTE. See SHUTE, NEVIL

NOTO, COSIMO

The Ideal City

Rooney, Charles J., Jr. *Dreams and Visions,* 30, 32, 68, 77, 194.

ODOEVSKII, VLADIMIR FEDOROVICH

General Criticism

Cornwell, Neil. *The Life, Times and Milieu of V. F. Odoyevsky, 1804–1869.* London: Athlone Press, 1986.

Russkie Nochi

Cornwell, Neil. "Utopia and Dystopia in Russian Fiction: The Contribution of V. F. Odoyevsky." *Renaissance and Modern Studies* 28 (1984): 59–71.

O'DUFFY, EIMAR ULTAN

General Criticism

Mercier, Vivian. "The Satires of Eimar O'Duffy." *The Bell* 12 (July 1946): 325–336.

King Goshawk and the Birds

Foster, J. W. *Fictions of the Irish Literary Revival: A Changeling Art.* Syracuse, NY: Syracuse University Press, 1987.

Hogan, Robert. *Eimar O'Duffy,* 51–57.

Mercier, Vivian. *The Irish Comic Tradition.* Oxford: Oxford University Press, 1962, pp. 205–207.

The Spacious Adventures of the Man in the Street

Hogan, Robert. *Eimar O'Duffy,* 57–59.

OLERICH, HENRY

A Cityless and Countryless World

Parrington, Vernon Louis, Jr. *American Dreams,* 136–139.

Roemer, Kenneth M. *The Obsolete Necessity,* 86, 131–132.

OLSEN, TILLIE

"Tell Me a Riddle"

Coles, Robert. *That Red Wheelbarrow: Selected Literary Essays.* Iowa City: University of Iowa Press, 1988, pp. 122–127.

Martin, Abigail. *Tillie Olsen.* Boise, ID: Boise State University, 1984, pp. 27–30.

Niehus, Edward L., and Teresa Jackson. "Polar Stars, Pyramids, and 'Tell Me a Riddle.' " *American Notes and Queries* 24 (January-February 1986): 77–83.

Nilsen, Helge Normann. "Tillie Olsen's 'Tell Me a Riddle': The Political Theme." *Etudes Anglaises* 37 (April-June 1984): 163–169.

Pearson, Carol, and Katherine Pope. *The Female Hero in American and British Literature.* New York: Bowker, 1981, pp. 44–45.

O'NEILL, JOSEPH

Land Under England

Crossley, Robert. "Dystopian Nights." *Science-Fiction Studies* 14 (March 1987): 93–98.

ORPEN, ADELIA ELIZABETH

Perfection City

Albinski, Nan Bowman. *Women's Utopias in British and American Fiction,* 52, 53, 54, 73.

Roemer, Kenneth M. *The Obsolete Necessity,* 52–53.

ORWELL, GEORGE

General Criticism

Dunn, Thomas P., and Richard D. Erlich. "A Vision of Dystopia: Beehives and Mechanization." *Journal of General Education* 33 (Spring 1981): 45–57.

Mezciems, Jenny. "Swift and Orwell: Utopia as Nightmare." In *Between Dream and Nature,* 91–112.

Muhlheim, Ulrike. "Utopie, Anti-Utopie and Science Fiction." In *Alternative Welten,* 315–328.

Sacks, Norman P. "Salvador de Madariaga and George Orwell: Parallels and Contrasts." In *Estudios en Honor de Rodolfo Oroz,* 285–297.

Woodcock, George. "Five Who Fear the Future." *New Republic* 134 (April 16, 1956): 17–19.

Animal Farm

Baker, Isadore L. *George Orwell: Animal Farm.* London: Brodie, 1961.

Colquitt, Betsey F. "Orwell: Traditionalist in Wonderland." *Discourse* 8 (Autumn 1965): 370–383.

Cook, Richard. "Rudyard Kipling and George Orwell." *Modern Fiction Studies* 7 (Summer 1961): 125–135.

Cooper, Nancy. "*Animal Farm*: An Explication for Teachers of Orwell's Novel." *California English Journal* 4 (1968): 59–69.

Gulbin, Suzanne. "Parallels and Contrasts in *Lord of the Flies* and *Animal Farm.*" *English Journal* 55 (January 1966): 86–90.

Harward, Timothy B. *European Patterns: Contemporary Patterns in European Writing.* Chester Springs, PA: DuFour, 1967, pp. 44–48.

Ho, Koon-Ki T. "Why Utopias Fail: A Comparative Study of the Modern Anti-Utopian Traditions in Chinese, English, and Japanese Literature." Ph.D. diss., University of Illinois at Urbana-Champaign, 1986.

Hopkinson, Tom. "*Animal Farm.*" *World Review* 16 (June 1950): 54–57.

Kubal, David L. *Outside the Whale,* 37–40, 122–130.

Lee, Robert A. "The Uses of Form: A Reading of *Animal Farm.*" *Studies in Short Fiction* 6 (Fall 1969): 557–573.

Lee, Robert E. *Orwell's Fiction.* Notre Dame, IN: Notre Dame University Press, 1969, pp. 105–127.

Meyers, Jeffrey. *A Reader's Guide to George Orwell.* London: Thames and Hudson, 1975, pp. 130–143.

———. "Orwell's Bestiary: The Political Allegory of *Animal Farm.*" *Studies in the Twentieth Century* 8 (1971): 65–84.

Oxley, B. T. *George Orwell,* 75–82.

Paden, Frances Freeman. "Narrative Dynamics in *Animal Farm.*" *Literature in Performance* 5 (April 1985): 49–55.

Schlesinger, Arthur, Jr. "Mr. Orwell and the Communists." *New York Times Book Review* (August 25, 1946): 1, 28.

Smyer, Richard I. *Animal Farm: Pastoralism and Politics.* Boston: Twayne, 1988.

Zwerdling, Alex. *Orwell and the New Left.* New Haven, CT: Yale University Press, 1974, pp. 88–96, 198–199, 203–207.

1984

Ainsa, Fernando. "Antes de *1984.*" *Plural* 15 (May 1986): 37–41.

Aldridge, A. *The Scientific World View in Dystopia,* 79–80.

Alldritt, Keith. *The Making of George Orwell: An Essay in Literary History.* New York: St. Martin's, 1969, pp. 150–178.

Allen, Francis A. "*Nineteen Eighty-Four* and the Eclipse of Private Worlds." In *The Future of Nineteen-Eighty Four,* edited by Ejner J. Jensen, 151–175. Ann Arbor, MI: University of Michigan Press, 1984.

Atkins, John A. *George Orwell: A Literary Study.* London: J. Calder, 1954, pp. 237–254.

Barr, Alan. "The Paradise Behind *1984.*" *English Miscellany* 19 (1968): 197–203.

Beauchamp, Gorman. "*1984*: Oceania as an Ideal State." *College Literature* 11 (Winter 1984): 1–12.

———. "Of Man's Last Disobedience: Zamiatin's *We* and Orwell's *1984.*" *Comparative Literature Studies* 10 (December 1973): 289–293.

Berger, Harold L. *Science Fiction and the New Dark Age,* 88–92.

Bergonzi, Bernard. "*Nineteen Eighty-Four* and the Literary Imagination." In *Between Dream and Nature,* 211–228. Amsterdam: Rodopi, 1987.

Blakemore, Stephen. "Language and Ideology in Orwell's *1984.*" *Social Theory & Practice* 10 (Fall 1984): 349–356.

Bonifas, Gilbert. "L'Anti-Utopie Face à l'Histoire: Le Cas de *Nineteen Eighty-Four.*" *Cycnos* 4 (1988): 107–117.

———. "*Nineteen Eighty-Four* and *Swastika Night.*" *Notes and Queries* 34 (March 1987): 59.

Borgmeier, Raimond. "Nature in Orwell's *Nineteen Eighty-Four.*" In *Essays from Oceania and Eurasia,* 111–119.

Brito, Manuel. "El Concepto de 'Doublethink' en *1984* y su Relacion con el Solipsismo Linguistico." *Revista de Filologia de la Universidad de la Laguna* 2 (1983): 101–107.

Brown, E. J. *'Brave New World,' '1984' and 'We.'*

Browning, Gordon. "Toward a Set of Standards for [evaluating] Anti-Utopian Fiction." *Cithara* 10 (December 1970): 18–32.

Buisson, R. "Anti-Utopie au Corruption d'un Idéal dans *1984.*" In *Autour de l'Idee de Nature,* 193–201.

Burgess, Anthony. *1985.* Boston: Little, Brown, 1978.

———. "Orwell's *1984.*" *Times* [London] (April 20 1977): 12.

———. "Utopia and Science Fiction." In *Essays from Oceania and Eurasia,* 3–18.

Burkhardt, Louis C. "G. K. Chesterton and *Nineteen Eighty-Four.*" In *George Orwell,* 5–10.

Calder, Jenni. *Chronicles of Conscience,* 229–253.

Casement, William. "Another Perspective on Orwellian Pessimism." *International Fiction Review* 15 (Winter 1988): 48–50.

Chilton, Paul. "Newspeak: It's the Real Thing." In *Nineteen Eighty-Four in 1984,* 33–44. London: Comedia, 1983.

Christensen, Bryce J. *Utopia Against the Family,* 8–9.

Connors, J. " 'Do It to Julia': Thoughts on Orwell's *1984.*" *Modern Fiction Studies* 16 (Winter 1970–1971): 463–473.

———. "Zamyatin's *We* and the Genesis of *1984.*" *Modern Fiction Studies* 21 (Spring 1975): 107–124.

Cooper, Thomas W. "Fictional 1984 and Factual 1984: Ethical Questions Regarding the Control of Consciousness by Mass Media." In *The Orwellian Moment,* 83–107.

Cory, Mark E. "Dark Utopia: *1984* and Its German Contemporaries." In *The Orwellian Moment,* 69–82.

Courtine, Jean-Jacques. "A Brave New Language: Orwell's Invention of Newspeak in *1984.*" Translated by Laura Willett. *Sub-Stance* 15 (1986): 69–74.

Crick, Bernard. "Reading *Nineteen Eighty-Four* as Satire." In *Reflections on America, 1984: An Orwell Symposium,* edited by Robert Mulvihill, 15–45. Athens: University of Georgia Press, 1986.

Deatherage, Scott. *From Plato to Orwell: Utopian Rhetoric in a Dystopian World.* Boston: Speech Communication Association, 1987. ERIC (290192).

Deutscher, Isaac. *Heretics and Renegades and Other Essays,* 35–50.

———. "*1984*: Le Mysticisme de la Cruaute." *Les Temps Modernes* 114–115 (June–July 1955): 2,205–2,218.

Dittmar, Kurt. "Die Fiktionalisierung der Wirklichkeit als Antiutopische Fiktion: Manipulative Realitatskontrolle in George Orwell's *Nineteen Eighty-Four.*" *Deutsche Vierteljahrsschrift fur Literaturwissenschaft und Geistesgeschichte* 58 (December 1984): 679–712.

Douglass, R. Bruce. "The Fate of Orwell's Warning." *Thought* 60 (September 1985): 263–274.

Dyson, Anthony E. *The Crazy Fabric: Essays in Irony.* New York: St. Martin's, 1965, pp. 197–219.

Elkins, Charles. "George Orwell, 1903–1950." In *Science Fiction Writers,* 233–241.

Elsbree, Langdon. "The Structured Nightmare of *1984.*" *Twentieth Century Literature* 5 (October 1959): 135–141.

Enteen, George M. "George Orwell and the Theory of Totalitarianism: A 1984 Retrospective." *Journal of General Education* 36, no. 3 (1984): 206–215.

Fink, Howard. "Newspeak: The Epitome of Parody Techniques in *Nineteen Eighty-Four.*" *Critical Survey* 5 (1971): 155–163.

————. "Orwell versus Koestler: *Nineteen Eighty-Four* as Optimistic Satire." In *George Orwell,* 101–109.

Fyvel, T. R. "Orwell as Friend and as Prophet." In *High Technology and Human Freedom,* edited by Lewis Lapham, 161–168. Washington, DC: Smithsonian Institute, 1985.

Geering, R. G. "*Darkness at Noon* and *Nineteen Eighty-Four*—A Comparative Study." *Australian Quarterly* 30, no. 3 (1958): 90–96.

Gerber, Richard. "The English Island Myth: Remarks on the English-ness of Utopian Fiction." *Critical Quarterly* 1 (Spring 1959): 36–43.

Gleckner, Robert F. "1984 or 1948?" *College English* 18 (November 1956): 95–99.

Gray, Russell. "*Nineteen Eighty-Four* and the Massaging of the Me-dia." In *George Orwell,* 111–117.

Greenland, Colin. "Images of *Nineteen Eighty-Four*: Fiction and Pre-diction." In *Storm Warnings,* 124–134.

Grossman, Kathryn M. " 'Through a Glass Darkly': Utopian Imagery in *Nineteen Eighty-Four.*" *Utopian Studies* 1 (1987): 52–60.

Gulati, Basia Miller. "Orwell's *Nineteen Eighty-Four*: Escape from Doublethink." *International Fiction Review* 12 (Summer 1985): 79–83.

Hadomi, Leah. "*Nineteen Eighty-Four* as Dystopia." In *George Orwell,* 119–125.

Harris, Harold J. "Orwell's Essay and *1984.*" *Twentieth Century Literature* 4 (January 1959): 154–161.

Hellemans, Karel. "Always the Eyes Watching You." In *Essays from Oceania and Eurasia,* 27–33.

Hewitt, Janice L. "More to Orwell: An Early Leap from *Utopia* to *Nineteen Eighty-Four.*" In *George Orwell,* 127–133.

Howard, Mary K. "Orwell and the Futurists." *Cuyahoga Review* 2 (Spring-Summer 1984): 17–21.

Howe, Irving. "The Fiction of Anti-Utopia." *New Republic* 146 (April 23, 1962): 13–16.

———. "Orwell: History as Nightmare." *American Scholar* 25 (Spring 1956): 193–207.

———. *Orwell's Nineteen Eighty-Four: Text, Sources, Criticism.* New York: Harcourt Brace, 1963.

Huerta, Alberto. "Politica Apocaliptica: Zamyatin, Koestler, Orwell y Milosz." *Religion y Culture* 30 (July-October 1984): 141–142.

Huntington, John. "Utopian and Anti-Utopian Logic: H. G. Wells and His Successors." *Science-Fiction Studies* 9 (July 1982): 122–146.

Hynes, Samuel L. *Twentieth Century Interpretations of 1984: A Collection of Critical Essays.* Englewood Cliffs, NJ: Prentice-Hall, 1971.

Jolicoeur, Claude. "Orwell et l'Utopie." *Cahiers du Centre d'Études et de Récherches sur les Littéraires de l'Imaginaire* 9 (1984): 111–120.

Jones, Joseph. "Utopias as Dirge." *American Quarterly* 2 (Fall 1950): 214–226.

Kampf, Louis. "*1984*: Why Read It?" *Radical Teacher* 28 (May 1985): 11–14.

Karl, Frederick R. "George Orwell: The White Man's Burden." In *A Reader's Guide to the Contemporary English Novel,* edited by Frederick Karl, 159–161, 163–165. New York: Octagon, 1972.

Kegel, Charles H. "*Nineteen Eighty-Four*: A Century of Ingsoc." *Notes and Queries* 10 (April 1963): 151–152.

Kessler, Martin. "Power and the Perfect State: A Study in Disillusionment as Reflected in Orwell's *Nineteen Eighty-Four* and Huxley's *Brave New World.*" *Political Science Quarterly* 72 (December 1957): 565–577.

Khouri, Nadia. "Reaction and Nihilism: The Political Genealogy of Orwell's *1984.*" *Science-Fiction Studies* 12 (July 1985): 136–147.

Knox, George. "The Divine Comedy in *1984.*" *Western Humanities Review* 9 (Autumn 1955): 371–372.

Kubal, David L. *Outside the Whale,* 43–47, 130–141.

Kumar, Krishan. *Utopia and Anti-Utopia in Modern Times,* 288–346.

Laborda, J. Javier. "1984, con Orwell y sin Koestler." *Quimera* (January 1984): 43–45.

Lang, Berel. "1984: Newspeak, Technology and the Death of Language." *Soundings* 72 (Spring 1989): 165–177.

Lange, Bernd-Peter. "Orwell und die Utopie." *Germanisch-Romanische Monatsschrift* 36, no. 2 (1986): 195–208.

Lee, Robert E. *Orwell's Fiction,* 128–157.

Le Roy, Gaylord C. "A. F. 632 to 1984." *College English* 12 (December 1950): 135–138.

Lewis, Florence, and Peter Moss. "The Tyranny of Language." In *Nineteen Eighty-Four in 1984,* 45–57.

Liebman, Arthur. "The Political Economic Problems of 1984." In *George Orwell and 1984,* 28–38.

Lief, Ruth Ann. *Homage to Oceania: The Prophetic Vision of George Orwell.* Columbus: Ohio State University Press, 1969.

Lyons, John O. "George Orwell's Opaque Glass in *1984.*" *Wisconsin Studies in Contemporary Literature* 2 (Fall 1961): 39–46.

Macey, Samuel L. "George Orwell's *1984*: The Future that Becomes the Past." *English Studies in Canada* 11 (December 1985): 450–458.

Maddison, Michael. "*1984:* A Burnhamite Fantasy?" *Political Quarterly* 32 (January-March 1961): 71–79.

Malak, Amin. "Margaret Atwood's *The Handmaid's Tale* and the Dystopian Tradition." *Canadian Literature* 112 (Spring 1987): 9–16.

Malkin, Lawrence. "Halfway to *1984.*" *Horizon* 12 (Spring 1970): 33–39.

Maslen, Elizabeth. "One Man's Tomorrow is Another's Today: The Reader's World and Its Impact on *Nineteen Eighty-Four.*" In *Storm Warnings,* 146–158.

Messerer, Azary. "Orwell and the Soviet Union." *ETC.* 41 (Summer 1984): 130–134.

Mettinger, Arthur. "Unendurable Unpersons Unmask Unexampled Untruths: Remarks on the Functions of Negative Prefixes in Orwell's *1984.*" In *A Yearbook of Studies in English Language and Literature 1985/86,* 109–118.

Meyer, Alfred G. "The Political Theory of Pessimism: George Orwell and Herbert Marcuse." In *The Future of Nineteen Eighty-Four,* edited by Ejner Jensen, 121–135. Ann Arbor, MI: University of Michigan Press, 1984.

Miller, Cecil. "Orwell and Literature." *American Scholar* 26 (Winter 1956–1957): 128.

New, Melvyn. "Ad Nauseam: A Satiric Device in Huxley, Orwell, and Waugh." *Satire Newsletter* 8 (Fall 1970): 24–28.

Nielsen, Joyce McCarl. "Women in Dystopia/Utopia: 1984 and Beyond." *International Journal of Women's Studies* 7 (March-April 1984): 144–154.

Nisbet, Robert. "1984 and the Conservative Imagination." In *1984 Revisited: Totalitarianism in our Century,* edited by Irving Howe, 180–206. New York: Harper & Row, 1983.

Nott, Kathleen. "Orwell's *Nineteen Eighty-Four.*" *Listener* 70 (October 31, 1963): 687–688.

Oxley, B. T. *George Orwell,* 112–125.

Parrinder, Patrick. "Updating Orwell? Burgess's Future Fictions." *Encounter* 56 (January 1981): 45–53.

Patai, Daphne. "Gamesmanship and Androcentrism in Orwell's *1984.*" *PMLA* 97 (October 1982): 856–870.

Plank, William. "Orwell and Huxley: Social Control through Standardized Eroticism." *Recovering Literature* 12 (1984): 29–39.

Rahv, Philip. "The Unfuture of Utopia." *Partisan Review* 16 (July 1949): 743–749.

Ranald, Ralph A. "George Orwell and the Mad World: The Anti-Universe of *1984.*" *South Atlantic Quarterly* 66 (Autumn 1967): 544–553.

Rankin, David. "Orwell's Intention in *1984.*" *English Language Notes* 12 (March 1975): 188–192.

Reszler, Andre. "Man as Nostalgia: The Image of the Last Man in Twentieth-century Postutopian Fiction." In *Visions of Apocalypse,* 196–215.

Richards, D. "Four Utopias." *Slavonic and East European Review* 40 (1962): 220–228.

Rodriguez Gonzalez, Felix. "Eufemismo y Propaganda Politica." *Revista Alicantina de Estudios Ingleses* 1 (November 1988): 153–170.

Roelofs, H. Mark. "George Orwell's Obscured Utopia." *Religion and Literature* 19 (Summer 1987): 11–33.

Ronnov-Jessen, Peter. "World Classics and Nursery Rhymes: Emblems of Resistance in Ray Bradbury's *Fahrenheit 451* and George Orwell's *1984.*" In *George Orwell and 1984,* 59–72.

Sanderson, Richard K. "The Two Narrators and Happy Ending of *Nineteen Eighty-Four.*" *Modern Fiction Studies* 34 (Winter 1988): 587–595.

Schwartz, Jonathan Matthew. "Two (Possible) Soviet Antecedents to Orwell's *1984:* Chayanov's *Peasant Utopia* and Zamiatin's *We.*" In *George Orwell and 1984,* 73–81.

Sheldon, Leslie E. "Newspeak and Nadsat: The Disintegration of Language in *1984* and *A Clockwork Orange.*" *Studies in Contemporary Satire* 6 (1979): 7–13.

Shippey, T. A. "Variations on Newspeak: The Open Question of *Nineteen Eighty-Four.*" In *Storm Warnings,* 171–193.

Sicher, Efraim. "By Underground to Crystal Palace: The Dystopian Eden." *Comparative Literature Studies* 22 (Fall 1985): 377–393.

Smith, Marcus. "The Wall of Blackness: A Psychological Approach to *1984*." *Modern Fiction Studies* 14 (Winter 1968–1969): 423–433.

Steinhoff, William. *George Orwell and the Orgins of 1984.* Ann Arbor, MI: University of Michigan Press, 1975.

————. "Utopia Reconsidered: Comments on *1984*." In *No Place Else*, 147–161.

Tampling, Victor. "Jack London and George Orwell: A Literary Kinship." In *George Orwell*, 171–175.

Thale, Jerome. "Orwell's Modest Proposal." *Critical Quarterly* 4 (Winter 1962): 365–368.

"To 1984 and Beyond." *Science-Fiction Studies* 12 (July 1985): 113–183.

Voorhees, Richard J. "*Nineteen Eighty-Four:* No Failure of Nerve." *College English* 18 (November 1956): 101–102.

Walsh, Chad. *From Utopia to Nightmare*, 106–112.

Warncke, Wayne. "A Note on *1984*." *Hartwick Review* 3 (Fall 1967): 60–61.

Watt, Alan. "George Orwell and Yevgeny Zamyatin." *Quadrant (Sydney, Australia)* 28 (July-August 1984): 110–111.

Weatherly, Joan. "The Death of Big Sister: Orwell's Tragic Message." *College Literature* 15, no. 3 (1988): 269–280.

Westlake, J. H. J. "Aldous Huxley's *Brave New World* and George Orwell's *Nineteen Eighty-Four:* A Comparative Study." *Die Neueren Sprachen* 21 (1971): 94–102.

Widgery, David. "Reclaiming Orwell." In *Nineteen Eighty-Four in 1984*, 15–23.

Willison, Ian. "Orwell's Bad Good Books." *Twentieth Century* 157 (April 1955): 354–366.

Woodcock, George. "Utopias in Negative." *Sewanee Review* 64 (Winter 1956): 81–97.

Zuckert, Michael P. "Orwell's Hopes, Orwell's Fears: *1984* as a Theory of Totalitarianism." In *The Orwellian Moment,* 45–67.

PALLEN, CONDE B.

Crucible Island

Walsh, Chad. *From Utopia to Nightmare,* 78–79.

PALTOCK, ROBERT

Peter Wilkins

Crossley, Robert. "Ethereal Ascents: Eighteenth-century Fantasies of Human Flight." *Eighteenth-Century Life* 7 (January 1982): 55–64.

Fortunati, Vita. "Utopia, Satira e Romance in *The Life and Adventures of Peter Wilkins* di Robert Paltock." *Il Lettore di Provincia* 15 (March 1984): 23–34.

Lemoine, Georges. "Deux Utopies du Dix-Huitième Siècle Chez les Hommes Volants: Quelques Aspects." *Littératures* 5 (Spring 1982): 7–18.

PANSHIN, ALEXEI

Rite of Passage

Jones, Anne Hudson. "Alexei Panshin's Almost Non-Sexist *Rite of Passage.*" In *Future Females,* 26–33.

Zaki, Hoda M. *Phoenix Renewed,* 61–63, 67, 73.

PAROTAUD, J. M. A.

La Ville Incertaine

Fondaneche, Daniel. "*La Ville Incertaine,* une Contre-Utopie Libértaire." *Cahiers du Centre d'Études et de Récherches sur les Littéraires de l'Imaginaire* 9 (1984): 99–107.

PAZ, OCTAVIO

General Criticism

Stabb, Martin S. "Utopia and Anti-Utopia; The Theme in Selected Essayistic Writings of Spanish Americans." *Revista de Estudios Hispanicus* 15 (October 1981): 377–393.

PECK, BRADFORD

The World a Department Store

Parrington, Vernon Louis, Jr. *American Dreams,* 153–155.

Rooney, Charles J., Jr. *Dreams and Visions,* 65, 81–82, 148, 194–195.

PERCY, WALKER

Love in the Ruins

Berrigan, J. "An Explosion of Utopias." *Moreana* 10 (1973): 21–26.

Bradford, Melvin E. "Dr. Percy's Paradise Lost: Diagnostics in Louisiana." *Sewanee Review* 81 (Autumn 1973): 839–844.

Brown, Ashley. "Walker Percy: The Novelist as Moralist." In *Walker Percy: Novelist and Philosopher,* edited by Jan Nordby Gretlund and Karl-Heinz Westarp, 173–174. Jackson: University Press of Mississippi, 1991.

Cogell, Elizabeth Cummins. "The Middle-Landscape Myth in Science Fiction." *Science-Fiction Studies* 5 (July 1978): 134–142.

Godshalk, William Leigh. "*Love in the Ruins:* Thomas More's Distorted Vision." In *The Art of Walker Percy,* 137–157.

———. "Walker Percy's Christian Vision." *Louisiana Studies* 13 (1974): 130–141.

Kennedy, J. Gerald. "The Sundered Self and the Riven World: *Love in the Ruins.*" In *The Art of Walker Percy,* 115–136.

Le Clair, T. "Walker Percy's Devil." *Southern Literary Journal* 10, no. 1 (1977): 3–13.

Ledbetter, T. Mark. "An Apocalyptic Cacophony: Music as Apocalypse Symbol in Walker Percy's *Love in the Ruins.*" *Literature & Theology* 1 (September 1987): 221–227.

Luschei, Martin. "The Ruins of Consensus: *Love in the Ruins.*" In *Walker Percy,* edited by Harold Bloom, 25–51. New York: Chelsea House, 1986.

Sivley, Sherry. "Percy's Down Home Version of More's *Utopia.*" *Notes on Contemporary Literature* 7, no. 4 (1977): 3–5.

Tharpe, Jac. *Walker Percy.* Boston: Twayne, 1983, pp. 78–87.

Weber, Brom. "The Mode of 'Black Humor.' " In *The Comic Imagination in American Literature,* edited by Louis Rubin, Jr., 361–371. New Brunswick, NJ: Rutgers University Press, 1973.

Young, R. V. "Catholic Science Fiction and the Comic Apocalypse: Walker Percy and Walker Miller." *Renascence* 40 (Winter 1988): 95–110.

PERSINGER, CHARLES EDMUND

Letters from a New America

Rooney, Charles J., Jr. *Dreams and Visions,* 34, 151, 156, 195.

PHELPS, CORWIN

An Ideal Republic

Rooney, Charles J., Jr. *Dreams and Visions,* 106, 195.

PHELPS, ELIZABETH STUART (WARD, ELIZABETH STUART PHELPS)

General Criticism

Kessler, Carol Farley. "The Heavenly Utopia of Elizabeth Stuart Phelps." In *Women and Utopia,* 85–95.

Beyond the Gates

Kessler, Carol Farley. *Elizabeth Stuart Phelps,* 33–36.

The Gates Ajar

Kessler, Carol Farley. *Elizabeth Stuart Phelps,* 29–34.

PHILOCTÉTE, RENÉ

Le Huitième Jour

Desroches, Rosny. "L'Utopie: Évasion on Anticipation?" In *France and North America,* 83–92.

PIERCY, MARGE

General Criticism

DuPlessis, Rachel. "The Feminist Apologues of Lessing, Piercy, and Russ." *Frontiers* 4 (Spring 1979): 1–8.

Russ, Joanna. "Recent Feminist Utopias." In *Future Females,* 71–75.

Dance the Eagle to Sleep

Berger, Harold L. *Science Fiction and the New Dark Age,* 142–143, 145.

Woman on the Edge of Time

Albinski, Nan Bowman. *Women's Utopias in British and American Fiction,* 165, 166, 168, 171–175, 177–178, 180.

Bartkowski, Frances. "Toward a Feminist Eros."

Burton, Dierdre. "Linguistic Innovation in Feminist Utopian Fiction." *Ilha do Desterro* 14, no. 2 (1985): 82–106.

Cranny-Francis, Anne. *Feminist Fiction,* 130–131, 134–140.

Devine, Maureen. "*Woman on the Edge of Time* and *The Wanderground:* Visions in Eco-Feminist Utopoias." In *Utopian Thought in American Literature,* 131–145.

Elshtain, Jean Bethke. *Public Man, Private Woman: Women in Social and Political Thought.* Princeton, NJ: Princeton University Press, 1981, pp. 201–255.

Ferns, Chris. "Dreams of Freedom: Ideology and Narrative Structure in the Utopian Fictions of Marge Piercy and Ursula Le Guin." *English Studies in Canada* 14 (December 1988): 453–466.

Fitting, Peter. "Positioning and Closure: On the 'Reading Effect' of Contemporary Utopian Fiction." *Utopian Studies* 1 (1987): 23–36.

Foster, David L. "Woman on the Edge of Narrative: Language in Marge Piercy's Utopia." In *Patterns of the Fantastic,* 47–56.

Freibert, Lucy M. "World Views in Utopian Novels by Women." In *Women and Utopia,* 67–84.

Gardiner, Judith Kegan. "Evil, Apocalypse, and Feminist Fiction." *Frontiers: A Journal of Women Studies* 7, no. 2 (1983): 74–80.

Huckle, Patricia. "Women in Utopias." In *The Utopian Vision,* 115–136.

Jones, Libby Falk. "Gilman, Bradley, Piercy, and the Evolving Rhetoric of Feminist Utopias." In *Feminism, Utopia, and Narrative,* 116, 119, 122–125.

Kessler, Carol Farley. "*Woman on the Edge of Time:* A Novel 'to be of Use.' " *Extrapolation* 28 (Winter 1987): 310–318.

Khouri, Nadia. "The Dialectic of Power: Utopia in the Science Fiction of Le Guin, Jeury, and Piercy." *Science-Fiction Studies* 7 (March 1980): 49–59.

Moylan, Tom. *Demand the Impossible,* 121–155.

———. "History and Utopia in Marge Piercy's *Woman on the Edge of Time.*" In *Science Fiction Dialogues,* 133–140.

Orth, Michael. "A Response to Kessler." *Extrapolation* 29 (Fall 1988): 295–296.

Sargent, Lyman Tower. "A New Anarchism: Social and Political Ideas in Some Recent Feminist Eutopias." In *Women and Utopia,* 3–33.

Sauter-Bailliet, Theresia. "Marge Piercy: *Woman on the Edge of Time.*" In *Die Utopie in der Angloamerikanischen Literatur,* 349–370.

Spector, Judith. "The Functions of Sexuality in the Science Fiction of Russ, Piercy, and Le Guin." In *Erotic Universe,* 197–207.

PLATO

General Criticism

Koppenfels, Werner von. "Thomas Morus und die Humanistische Utopie der Renaissance." In *Alternative Welten,* 96–113.

Pons, Alain. "Vico, Marx, Utopia, and History." In *Vico and Marx,* 20–37.

Saunders, Trevor J. "Plato's Clockwork Orange." *Durham University Journal* 68 (June 1976): 113–117.

Voegelin, Eric. *Plato.* Baton Rouge: Louisiana State University Press, 1966.

Wells, Arvin R. "Huxley, Plato and the Just Society." *Centennial Review* 24 (1980): 475–491.

The Republic

Allen, V. R. E. "Argument from Opposites in *Republic.*" *Review of Metaphysics* 15 (December 1961): 325–335.

Baker-Smith, Dominic. "The Escape from the Cave: Thomas More and the Vision of Utopia." *Dutch Quarterly Review of Anglo-American Letters* 15, no. 3 (1985): 148–161.

Beauchamp, Gorman. "Gulliver's Return to the Cave: Plato's *Republic* and Book IV of *Gulliver's Travels*." *Michigan Academician* 7 (1974): 201–209.

Berneri, Marie Louise. *Journey Through Utopia*, 10–33.

Bradshaw, David. "Thomas White on Plato and *Utopia*." *Moreana* 21 (December 1984): 51–53.

Brumbaugh, R. S. "New Interpretation of Plato's *Republic*." *Journal of Philosophy* 64 (October 26, 1967): 661–670.

Calvert, B. "Slavery in Plato's *Republic*." *Classical Quarterly* 37, no. 2 (1987): 267–272.

Cassirer, E. *Myth of the State*. New Haven, CT: Yale University Press, 1946, pp. 61–77.

Christensen, Bryce J. *Utopia Against the Family*, 3–4.

Deatherage, Scott. *From Plato to Orwell: Utopian Rhetoric in a Dystopian World*. Boston: Speech Communication Association, 1987. ERIC (ED 290192).

Dunham, B. *Man Against Myth*. New York: Little, Brown, 1947, pp. 210–214.

Elshtain, Jean Bethke. "Response." In *Feminism, Utopia, and Narrative*, 201–202.

Faris, J. A. "Is Plato's Caste State Based on Racial Differences?" *Classical Quarterly* 44 1950): 38–43.

Fireman, P. *Justice in Plato's Republic*. New York: Philosophical Library, 1957.

Frye, Northrop. "Varieties of Literary Utopias." In *Utopias and Utopian Thought*, 27, 32–34, 36–39.

Hourani, G. F. "The Education of the Third Class in Plato's *Republic*." *Classical Quarterly* 43 (January/April 1949): 58–60.

Jaeger, W. W. *Paideia: The Ideals of Greek Culture.* Volume 2. London: Oxford University Press, 1943, pp. 198–370.

Joseph, H. W. B. *Essays in Ancient and Modern Philosophy.* Oxford: Clarendon, 1935, pp. 1–40, 82–121.

Mabbott, J. D. "Is Plato's *Republic* Utilitarian?" *Mind* 46 (October 1937): 468–474.

Maguire, J. P. "The Individual and the Class in Plato's *Republic.*" *Classical Journal* 60 (January 1965): 145–150.

Masso, Gildo. *Education in Utopias,* 2, 8, 19, 20, 58, 63–64, 71, 79–82, 99–100, 140.

Miething, Christoph. "Platon, Dante et More: Esquisse d'Une Théorie de l'Utopie Littéraire." In *De l'Utopie à l'Uchronie,* 143–148.

———. "Politeia und Utopia: Zur Epistemologie der Literarischen Utopie." *Germanisch-Romanische Monatsschrift* 37, no. 3 (1987): 247–263.

Morrison, J. "The Origins of Plato's Philosopher-Statesman." *Classical Quarterly* 8 (1958): 198–218.

Mumford, Lewis. *The Story of Utopias,* 27–56.

Murley, C. "Plato's *Republic,* Totalitarian or Democratic?" *Classical Journal* 36 (April 1941): 413–420.

Murphy, N. R. *Interpretation of Plato's Republic.* Oxford: Clarendon Press, 1951.

Nettleship. R. L. *Lectures on the Republic of Plato.* New York: St. Martin's, 1962.

Notopolus, J. A. "Socrates and the Sun." *Classical Journal* 37 (February 1942): 260–274.

———. "The Symbolism of the Sun and Light in the *Republic* of Plato. I" *Classical Philology* 39 (July 1944): 163–172.

———. "The Symbolism of the Sun and Light in the *Republic* of Plato. II" *Classical Philology* 39 (October 1944): 223–240.

Rosen, S. "Role of Eros in Plato's *Republic.*" *Review of Metaphysics* 18 (March 1965): 452–475.

Ross, Harry. *Utopias Old and New,* 31–46.

Russell, B. *History of Western Philosophy.* New York: Simon and Schuster, 1945, pp. 108–119.

Sachs, D. "Fallacy in Plato's *Republic.*" *Philosophical Review* 72 (April 1963): 141–158.

Sesonske, A., ed. *Plato's Republic: Interpretation and Criticism.* Belmont, CA: Wadsworth, 1966.

Tarrant, D. "Imagery in Plato's *Republic.*" *Classical Quarterly* 40 (January 1946): 27–34.

Taylor, A. E. "Decline and Fall of the State in *Republic,* VIII." *Mind* 48 (January 1939): 23–38.

Vlastos, G. "Argument in the *Republic* that Justice Pays." *Journal of Philosophy* 65 (November 7, 1968): 665–674.

———. "Does Slavery Exist in Plato's *Republic.*" *Classical Philology* 63 (October 1968): 291–295.

———. "Justice and Psychic Harmony in the *Republic.*" *Journal of Philosophy* 66 (August 21, 1969): 505–521.

Walsh, Chad. *From Utopia to Nightmare,* 32, 37–39.

White, T. I. "Pride and the Public Good: Thomas More's Use of Plato in *Utopia.*" *Journal of the History of Philosophy* 20 (October 1982): 329–354.

Whitman, John Pratt. *Utopia Dawns,* 29–33.

PLATONOV, ANDREI

Chevengur

Bethea, D. M. *The Shape of Apocalypse in Modern Russian Fiction.* Princeton, NJ: Princeton University Press, 1989, pp. 145–185.

Gunther, Hans. "Andrej Platonov: Unterwegs Nach Tschevengur." In *Literarische Utopien von Morus bis zur Gegenwart,* 191–202.

Karlinsky, Simon. "Andrei Platonov, 1899–1951: An Early Soviet Master." *New Republic* 180 (March 31, 1979): 25–30.

Striedter, Jurij. "Three Postrevolutionary Russian Utopian Novels." In *The Russian Novel from Pushkin to Pasternak,* 177–201.

Teskey, Ayleen. *Platonov and Fyodorov: The Influence of Christian Philosophy on a Soviet Writer.* England: Avebury, 1982, pp. 52–74.

Vasil'ev, Vladimir. "Natsional'naia Tragedita: Utopiia i Real'nost': Roman Andreia Platonova *Chevengur* v Kontekste ego Vremeni." *Nash Sovremennik* 3 (1989): 172–182.

Yakushev, Henryka. "Andrei Platonov's Artistic Model of the World." *Russian Literature Triquarterly* 16 (1979): 171–188.

Yevtushenko, Yevgeny. "Introduction: 'Without Me, the Country's Not Complete.' " *The Fierce and Beautiful World: Stories by Andrei Platonov.* By Andrei Platonov. Translated by Joseph Barnes. New York: Dutton, 1970, pp. 7–18.

PLUTARCH

General Criticism

Gianaharis, C. J. *Plutarch.* New York: Twayne, 1970.

Halewood, W. H. "Plutarch in Houyhnhnmland: A Neglected Source for Gulliver's Fourth Voyage." *Philological Quarterly* 44 (April 1965): 185–194.

Russell, Donald Andrew. *Plutarch.* London: Duckworth, 1973.

Life of Lycurgus

Berneri, Marie Louise. *Journey Through Utopia,* 33–45.

POE, EDGAR ALLAN

"Mellonta Tauta"

Franklin, H. Bruce. *Future Perfect: American Science Fiction of the Nineteenth Century.* New York: Oxford University Press, 1966, pp. 100–101.

Hoffman, Daniel G. *Poe Poe Poe Poe Poe Poe Poe.* Garden City, NJ: Doubleday, 1972, pp. 193–195.

Pollin, Burton. "Politics and History in Poe's 'Mellonta Tauta': Two Allusions Explained." *Studies in Short Fiction* 8 (Fall 1971): 627–631.

Taft, Kendall. "The Identity of Martin van Buren Mavis." *American Literature* 26 (January 1954): 562–563.

POHL, FREDERIK

General Criticism

"Science Fiction: Predicting the Future or a Warning to Mankind?" *Soviet Literature* 12 (1987): 180–182.

Gateway

Bartter, Martha. "Times and Spaces: Exploring *Gateway.*" *Extrapolation* 23 (Summer 1982): 189–199.

Dunn, Thomas P. "Theme and Narrative Structure in Ursula K. Le Guin's *The Dispossessed* and Frederik Pohl's *Gateway.*" *Reflections on the Fantastic,* 87–95.

Paul, Terri. " 'Sixty Billion Gigabits': Liberation through Machines in Frederik Pohl's *Gateway* and *Beyond the Blue Event Horizon.*" In *The Mechanical God,* 53–62.

Zaki, Hoda M. *Phoenix Renewed,* 67, 71, 73.

Man Plus

Zaki, Hoda M. *Phoenix Renewed,* 71, 73.

Midas Plague

Amis, Kingsley. *New Maps of Hell,* 119–121, 127, 130–131, 148.

Berger, Harold L. *Science Fiction and the New Dark Age,* 19–20.

"The Wizards of Pung's Corners"

Berger, Harold L. *Science Fiction and the New Dark Age,* 117–118.

POHL, FREDERIK and KORNBLUTH, C. M.

Gladiator-at-Law

Berger, Harold L. *Science Fiction and the New Dark Age,* 120.

Erlich, Richard D. "Odysseus in Grey Flannel: The Heroic Journey in Two Dystopias by Pohl and Kornbluth." *Par Rapport* 1 (1978): 126–131.

The Space Merchants

Amis, Kingsley. *New Maps of Hell,* 124–133.

Berger, Harold L. *Science Fiction and the New Dark Age,* 118–122.

Erlich, Richard D. "Odysseus in Grey Flannel: The Heroic Journey in Two Dystopias by Pohl and Kornbluth." *Par Rapport* 1 (1978): 126–131.

Walsh, Chad. *From Utopia to Nightmare,* 164.

PRÉVOST, ANTOINE FRANÇOIS, L'ABBÉ

Cleveland

Cherpack, Clifton. "Literature and Belief: The Example of Prévost's *Cleveland.*" *Eighteenth-Century Studies* 6 (Winter 1972–1973): 186–202.

Cooper, Bernice. "An Eighteenth Century Dictatorship." *Transactions of the Wisconsin Academy of Sciences, Arts, and Letters* 34 (1942): 231–236.

Decobert, Jacques. "Au Procès de l'Utopie, un 'Roman des Illusions Perdues': Prévost et la 'Colonie Rochelloise.' " *Revue des Sciences Humaines* 39 (1974): 493–504.

Francis, R. A. "Prévost's *Cleveland* and Its Anonymous Continuation." *Nottingham French Studies* 23 (May 1984): 12–23.

———. "Prévost's *Cleveland* and Voltaire's *Candide*." *Studies on Voltaire and the Eighteenth Century* 191 (1980): 671–672.

———. "Prévost's *Cleveland* and Voltaire's *Candide*." *Studies on Voltaire and the Eighteenth Century* 208 (1982): 295–303.

Gilroy, James P. "Peace and the Pursuit of Happiness in the French Utopian Novel: Fénelon's *Télémaque* and Prévost's *Cleveland*." *Studies on Voltaire and the Eighteenth Century* 176 (1979): 169–187.

Haac, O. A. "Comedy in Utopia: The Literary Imagination of Marivaux and the Abbé Prévost." *Studies on Voltaire and the Eighteenth Century* 191 (1980): 684–685.

Lewis, B. "The Influence of Chasle's *Illustrés Françoises* on Prévost's *Cleveland*. *Studies on Voltaire and the Eighteenth Century* 219 (1983): 153–158.

Smernoff, Richard A. *L'Abbé Prévost.* Boston: Twayne, 1985, pp. 60–81.

Stewart, Philip. "Utopias that Self-Destruct." *Studies in Eighteenth-Century Culture* 9 (1979): 15–24.

———. "Vox Naturae: A Reading of Prévost." *Romanic Review* 71 (March 1980): 141–148.

Trousson, R. "L'Utopie en Procès au Siècle des Lumières." In *Essays on the Age of Enlightenment in Honour of Ira O. Wade,* edited by J. Macary, 313–327. Geneva: Droz, 1977.

PRIBER, CHRISTIAN

General Criticism

Crane, Verner W. "A Lost Utopia to the First American Frontier." *Sewanee Review* 27 (January 1919): 48–61.

RABELAIS, FRANÇOIS

General Criticism

Desroches, Rosny. "L'Utopie: Évasion ou Anticipation?" In *France and North America,* 83–92.

Febvre, Lucien. *The Problem of Unbelief in the Sixteenth Century: The Religion of Rabelais.* Translated by Beatrice Gottlieb. Cambridge, MA: Harvard University Press, 1982.

Koppenfels, Werner von. "*Mundus Alter et Idem*: Utopiefiktion und Menippeische Satire." *Poetica* 13, nos. 1–2 (1981): 16–66.

Gargantua and Pantagruel

Auerbach, Erich. *Mimesis: The Representation of Reality in Western Literature.* Translated by Willard Trask. Princeton, NJ: Princeton University Press, 1953, pp. 229–249.

Bakhtin, Mikhail. *Rabelais and His World.* Cambridge, MA: MIT Press, 1968, pp. 158–179, 326–340.

Berneri, Marie Louise. *Journey Through Utopia,* 137–142.

Bowen, Barbara C. *Age of Bluff: Paradox and Ambiguity in Rabelais and Montaigne.* Urbana: University of Illinois Press, 1972.

Chappell, A. F. *The Enigma of Rabelais.* Cambridge, England: Cambridge University Press, 1924, pp. 45–90, 120–191.

Cholakian, Rouben C. "A Re-Examination of the Tempest Scene in the *Quart Livre.*" *French Studies* 21 (April 1967): 104–109.

Coleman, D. G. *Rabelais: A Critical Study in Prose Fiction.* Cambridge, England: Cambridge University Press, 1971.

Eddy, William A. "Rabelais—A Source for *Gulliver's Travels.*" *Modern Language Notes* 37 (November 1922): 416–418.

Eskin, Stanley G. "Mythic Unity in Rabelais." *PMLA* 79 (December 1964): 548–553.

Frame, Donald M. *François Rabelais: A Study*. New York: Harcourt Brace Jovanovich, 1977, pp. 20–46.

Francon, Marcel. "Cannibales, Rabelais et Montaigne." *Bulletin de la Société des Amis de Montaigne* 13–14 (1983): 106–108.

Frautschi, R. L. "The 'Enigme en Prophetie' and the Question of Authorship." *French Studies* 17 (October 1963): 331–339.

Freccero, Carla. "Rabelais's 'Abbaye de Thélème': Utopia as Supplement." *L'Ésprit Créateur* 25 (Spring 1985): 73–87.

Gray, Floyd. "Ambiguity and Point of View in the Prologue to *Gargantua*." *Romanic Review* 56 (February 1965): 12–21.

Greene, Thomas M. *Rabelais: A Study in Comic Courage*. Englewood Cliffs, NJ: Prentice-Hall, 1970.

Helgerson, Richard. "Inventing Noplace, or the Power of Negative Thinking." *Genre* 15 (Spring-Summer 1982): 101–121.

Herrmann, Leon. "La Langue Lilliputienne et Lemuel Gulliver d'Après Swift." *Revue de Littérature Comparée* 57 (January–March 1983): 95–100.

Ianziti, Gary. "Rabelais and Machiavelli." *Romance Notes* 16 (Winter 1975): 460–473.

Keller, Abraham C. "Absurd and Absurdity in Rabelais." *Kentucky Romance Quarterly* 19, no. 2 (1972): 149–157.

———. "The Books and Stories of Rabelais." *Romanic Review* 53 (December 1963): 241–259.

———. "The Idea of Progress in Rabelais." *PMLA* 66 (March 1951): 235–243.

———. *The Telling of Tales in Rabelais: Aspects of His Narrative Art*. Frankfurt, Germany: Klostermann, 1963.

Kinser, Samuel. *Rabelais's Carnival: Text, Context, Metatext*. Berkeley: University of California Press, 1990, pp. 200–213.

Kleis, Charlotte C. "Structural Parallels and Thematic Unity in Rabelais." *Modern Language Quarterly* 31 (December 1970): 403–423.

Kotin, A. "*Pantagruel*: Language vs. Communication." *Modern Language Notes* 87 (November 1972): 691–709.

La Charite, Raymond C. "The Unity of Rabelais' *Pantagruel*." *French Studies* 26 (1972): 257–265.

Lewis, Dominic B. *Doctor Rabelais*. Westport, CT: Greenwood, 1969.

McFarlane, I. D. *A Literary History of France: Renaissance France 1470–1589*. New York: Barnes & Noble, 1974, pp. 171–189.

Masters, G. Mallary. *Rabelaisian Dialectic and the Platonic-Hermetic Tradition*. Albany: State University of New York Press, 1969.

Morrison, I. R. "Ambiguity, Detachment and Joy in *Gargantua*." *Modern Language Review* 71 (July 1976): 513–522.

Muir, Edwin. *Essays on Literature and Society*. Cambridge, MA: Harvard University Press, 1965, pp. 166–181.

Muir, Lynette R. "The Abbey and the City: Two Aspects of the Christian Community." *Australian Journal of French Studies* 14 (January-April 1977): 32–38.

Mumford, Lewis. *The Story of Utopias*, 199–201.

Rebhorn, W. A. "The Burdens and Joys of Freedom: An Interpretation of the Five Books of Rabelais." *Études Rabelaisiennes* 9 (1971): 71–90.

Regosin, Richard L. "The Artist and the 'Abbaye.'" *Studies in Philology* 68 (April 1971): 121–129.

Russell, Daniel. "Some Reflexions on the Abbey of Thelema." *Etudes Rabelaisiennes* 8 (1969): 109–114.

Sanford, Charles L. *The Quest for Paradise*, 45–46.

Schwartz, Jerome. "Gargantua's Device and the Abbey of Thélème: A Study in Rabelais Iconography." *Yale French Studies* 47 (1972): 232–242.

————. *Irony and Ideology in Rabelais: Structures of Subversion.* New York: Cambridge University Press, 1990, pp. 82–85.

Screech, M. A. *Rabelais.* London: Duckworth, 1979, pp. 39–40.

————. *The Rabelaisian Marriage.* London: Arnold, 1958.

————. ''The Sense of Rabelais's 'Enigme en Propetie.' '' *Bibliotheque d'Humanisme et Renaissance* 18 (September 1956): 392–404.

————. ''Some Stoic Elements in Rabelais's Religious Thought.'' *Etudes Rabelaisiennes* 1 (1956): 73–87.

Stevens, Linton C. ''Rabelais and Aristophanes.'' *Studies in Philology* 55 (January 1958): 24–30.

Tetel, Marcel. *Rabelais.* New York: Twayne, 1967, pp. 45–48.

Tilley, Arthur. *Francois Rabelais.* Port Washington, NY: Kennikat Press, 1970, pp. 151–160.

Tournon, Andre. ''Ce qui Devait se Dire en Utopien.'' In *Croisements Culturels,* 115–135.

Weinberg, Florence M. *The Wine and the Will: Rabelais's Bacchic Christianity.* Detroit: Wayne State University Press, 1972.

White, Frederic R. *Famous Utopias of the Renaissance,* 121–136.

Wortley, W. Victor. ''From *Pantagruel* to *Gargantua*: The Development of an Action Scene.'' *Romance Notes* 10 (Autumn 1968): 129–138.

Zeldin, Jesse. ''The Abbey and the Battle.'' *L'Ésprit Créateur* 3 (Summer 1963): 68–74.

RAND, AYN

General Criticism

Rimmer, Robert H. ''Alternative Lifestyles on the Road to Utopia.'' In *France and North America,* 149–163.

Walsh, Chad. *From Utopia to Nightmare,* 81–82.

Anthem

Albinski, Nan Bowman. *Women's Utopias in British and American Fiction,* 115, 118–120, 129.

Berger, Harold L. *Science Fiction and the New Dark Age,* 94–95.

Branden, Barbara. *The Passion of Ayn Rand.* Garden City, NY: Doubleday, 1986, pp. 142–143, 187–188.

Atlas Shrugged

Branden, Nathaniel. *Who Is Ayn Rand?* New York: Random House, 1962, pp. 3–65.

Hunt, R. "Science Fiction for the Age of Inflation: Reading *Atlas Shrugged* in the 1980's." In *Coordinates,* 80–98.

Rand, Ayn. *For the New Intellectual: The Philosophy of Ayn Rand.* New York: Random House, 1961, pp. 104–242.

Rolo, Charles. *"Atlas Shrugged." Atlantic* 200 (November 1957): 249.

RANDALL, ROBERT

A Time for Changes

Zaki, Hoda M. *Phoenix Renewed,* 63–64, 67, 73.

RAULIN, ANDRÉ

L'Utopiste

Smith, C. N. "André Raulin's *L'Utopiste." Moreana* 21 (December 1984): 44.

REHM, WARREN S.

The Practical City

Rooney, Charles J., Jr. *Dreams and Visions,* 66, 130–132, 195.

RESTIF DE LA BRETONNE, NICOLAS EDME

General Criticism

Knight, I. F. "Utopian Dreams as Psychic Reality." *Studies in Eighteenth Century Culture.* Volume 6, pp. 427–438.

Porter, Charles A. *Restif's Novels: Or an Autobiography in Search of an Author.* New Haven, CT: Yale University Press, 1967.

Poster, Mark. *The Utopian Thought of Restif de la Bretonne.* New York: New York University Press, 1971.

Wagstaff, Peter. "A Better Country: Restif's Later Utopias." *Modern Language Review* 81 (January 1986): 64–70.

La Decouverte Australe

Lamoine, Georges. "Deux Utopies de Dix-Huitième Siècle Chez les Hommes Volants: Quelques Aspects." *Littératures* 5 (Spring 1982): 7–18.

REYES, ALFONSO

General Criticism

Gutierrez Girardot, Rafael. *La Imagen de America en Alfonso Reyes.* Madrid: Insula, 1955, pp. 45–55.

Stabb, Martin S. "Utopia and Anti-Utopia: The Theme in Selected Essayistic Writings of Spanish Americans." *Revista de Estudios Hispanicos* 15 (October 1981): 377–393.

REYNOLDS, JAMES

Equality—A Political Romance

Nydahl, Joel. Introduction. *An Experiment in Marriage,* xvii.

RICE, ELMER

A Voyage to Purilia

Palmieri, Anthony F. R. *Elmer Rice: A Playwright's Vision of America.*
Cranbury, NJ: Associated University Presses, 1980, p. 106.

RICHTER, EUGENE

Pictures of the Socialistic Future

Asholt, Wolfgang. "Sozialistische Irrlehren und Liberale Zerrbilder:
Die Anfange der Anti-Utopie." *Germanisch-Romanische Monatsschrift
Grundzuge* 35, no. 4 (1985): 369–381.

Berneri, Marie Louise. *Journey Through Utopia,* 281–292.

RICHTER, JOHANN PAUL FRIEDRICH. See JEAN PAUL

RIMMER, ROBERT H.

General Criticism

Rimmer, Robert H. "Alternative Lifestyles on the Road to Utopia."
France and North America, 149–163.

———. "I Write Eutopian Novels." In *America as Utopia,* 43–51.

RIVERA, TOMAS

"And the Earth Did Not Part"

Reed, Michael D. "Structural Motif in the Stories of Tomas Rivera."
Journal of the American Studies Association of Texas 18 (1987): 40–45.

Rodriguez, Alfonso. "Time as a Structural Device in Tomas Rivera's '. . . Y no se lo Trago la Tierra.' " In *Contemporary Chicano Fiction*, 126–130.

Rodriquez, Joe. "The Chicano Novel and the North American Narrative of Survival." *Denver Quarterly* 16 (Fall 1981): 63–70.

Saldivar, Jose David. "The Ideological and the Utopian in Tomas Rivera's '. . . Y no se lo Trago la Tierra' and Ron Arias' *The Road to Tamazunchale*." In *Missions in Conflict*, 203–214.

Saldivar, Ramon. *Chicano Narrative*, 74–90.

ROBERTS, J. W.

Looking Within

Egbert, Nelson Norris. "Problems of Form and Content in Six Utopian Responses to Edward Bellamy's *Looking Backward: 2000–1887*."

ROBIDA, ALBERT

General Criticism

Angenot, Marc. "The Emergence of the Anti-Utopian Genre in France: Souvestre, Giraudeau, Robida, *et al.*" Translated by R[obert] P[hilmus]. *Science-Fiction Studies* 12 (July 1985): 129–135.

ROCHEFORT, CHRISTIANE

General Criticism

Arbour, Kathryn Mary. "French Feminist Re-visions."

Hirsch, Marianne, Mary Jean Green, and Lynn Higgins. "An Interview with Christiane Rochefort." *L'Espirt Createur* 19 (Summer 1979): 107–120.

Archaos

Bartkowski, Frances. "Toward a Feminist Eros."

ROLFE, FREDERICK WILLIAM SEFAFINO AUSTIN LEWIS
MARY

Hadrian the Seventh

Benkovitz, Miriam J. *Frederick Rolfe: Baron Corvo.* London: Hamish
Hamilton, 1977, pp. 158–164.

Lawrence, D. H. *Selected Literary Criticism.* Edited by Anthony Beal.
New York: Viking, 1956, pp. 149–153.

Weeks, Donald. "More Light on *Hadrian the Seventh.*" *Antigonish
Review* 1, no. 1 (1970): 54–69.

ROSEWATER, FRANK

'96: A Romance of Utopia

Pfaelzer, Jean. *The Utopian Novel in America, 1886–1896,* 117–118.

ROUSSEAU, JEAN-JACQUES

General Criticism

Granderoute, Robert. *Le Roman Pédagogique de Fénelon à Rousseau.*

Gury, Jacques. "Thomas More Traduit par Thomas Rousseau; ou une
Utopie pour le Club des Jacobins." *Moreana* 13 (1976): 79–86.

Lypp, Bernhard. "Rousseaus Utopien." In *Utopieforschung: Interdisziplinare Studienzur Neuzeitlichen Utopie,* Volume 3, pp. 113–124.

Émile

Blanchard, William H. *Rousseau and the Spirit of Revolt: A Psychological Study.* Ann Arbor: University of Michigan Press, 1967, pp. 147–163.

Bloom, Allan. "The Education of a Democratic Man: *Émile.*" In *Jean-Jacques Rousseau,* 149–171.

Burgelin, Pierre. "The Secondary Education of Émile." *Yale French Studies* 28 (Fall-Winter 1961): 106–111.

Coleman, Patrick. "Characterizing Rousseau's *Émile.*" *MLN* 92 (May 1977): 761–778.

Compayre, Gabriel. *Jean-Jacques Rousseau and Education from Nature.* New York: Burt Franklin, 1971.

Dobinson, C. H. *Jean-Jacques Rousseau: His Thought and Its Relevance Today.* London: Methuen, 1969, pp. 70–127.

Ellis, Madeleine B. *Rousseau's Socratic Aemilian Myth.* Columbus: Ohio State University Press, 1977.

Green, F. C. *Jean-Jacques Rousseau: A Critical Study of His Life and Writings.* Cambridge, England: Cambridge University Press, 1955, pp. 225–264.

Havens, George R. *Jean-Jacques Rousseau,* 93–99.

Hudson, William Henry. *Rousseau and Naturalism in Life and Thought,* 180–206.

Jordan, R. J. P. "A New Look at Rousseau as Educator." *Studies on Voltaire and the Eighteenth Century* 182 (1979): 59–72.

Kaplan, Cora. "Pandora's Box: Subjectivity, Class, and Sexuality in Socialist Feminist Criticism." In *Making a Difference: Feminist Literary Criticism,* edited by Gayle Greene and Coppelia Kahn, 146–176. London: Methuen, 1985.

Mercken-Spaas, Godelieve. "The Social Anthropology of Rousseau's *Émile.*" *Studies on Voltaire and the Eighteenth Century* 132 (1975): 137–181.

Meyer, Paul H. "The Individual and Society in Rousseau's *Émile.*" *Modern Language Quarterly* 19 (June 1958): 99–114.

Politzer, Robert L. "Rousseau on Language Education." *Modern Language Forum* 41 (June 1956): 23–34.

Rosenow, Eliyah. "Rousseau's *Émile*, an Anti-Utopia." *British Journal of Educational Studies* 28 (October 1980): 212–224.

Sahakian, Mabel Lewis, and William S. Sahakian. *Rousseau as Educator.* New York: Twayne, 1974, pp. 78–106.

Scanlan, Timothy M. "A Biblical Allusion in Rousseau's *Émile.*" *Language Quarterly* 14 (Fall–Winter 1975): 12–14.

Vulliamy, C. E. *Rousseau,* 212–225.

Warner, James H. "Émile in Eighteenth-Century England." *PMLA* 59 (September 1944): 773–791.

Wexler, Victor G. " 'Made for Man's Delight': Rousseau as Antifeminist." *American Historical Review* 81 (April 1976): 270–275.

Winwar, Frances. *Jean-Jacques Rousseau,* 263–265.

The New Heloise

Anderson, David L. "Aspects of Motif in *La Nouvelle Héloise.*" *Studies on Voltaire and the Eighteenth Century* 94 (1972): 25–72.

Blum, Carol. "Styles of Cognition as Moral Options in *La Nouvelle Héloise* and *Les Liaisons Dangereuses.*" *PMLA* 88 (March 1973): 289–298.

Brown, F. Andrew. "Rousseau's Bomston and Muralt." *Modern Language Forum* 39 (December 1954): 126–129.

Duckworth, Colin. "Georgiana Spencer in France: Or the Dangers of Reading Rousseau." *Eighteenth-Century Life* 7 (May 1982): 85–91.

Frayling, Christopher. "The Composition of *La Nouvelle Héloise.*" In *Reappraisals of Rousseau,* 181–214.

Gelley, Alexander. "The Two Julies: Conversion and Imagination in *La Nouvelle Héloise.*" *Modern Language Notes* 92 (May 1977): 749–760.

Green, F. C. "Medieval and Modern Sensibility." *Modern Language Review* 32 (October 1937): 553–570.

Grimsley, Ronald. "The Human Problem in *La Nouvelle Héloise.*" *Modern Language Review* 53 (April 1958): 171–184.

Hall, H. Gaston. "The Concept of Virtue in *La Nouvelle Héloise.*" *Yale French Studies* 28 (Fall-Winter 1961): 20–33.

Havens, George R. *Jean-Jacques Rousseau,* 80–89.

―――. "The Sources of Rousseau's Edouard Bromston." *Modern Philology* 17 (1919–1920): 13–27.

―――. "The Theory of 'Natural Goodness' in Rousseau's *Nouvelle Héloise.*" *Modern Language Notes* 36 (November 1921): 385–394.

Hoffding, Harald. *Jean Jacques Rousseau and His Philosophy.* New Haven, CT: Yale University Press, 1930, pp. 83–89.

Hudson, William Henry. *Rousseau and Naturalism in Life and Thought,* 153–179.

Jones, James F., Jr. *La Nouvelle Héloise: Rousseau and Utopia.* Geneve: Droz, 1978.

―――. "Rousseau's Answer to Crime: The Utopia at Clarens." *Eighteenth-Century Life* 2 (1976): 68–71.

Kusch, Manfred. "Landscape and Literary Form: Structural Parallels in *La Nouvelle Héloise.*" *L'Ésprit Créateur* 17 (Winter 1977): 349–360.

―――. "The River and the Garden: Basic Spatial Models in *Candide* and *La Nouvelle Héloise.*" *Eighteenth-Century Studies* 12 (Fall 1978): 8–14.

Macklem, Michael. "Rousseau and the Romantic Ethic." *French Studies* 4 (October 1950): 325–332.

Mall, James P. "La Nouvelle Héloise: Rousseau's Fiction and the Impossibility of Utopia." Ph.D. diss., University of Illinois, 1969.

Mead, William. "*La Nouvelle Héloise* and The Public of 1761." *Yale French Studies* 28 (Fall-Winter 1961): 13–19.

Mille, Pierre. *The French Novel.* Philadelphia: Lippincott, 1930, pp. 49–55.

Mylne, Vivienne. *The Eighteenth-Century French Novel*, 166–191.

Scanlan, Timothy M. "The Notion of 'Paradis sur la Terre' in Rousseau's *La Nouvelle Héloise*." *Nottingham French Studies* 13 (May 1974): 12–22.

————. "*La Nouvelle Héloise*: The Story of a Failure and the Success of a Story." *Modern Languages* 61 (June 1980): 71–80.

Showalter, English, Jr. *The Evolution of the French Novel, 1641–1782*. Princeton, NJ: Princeton University Press, 1972, pp. 301–306, 316–322.

Starobinski, Jean. "Les Déscriptions de Journées dans *La Nouvelle Héloise*." In *Reappraisals of Rousseau*, 46–62.

Tanner, Tony. "Julie and 'La Maison Paternelle': Another Look at Rousseau's *La Nouvelle Héloise*." In *Jean-Jacques Rousseau*, 119–147.

Vance, Christie McDonald. "The Extravagant Shepherd: A Study of the Pastoral Vision in Rousseau's *Nouvelle Héloise*." *Studies on Voltaire and the Eighteenth Century* 105 (1973): 13–179.

Vartanian, Aram. "The Death of Julie: A Psychological Post-Mortem." *L'Ésprit Créateur* 6 (Summer 1966): 77–84.

Vulliamy, C. E. *Rousseau*, 181–197.

Warner, James H. "Eighteenth-Century English Reactions to the *Nouvelle Héloise*." *PMLA* 52 (September 1937): 803–819.

Webb, Donald P. "Did Rousseau Bungle the Nuit d'Amour?" *Kentucky Romance Quarterly* 17, no. 1 (1970): 3–8.

Weightman, John. "The Conflict of Values in *La Nouvelle Héloise*." *Forum for Modern Language Studies (Univ. of St. Andrews, Scotland)* 4 (October 1968): 309–321.

Wexler, Victor G. " 'Made for Man's Delight': Rousseau as Antifeminist." *American Historical Review* 81 (April 1976): 275- 281.

Winwar, Frances. *Jean-Jacques Rousseau*, 248–254.

Wolpe, Hans. "Psychological Ambiguity in *La Nouvelle Héloise*." *University of Toronto Quarterly* 28 (April 1959): 279–290.

RUSS, JOANNA

General Criticism

Duplessis, Rachel. "The Feminist Apologues of Lessing, Piercy, and Russ." *Frontiers* 4 (Spring 1979): 1–8.

The Female Man

Albinski, Nan Bowman. *Women's Utopias in British and American Fiction,* 164, 171–172, 177, 184.

Bartkowski, Frances. "Toward a Feminist Eros."

Cranny-Francis, Anne. *Feminist Fiction,* 131–135, 138–140.

Fitting, Peter. "Positioning and Closure: On the 'Reading Effect' of Contemporary Utopian Fiction." *Utopian Studies* 1 (1987): 23–36.

Howard, June. "Widening the Dialogue on Feminist Science Fiction." In *Feminist Re-Visions,* 64–96.

Huckle, Patricia. "Women in Utopias." In *The Utopian Vision,* 115–136.

Moylan, Tom. *Demand the Impossible,* 55–90.

Rosinsky, Natalie M. "A Female Man? The 'Medusan' Humor of Joanna Russ." *Extrapolation* 23 (Spring 1982): 31–36.

Sargent, Lyman Tower. "A New Anarchism: Social and Political Ideas in Some Recent Feminist Eutopias." In *Women and Utopia,* 3–33.

Schuyler, W. M. "Sexes, Genders, and Discrimination." In *Erotic Universe,* 45–60.

Spector, Judith. "The Functions of Sexuality in the Science Fiction of Russ, Piercy, and Le Guin." In *Erotic Universe,* 197–207.

RUSSELL, ADDISON PEALE

Sub-Coelum

Pfaelzer, Jean. *The Utopian Novel in America, 1886–1896*, 102.

RUSSELL, GEORGE WILLIAM
(AE)

The Avatars

Davis, Robert Bernard. *George William Russell ("AE")*. Boston: Twayne, 1977, pp. 83–89.

SAAVEDRA FAJARDO, DIEGO DE

The Royal Politician

Dowling, John. *Diego De Saavedra Fajardo*. Boston: Twayne, 1977, pp. 78–113.

SADE, DONATIEN ALPHONSE FRANÇOIS, COMTE DE
(MARQUIS DE SADE)

General Criticism

Barthes, Roland. *Sade, Fourier, Loyola*. Translated by Richard Miller. New York: Hill and Wang, 1976, pp. 77–120.

Berneri, Marie Louise. *Journey Through Utopia*. pp. 178–182.

Aline et Valcour

Dolan, John C. "Source and Strategy in Sade: Creation of 'Natural' Landscapes in *Aline et Valcour*." *French Forum* 11 (September 1986): 301–316.

Glaser, Horst Albert. "Utopie und Gegen-Utopie: Zu Sades *Aline et Valcour*." *Poetica* 13, nos. 1–2 (1981): 67–81.

Lynch, Lawrence. *The Marquis de Sade*. Boston: Twayne, 1984, pp. 3–4, 80–90, 99–100.

Manfredi, Pierrette. "Sade, L'Art de la Subversion dans *Aline et Valcour*." Ph.D. diss., University of California, Irvine, 1986.

Miller, C. L. *Blank Darkness: Africanist Discourse in French*. Chicago: University of Chicago Press, 1985, pp. 184–200.

Roger, Philippe. "La Trace de Fénelon." In *Sade,* 149–173.

La Philosophie dans le Boudoir

Bloch, Iwan. *Le Marquis de Sade et Son Temps*. Geneva: Statkine, 1970.

ST. AUGUSTINE OF HIPPO

General Criticism

Bonner, Gerald. *God's Decree and Man's Destiny: Studies on the Thought of Augustine of Hippo*. London: Variorum Reprints, 1987.

City of God

Barker, E. *Essays on Government*. New York: Oxford University Press, 1951, pp. 234–269.

Baynes, N. H. *Byzantine Studies and Other Essays*. London: Athlone Press, 1955, pp. 288–306.

Brookes, Edgar H. *The City of God and the Politics of Crisis*. Westport, CT: Greenwood Press, 1980.

Burleigh, J. H. *The City of God: A Study of St. Augustine's Philosophy*. London: Nisbet, 1949.

Cranz, F. E. "*De Civitate Dei,* XV, 2, and Augustine's Idea of the Christian Society." *Speculum* 25 (April 1950): 215–225.

Figgis, J. N. *The Political Aspects of St. Augustine's City of God*. London: Peter Smith, 1963.

Guy, Jean-Claude. *Unité et Structure Logique de la 'Cité de Dieu' de Saint Augustin.* Paris: Etudes Augustiniennes, 1961.

Markus, R. A. "Two Conceptions of Political Authority: Augustine, *De Civitate Dei,* 19, 14–15, and Some Thirteenth-Century Interpretations." *Journal of Theological Studies* 16 (April 1965): 68–100.

Mommsen, T. E. *Medieval and Renaissance Studies.* Ithaca, NY: Cornell University Press, 1959, pp. 265–298.

Niebuhr, R. *Christian Realism and Political Problems.* New York: Scribner, 1953, pp. 119–145.

Roemer, Kenneth M. *The Obsolete Necessity,* 50, 88.

Silverstein, Theodore. "On the Genesis of *De Monarchia,* II, v." In *Dante in America,* 187–218.

Versfeld, M. *Guide to the City of God.* New York: Sheed & Ward, 1958.

SAINT-PIERRE, JACQUES-HENRI BERNARDIN DE

Paul and Virginia

Donovan, John. Introduction. *Paul and Virginia.* By Jacques-Henri Bernardin de Saint-Pierre. London: Peter Owen, 1982, pp. 9–33.

Guitton, Edouard. "Entre la Norme et la Trangression: L'Érotisme dans *Paul et Virginie.*" *Textes & Langages* 12 (1986): 191–203.

Jordanova, L. J. "Natural Facts: A Historical Perspective on Science and Sexuality." In *Nature, Culture, and Gender,* edited by Carol MacCormack and Marilyn Strathern, 42–69. Cambridge, England: Cambridge University Press, 1980.

Mylne, Vivienne. *The Eighteenth-Century French Novel,* 245–262.

Racault, Jean-Michel. "Bernardin de Saint-Pierre et les *Vies des Saints*: Sur Quelques Reminiscences Hagiographiques dans *Paul et Virginie.*" *Revue d'Histoire Littéraire de la France* 86, no. 2 (1986): 179–188.

———. "*Paul et Virginie* et l'Utopie: De la 'Petite Société' au Mythe Collectif." *Studies on Voltaire and the Eighteenth Century* 242 (1986): 419–471.

SALISBURY, HENRY BARNARD

The Birth of Freedom

Pfaelzer, Jean. *The Utopian Novel in America, 1886–1896*, 114–115.

SARGENT, PAMELA

The Shore of Women

Albinski, Nan Bowman. *Women's Utopias in British and American Fiction*, 162, 164, 175, 185.

Barr, Marleen. "Food for Postmodern Thought: Isak Dinesen's Female Artists as Precursors to Contemporary Feminist Fabulators." In *Feminism, Utopia, and Narrative*, 26–27.

SATTERLEE, W. W.

Looking Backward and What I Saw

Egbert, Nelson Norris. "Problems of Form and Content in Six Utopian Responses to Edward Bellamy's *Looking Backward: 2000–1887*."

SCHILLER, JOHANN VON

The Maid of Orleans

Crosby, Donald H. "Freedom through Disobedience: *Die Jungfrau von Orleans*, Heinrich von Kleist, and Richard Wagner." In *Friedrich von Schiller and the Drama of Human Existence*, edited by Alexej Ugrinsky, 37–42. New York: Greenwood, 1988.

Evans, M. "*Die Jungfrau von Orleans*: A Drama of Philosophical Idealism." *Monatshefte* 35 (April 1943): 188–194.

Hadley, Michael. "Moral Dichotomies in Schiller's *Die Jungfrau von Orleans*: Reflections on the Prologue." In *Crisis and Commitment: Studies in German and Russian Literature in Honour of J. W. Dyck*, edited by John Whiton and Harry Loewen, 56–68. Waterloo, Ontario, Canada: University of Waterloo Press, 1983.

SCHINDLER, SOLOMON

Young West

Egbert, Nelson Norris. "Problems of Form and Content in Six Utopian Responses to Edward Bellamy's *Looking Backward: 2000–1887.*"

Parrington, Vernon Louis, Jr. *American Dreams,* 92–94, 179.

SHAKESPEARE, WILLIAM

The Tempest

Amis, Kingsley. *New Maps of Hell,* 29–30.

Berneri, Marie Louise. *Journey Through Utopia,* 4, 10.

Cohen, Walter. "Shakespeare and Calderon in an Age of Transition." *Genre* 15 (Spring-Summer 1982): 123–137.

Evans, John X. "Utopia on Prospero's Island." *Moreana* 18 (March 1981): 81–83.

Gatter, Frank Thomas. "Zur Utopie im *Tempest.*" *Gulliver: Deutsch-Englische Jhrb* 6 (1979): 80–99.

Knox-Shaw, Peter. " 'The Man in the Island': Shakespeare's Concern with Projection in *The Tempest.*" *Theoria* 61 (October 1983): 23–36.

Koppenfels, Werner von. "Thomas Morus und die Humanistische Utopie der Renaissance." In *Alternative Welten,* 96–113.

LeVay, John. "Shakespeare's *The Tempest.*" *Explicator* 46 (Summer 1988): 9–11.

Meckier, Jerome. "Shakespeare and Aldous Huxley." *Shakespeare Quarterly* 22 (Spring 1971): 129–135.

Paster, Gail Kern. "Montaigne, Dido, and the *Tempest*: 'How Came That Window In?'." *Shakespeare Quarterly* 35 (Spring 1984): 91–94.

Sanford, Charles L. *The Quest for Paradise,* 46, 65.

Tovey, Barbara. "Shakespeare's Apology for Imitative Poetry: *The Tempest* and *The Republic.*" *Interpretation* 11 (September 1983): 275–316.

Van Eeden, Janet. "The Monastery Months." *Crux* 21 (February 1987): 22–25.

Wilson, Robert. "Brave New World as Shakespeare Criticism." *Shakespeare Association Bulletin* 21 (July 1946): 99–107.

SHAW, GEORGE BERNARD

General Criticism

Coleman, D. C. "Bernard Shaw and *Brave New World.*" *Shaw Review* 10 (January 1967): 6–8.

Knepper, B. G. "*The Coming Rave*: Hell? Or Paradise Foretasted?" In *No Place Else,* 11–32.

Woodcock, George. "Five Who Fear the Future." *New Republic* 134 (April 16, 1956): 17–19.

Back To Methuselah

Armstrong, Daniel. "*Back to Methuselah*: Shaw's Debt to Swift." *Cahiers Victoriens et Edouardiens* 21 (April 1985): 63–71.

Bentley, Eric. *Bernard Shaw.* Norfolk, CT: New Directions, 1947, pp. 52–55, 58–60.

Bloomfield, Paul. *Imaginary Worlds, or the Evolution of Utopia,* 220–236.

Brustein, Robert. *The Theatre of Revolt.* Boston: Little, Brown, 1964, pp. 18–21, 195–204.

Carr, Pat M. *Bernard Shaw.* New York: Frederick Ungar, 1976, pp. 107–120.

Crompton, Louis. *Shaw the Dramatist.* Lincoln: University of Nebraska Press, 1969.

Ganz, Arthur. "The Ascent to Heaven: A Shavian Pattern." *Modern Drama* 14 (December 1971): 253–263.

Hamilton, Robert. "Philosophy of Bernard Shaw: A Study of *Back to Methuselah.*" *London Quarterly Review* 170 (July 1945): 333–341.

Hugo, Leon. *Bernard Shaw: Playwright and Preacher.* London: Methuen, 1971, pp. 206–208.

Hummert, Paul A. *Bernard Shaw's Marxian Romance.* Lincoln: University of Nebraska Press, 1973, pp. 135–147.

Irvine, William. *Universe of George Bernard Shaw.* New York: McGraw-Hill, 1949, pp. 316–320.

Leary, Daniel, and Richard Foster. "Adam and Eve: Evolving Archetypes in *Back to Methuselah.*" *Shaw Review* 4 (May 1961): 12–24.

MacCarthy, Desmond. *Shaw: The Plays.* Newton Abbot, England: David and Charles, 1973, pp. 134–142.

Morgan, Margery M. *The Shavian Playground: An Exploration of the Art of Bernard Shaw.* London: Methuen, 1972, pp. 221–238.

Sedlak, Werner. "Utopie und Darwinismus." In *Alternative Welten,* 216–238.

Tanzy, Eugene. "Contrasting Views of Man and Evolutionary Process: *Back to Methuselah* and *Childhood's End.*" In *Arthur C. Clarke,* 172–195.

Thornton-Duesbery, J. P. "The Electric Hedge." *Notes and Queries* 6 (September 1959): 338.

Valency, Maurice. *The Cart and the Trumpet: The Plays of George Bernard Shaw.* New York: Oxford University Press, 1973, pp. 349–368.

Webster, Margaret. "Soliloquy on Methuselah Shaw." *Theatre Arts* 42 (April 1958): 70–72.

Wisenthal, J. L. *The Marriage of Contraries: Bernard Shaw's Middle Plays.* Cambridge, MA: Harvard University Press, 1974, pp. 193–217.

SHELDON, ALICE HASTINGS. See TIPTREE, JAMES, JR.

SHELDON, CHARLES MONROE

In His Steps

Boyer, Paul S. "*In His Steps*: A Reappraisal." *American Quarterly* 23 (Spring 1971): 60–78.

Cazemajou, Jean. "Le Roman de l'Évangile Social: L'Exemple de *In His Steps*." In *Le Facteur Religieux en Amerique du Nord, No. 3: Millenium, République Chrétienne aux États-Unis; Religions et Société au Canada,* edited by Jean Beranger and Pierre Guillaume, 11–30. [Talence]: [Publs. de la Maison des Sciences de l'Homme d'Aquitaine, Univ. de Bordeaux III], 1982.

Ferre, John Patrick. "A Social Gospel for Millions: The Religious Bestsellers of Charles Sheldon, Charles Gordon, and Harold Bell Wright." Ph.D. diss., University of Illinois at Urbana-Champaign, 1986.

Parrington, Vernon Louis, Jr. *American Dreams,* 166–170, 179.

SHELLEY, MARY [GODWIN] WOLLSTONECRAFT

The Last Man

Aldiss, Brian W. *Billion Year Spree: The True History of Science Fiction.* New York: Doubleday, 1973, pp. 31–34.

———. "Mary Wollstonecraft Shelley." In *Science Fiction Writers,* 8.

El-Shater, Safaa. *The Novels of Mary Shelley.* Salzburg: Institut fur Englische Sprache und Literatur, Universitat Salzburg, 1977, pp. 67–110.

Franci, Giovanna. "Lo Specchio del Futuro: Vi Sione e Apocalisse in *The Last Man* di Mary Shelley." *Quaderni di Filologia Germanica* 1 (1980): 75–84.

Kuczynski, Ingrid. "Katastrophe und Hoffnung; Eine Gesellschaftsvision der Romantik: Mary Shelleys Roman *The Last Man.*" In *Literarische Diskurse und Historischer Prozess: Beitrage zur Englischen und Amerikanischen Literatur und Geschichte,* edited by Brunhild de Motte, 139–150. Potsdam, GDR: Padagogische Hochschule 'Karl Liebkneckt', 1988.

Neumann, Bonnie Rayford. *The Lonely Muse: A Critical Biography of Mary Wollstonecraft Shelley.* Salzburg: Institut fur Anglistik und Amerikanistik, Universitat Salzburg, 1979, pp. 173–194.

Palacio, Jean de. *Mary Shelley dans Son Oeuvre: Contribution aux Études Shelleyennes.* Paris: Klincksieck, 1969, pp. 585–592.

Powers, Katherine Richardson. *The Influence of William Godwin on the Novels of Mary Shelley.* New York: Arno, 1980, pp. 58–60, 79–82, 97–101.

Snyder, Robert Lance. "Apocalypse and Indeterminacy in Mary Shelley's *The Last Man.*" *Studies in Romanticism* 17 (Fall 1978): 435–452.

Spatt, Hartley S. "Mary Shelley's Last Men: The Truth of Dreams." *Studies in the Novel* 7 (Winter 1975): 534–536.

Sterrenburg, Lee. "*The Last Man*: Anatomy of Failed Revolution." *Nineteenth-Century Fiction* 33 (December 1978): 324–347.

SHUTE, NEVIL (NORWAY, NEVIL SHUTE)

On the Beach

Higdon, David Leon. " 'Into the Vast Post-Holocaust Novel." In *War and Peace,* 117–124.

Smith, Julian. *Nevil Shute (Nevil Shute Norway).* Boston: Twayne, 1976, pp. 124–134.

Zaki, Hoda M. *Phoenix Renewed,* 29.

SILLITOE, ALAN

Travels in Nihilon

Atherton, Stanley S. *Alan Sillitoe: A Critical Assessment.* London: W. H. Allen, 1979, pp. 185–186.

SILONE, IGNAZIO

General Criticism

Arnone, Vincenzo. *Ignazio Silone.* Rome: Edizioni e Dell'Ateneo & Bizzarri, 1980, pp. 55–56.

Berneri, Marie Louise. *Journey Through Utopia,* 311–312.

Fontamara

Laborda, J. Javier. "1984, con Orwell y sin Koestler." *Quimera* 35 (January 1984): 43–45.

Rawson, Judy. *"Che Fare?* Silone and the Russian *Chto Delat?* Tradition." *Modern Language Review* 76 (July 1981): 556–565.

SILVERBERG, ROBERT

A Time of Changes

Silverberg, Robert. Introduction. *A Time of Changes.* By Robert Silverberg. New York: Berkley, 1979, vii-x.

The World Inside

Abrash, Merritt. "Robert Silverberg's *The World Inside.*" In *No Place Else,* 225–243.

SIMPSON, WILLIAM

The Man from Mars

Rooney, Charles J., Jr. *Dreams and Visions,* 23–24, 51, 60, 64–65, 79, 150, 196–197.

SINCLAIR, UPTON

General Criticism

Creel, George. "Utopia Unlimited." *Saturday Evening Post* 207 (November 24, 1934): 5–7.

Mencken, H. L. "Storm Damage in Utopia." *Baltimore Evening Sun* (January 28, 1934).

Parrington, Vernon Louis, Jr. *American Dreams,* 153, 184–186, 195–196, 199–202.

SKINNER, BURRHUS FREDERIC

General Criticism

Burgess, Anthony. "A Fable for Social Scientists." *Horizon* 15 (Winter 1973): 12–15.

Farrelly, James P. "The Promised Land: Moses, Nearing, Skinner, Le Guin." *Journal of General Education* 33 (Spring 1981): 15–23.

K[arp], W[alter]. "The Clockwork Society." *Horizon* 15 (Winter 1973): 2–3.

Walden Two

Barnsley, John H. "*Island, Walden Two,* and the Utopian Tradition." *World Future Society Bulletin* 16 (September–October 1982): 1–7.

Berger, Harold L. *Science Fiction and the New Dark Age,* 51–55, 58, 59–64.

Christensen, Bryce J. *Utopian Against the Family,* 7–8, 15–16.

Elliott, Robert C. *The Shape of Utopia,* 123, 129–137, 144–146, 150–153.

Elms, Alan C. "Skinner's Dark Year and *Walden Two.*" *American Psychologist* 36, no. 5 (1981): 470–479.

Evans, Richard I. *Dialogue with B. F. Skinner.* New York: Praeger, 1981, pp. 46–47.

Howard, Mary K. "Orwell and the Futurists." *Cuyahoga Review* 2 (Spring–Summer 1984): 17–21.

Jehmlich, Reimer. "Cog-Work: The Organization of Labor in Edward Bellamy's *Looking Backward* and in Later Utopian Fiction." In *Clockwork Worlds,* 27–46.

Krutch, Joseph Wood. *The Measure of Man: On Freedom, Human Values, Survival, and the Modern Temper.* New York: Bobbs-Merrill Co., 1954, pp. 55–76.

Kumar, Krishan. *Utopia and Anti-Utopia in Modern Times,* 347–379.

Plank, Robert. "The Modern Shrunken Utopia." In *America as Utopia,* 206–230.

Roemer, Kenneth M. "Mixing Behaviorism and Utopia: The Transformations of *Walden Two.*" In *No Place Else,* 125–146.

Schaller, Hans-Wolfgang. "B. F. Skinner: *Walden Two.*" In *Die Utopie in der Angloamerikanischen Literatur,* 219–234.

Schwarz, Egon. "B. F. Skinner: *Walden Two.*" In *Literarische Utopien von Morus bis zur Gegenwart,* 218–232.

Sitwell, Robert L. "Literature and Utopia: B. F. Skinner's *Walden Two.*" *Western Humanities Review* 18 (Autumn 1964): 331–341.

Sullivan, E. D. S. "Place in No Place: Examples of the Ordered Society in Literature." In *The Utopian Vision,* 24–49.

Ziemba, Margaret Mary. "Contrasting Social Theories of Utopia."

SMITH, TITUS KEIPER

Altruria

Rooney, Charles J., Jr. *Dreams and Visions,* 105, 197.

Federal I.D. No. 13-566-66-49   Canadian GST No. 125663005

PLEASE USE ACCOUNT NUMBER FOR NEW ORDERS

8600

ACCOUNT NUMBER	PLEASE REFERENCE BOTH NUMBERS WHEN MAKING PAYMENTS	INVOICE NUMBER
53		484741

SHIP TO:

SHIPPED	CUSTOMER P.O. NUMBER	SHIP DATE	
h Class	REVIEW		
		PRICE	AMOUNT
LITERATURE /HASCHAK		52.50	S Free

		SHIPPING & HANDLING	Free
		INVOICE TOTAL	.00

OUR ORIGINAL INVOICE

omissions

Robert Herrick

Topper

C. Smith

SMOLLETT, TOBIAS GEORGE

The History and Adventures of an Atom

Bouce, Paul-Gabriel. *The Novels of Tobias Smollett*. London: Longman, 1976, pp. 37–38.

Day, Robert Adams. "Sex, Scatology, Smollett." In *Sexuality in Eighteenth Century Britain*, edited by Paul-Gabriel Bouce, 229–241. Totowa, NJ: Barnes & Noble, 1982.

Douglass, Wayne J. "Done After the Dutch Taste: Political Prints and Smollett's *Atom*." *Essays in Literature* 9 (Fall 1982): 170–179.

Grant, Damian. *Tobias Smollett: A Study in Style*. Totowa, NJ: Rowman and Littlefield, 1977, pp. 56–59, 80–82, 175–177.

Link, Viktor. *Die Tradition der Aussermenschlichen Erzahlperspektive in der Englischen und Amerikanischen Literatur*. Heidelberg: Carl Winter, 1980, pp. 128–132.

Sekora, John. *Luxury: The Concept in Western Thought, Eden to Smollett*. Baltimore: Johns Hopkins University Press, 1977, pp. 207–211.

SOUVESTRE, ÉMILE

Le Monde tel Qu'il Sera

Angenot, Marc. "The Emergence of the Anti-Utopian Genre in France: Souvestre, Giraudeau, Robida, *et al*." Translated by R[obert] P[hilmus]. *Science-Fiction Studies* 12 (July 1985): 129–135.

Crossley, Ceri. "Emile Souvestre's Anti-Utopia: *Le Monde tel qu'il Sera*." *Nottingham French Studies* 24 (October 1985): 28–40.

SPENCE, CATHERINE HELEN

Handfasted

Albinski, Nan Bowman. "*Handfasted*: An Australian Feminist's American Utopia." *Journal of Popular Culture* 23 (Fall 1989): 15–31.

Margarey, Susan. "Feminist Visions Across the Pacific: Catherine Helen Spence's *Handfasted." Antipodes* 3 (Spring 1989): 31–33.

Thomson, Helen. "Catherine Helen Spence: Pragmatic Utopian." In *Who Is She: Images of Woman in Australian Fiction,* edited by Shirley Walker, 12–25. St. Lucia: University of Queensland Press, 1983.

————. "Introduction." *Catherine Helen Spence.* St. Lucia: University of Queensland Press, 1987, p. xx.

SPENCE, THOMAS

General Criticism

Mumford, Lewis. *The Story of Utopias,* 134–137.

STAPLEDON, OLAF

General Criticism

Crossley, Robert. "Famous Mythical Beasts: Olaf Stapledon and H. G. Wells." *Georgia Review* 36 (Fall 1982): 619–635.

Last and First Men

Ash, Brian. *Faces of the Future,* 138–140.

Bailey, J. O. *Pilgrims Through Space and Time,* 138–143.

Campbell, James L., Sr. "Olaf Stapledon." In *Science Fiction Writers,* 95–98.

Elkins, Charles. " 'Seeing it Whole': Olaf Stapledon and the Issue of Totality." In *The Legacy of Olaf Stapledon: Critical Essays and an Unpublished Manuscript,* edited by Patrick McCarthy, Charles Elkins, and Martin Greenberg, 53–66. New York: Greenwood Press, 1989.

Fiedler, Leslie A. *Olaf Stapledon: A Man Divided.* Oxford: Oxford University Press, 1983, pp. 50–61.

Garrett, J. C. *Utopias in Literature Since the Romantic Period,* 49–50, 55.

Goodheart, Eugene. "Olaf Stapledon's *Last and First Men.*" In *No Place Else,* 78–93.

Huntington, John. "Olaf Stapledon and the Novel about the Future." *Contemporary Literature* 22 (Summer 1981): 351–365.

———. "Remembrance of Things to Come: Narrative Technique in *Last and First Men.*" *Science-Fiction Studies* 9 (1982): 257–264.

Kinnaird, John. *Olaf Stapledon.* San Bernardino, CA: Borgo Press, 1986, pp. 39–53.

Lem, Stanislaw, and Istvan Csicsery-Ronay, Jr. "On Stapledon's *Last and First Men.*" *Science-Fiction Studies* 13 (November 1986): 272–291.

McCarthy, Patrick A. *Olaf Stapledon.* Boston: Twayne, 1982, pp. 33–47.

Shelton, Robert Frederick. "Forms of Things Unknown."

Smith, Curtis C. "Olaf Stapledon and the Immortal Spirit." In *Death and the Serpent,* 107–109.

———. "Olaf Stapledon's Dispassionate Objectivity." In *Voices for the Future: Essays on Major Science Fiction Writers,* edited by Thomas D. Clareson, 44–49. Bowling Green, OH: BG University Popular Press, 1976.

Stableford, Brian. *Scientific Romance in Britain, 1890–1950.* New York: St. Martin's 1985, pp. 200–203.

Trousson, R. *Voyages anx Pays de Nulle Part,* 240–241.

Wagar, W. Warren. "Round Trips to Doomsday." In *The End of the World,* 93–94.

STATON, MARY

From the Legend of Biel

Albinski, Nan Bowman. *Women's Utopias in British and American Fiction*, 165, 169, 184.

Pearson, Carol. "Coming Home: Four Feminist Utopias and Patriarchal Experience." In *Future Females*, 63–70.

Sargent, Lyman Tower. "A New Anarchism: Social and Political Ideas in Some Recent Feminist Eutopias." In *Women and Utopia*, 3–33.

STEERE, C. A.

When Things Were Doing

Rideout, Walter B. *The Radical Novel in the United States, 1900–1954*, 53, 77, 79, 97.

STEVENS, FRANCIS

The Heads of Cerberus

Albinski, Nan Bowman. *Women's Utopias in British and American Fiction*, 69, 74.

Eshbach, Lloyd Arthur. Introduction. *The Heads of Cerberus*. By Francis Stevens. Reading, PA: Polaris Press, 1952. 13–16.

STOCKTON, FRANK R.

The Great War Syndicate

Griffin, Martin. *Frank R. Stockton: A Critical Biography*. Port Washington, NY: Kennikat Press, 1965, pp. 102–104.

STONE, C. H.

One of "Berrian's" Novels

Albinski, Nan Bowman. *Women's Utopias in British and American Fiction*, 73.

Parrington, Vernon Louis, Jr. *American Dreams*, 89–90.

STOWE, HARRIET BEECHER

General Criticism

Berkson, Dorothy. " 'So We All Become Mothers': Harriet Beecher Stowe, Charlotte Perkins Gilman, and the New World of Women's Culture." In *Feminism, Utopia, and Narrative*, 100–107.

Oldtown Folks

Adams, John R. *Harriet Beecher Stowe*. New York: Twayne, 1963, pp. 93–95, 101–102.

The Pearl of Orr's Island

Gerson, Noel B. *Harriet Beecher Stowe: A Biography*. New York: Praeger, 1976, pp. 154–158.

STRONG, JOSIAH

The New Era

Texada, David Ker. "Nineteenth Century Anglo-Saxonism in the United States with Special Reference to John Fiske, John William Burgess and Josiah Strong." M.A. thesis, Louisiana State University, 1958, pp. 60–74.

STRUGATSKY, ARKADY and BORIS

General Criticism

McGuire, Patrick L. "Future History, Soviet Style: The Work of the Strugatsky Brothers." In *Critical Encounters II: Writers and Themes in Science Fiction,* edited by Tom Staicar, 104–124. New York: Ungar, 1982.

Serebinenko, V. "Tri Veka Skitanii v Mire Utopii." *Novyi Mir* 5 (May 1989): 242–255.

STUMP, D. L.

From World to World

Rooney, Charles, J., Jr. *Dreams and Visions,* 110–111, 197.

SULLIVAN, J. W.

"A Modern Cooperative Colony"

Rooney, Charles J., Jr. *Dreams and Visions,* 104, 198.

SWEVEN, GODFREY

Limanora, The Island of Progress

Garrett, J. C. *Utopias in Literature Since the Romantic Period,* 7, 33.

Walsh, Chad. *From Utopia to Nightmare,* 89.

SWIFT, JONATHAN

General Criticism

Koppenfels, Werner von. "*Mundus Alter et Idem*: Utopiefiktion und Menippeische Satire." *Poetica* 13, nos. 1–2 (1981): 16–66.

Gulliver's Travels

Amis, Kingsley. *New Maps of Hell,* 30–32.

Anderson, William. "Paradise Gained by Horace, Lost by Gulliver." In *English Satire and the Satiric Tradition,* edited by Claude Rawson, 151–166. Oxford: Blackwell, 1984.

Armstrong, Daniel. *"Back to Methuselah*: Shaw's Debt to Swift." *Cahiers Victoriens et Edouariens* 21 (April 1985): 63–71.

Beauchamp, Gorman. "Gulliver's Return to the Cave: Plato's *Republic* and Book IV of *Gulliver's Travels." Michigan Academician* 7 (1974): 201–209.

Bentman, Raymond. "Satiric Structure and Tone in the Conclusion of *Gulliver's Travels." Studies in English Literature, 1500–1900* 11 (1971): 535–548.

Berman, David. "Gulliver's Dilemma." *Durham University Journal* 19 (June 1987): 247–248.

Bolanka, Mary. "Swift's *Gulliver's Travels." Explicator* 47 (Fall 1988): 11–12.

Brink, J. R. "From the Utopians to the Yahoos: Thomas More and Jonathan Swift." *Journal of the Rutgers University Libraries* 42 (1980): 59–66.

Bruce, Susan. "The Flying Island and Female Anatomy: Gynecology and Power in *Gulliver's Travels." Genders* 2 (July 1988): 60–76.

Carnochan, W. B. "The Complexity of Swift: Gulliver's Fourth Voyage." *Studies in Philology* 60 (January 1963): 23–44.

Champion, Larry S. "Gulliver's Voyages: The Framing Events as a Guide to Interpretation." *Texas Studies in Literature and Language* 10 (Winter 1969): 529–536.

Clark, John R. "Swift's *Gulliver's Travels." Explicator* 47 (Summer 1989): 9–21.

Dircks, Richard J. "Gulliver's Tragic Rationalism." *Criticism* 2 (1960): 134–149.

Ducrocq, Jean. "Relations de Voyages et recits Symboliques: Robinson et Gulliver." *Studies on Voltaire and the Eighteenth Century* 215 (1982): 1–8.

Eddy, William A. "Rabelais—A Source for *Gulliver's Travels.*" *Modern Language Notes* 37 (November 1922): 416–418.

Elliott, Robert C. *The Shape of Utopia,* 43, 50, 52–67, 108.

Fitzgerald, Robert P. "Science and Politics in Swift's Voyage to Laputa." *Journal of English and Germanic Philology* 87 (April 1988): 213–229.

————. "The Structure of *Gulliver's Travels.*" *Studies in Philology* 71 (April 1974): 247–263.

Frese, Jerry. "Swift's Houyhnhnms and Utopian Law." *University of Hartford Studies in Literature* 9 (1977): 187–195.

Frye, Northrop. "Varieties of Literary Utopias." In *Utopias and Utopian Thought,* 40, 43.

Gill, James E. "Beast over Man: Theriophilic Paradox in Gulliver's 'Voyage to the Country of the Houyhnhnms.' " *Studies in Philology* 67 (October 1970): 532–549.

————. "Man and Yahoo: Dialectic and Symbolism in Gulliver's 'Voyage to the Country of the Houyhnhnms.' " In *The Dress of Words: Essays on Restoration and Eighteenth Century Literature in Honor of Richmond P. Bond,* edited by Robert White, Jr., 67–90. Lawrence: University of Kansas Libraries, 1978.

Gottlieb, Sidney. "The Emblematic Background to Swift's Flying Island." *Swift Studies* 1 (1986): 24–31.

Halewood, W. H. "Plutarch in Houyhnhnmland: A Neglected Source for Gulliver's Fourth Voyage." *Philological Quarterly* 44 (April 1965): 185–194.

Hammond, Brean S. "Allegory in Swift's 'Voyage to Laputa.' " In *KM 80: A Birthday Album for Kenneth Muir, Tuesday, 5 May 1987,* 65–67. Liverpool: Liverpool University Press, n.d.

Hammond, Eugene R. "Nature-Reason-Justice in *Utopia* and *Gulliver's Travels.*" *Studies in English Literature, 1500–1900* 22 (1982): 445–468.

Harlow, Benjamin C. "Houyhnhnmland: A Utopian Satire." *McNeese Review* 13 (1962): 44–58.

Hazenstat, Steven F. "Swift's *Gulliver's Travels.*" *Explicator* 47 (Winter 1989): 14–16.

Herrmann, Leon. "La Langue Lilliputienne et Lemuel Gulliver d'Après Swift." *Revue de Littérature Comparée* 57 (January–March 1983): 95–100.

Jones, Horace Perry. "Swift's *Gulliver's Travels.*" *Explicator* 47 (Fall 1988): 11.

Kelly, Ann Cline. "Swift's Explorations of Slavery in Houyhnhnmland and Ireland." *PMLA* 91 (October 1976): 846–855.

Kennelly, Laura B. "Swift's Yahoo and King Jehu: Genesis of an Allusion." *English Language Notes* 26 (March 1989): 37–45.

Keyser, Elizabeth. "Looking Backward: From *Herland* to *Gulliver's Travels.*" *Studies in Science Fiction* 11 (Spring 1983): 31–46.

Landa, Louis. "The Dismal Science in Houyhnhnmland." *Novel* 13 (1979): 38–49.

Leddy, Annette Cecile. "Swift, Carroll, Borges."

Leonard, David Charles. "Swift, Whiston, and the Comet." *English Language Notes* 16 (June 1979): 284–287.

McWhir, Anne. "Animal Religiosum and the Witches in 'A Voyage to the Houyhnhnms.'" *English Studies in Canada* 12 (December 1986): 375–386.

Martins, Mario. "A Imagem do Homen Portugues nas *Viagens* de *Gulliver,* en *Robinson Crusoe* e no *Utopia.*" *Memorias da Academia das Ciencias de Lisboa, Classe de Letras* 21 (1980): 287–322.

Mezciems, Jenny. "Swift and Orwell: Utopia as Nightmare." In *Between Dream and Nature,* 91–112.

————. "Swift's Praise of Gulliver: Some Renaissance Background to the *Travels.*" In *The Character of Swift's Satire,* 245–281.

————. "The Unity of Swift's 'Voyage to Laputa': Structure as Meaning in Utopian Fiction." *Modern Language Review* 72 (January 1977): 1–21.

————. "Utopia and 'The Thing Which Is Not': More, Swift, and other Lying Idealists." *University of Toronto Quarterly* 52 (Fall 1982): 45–46, 48–54, 57–58.

Morris, John N. "Wishes as Horses: A Word for the Houyhnhnms." *Yale Review* 62 (March 1973): 355–371.

Passmann, Dirk F. "Mud and Slime: Some Implications of the Yahoos' Genealogy and the History of an Idea." *British Journal for Eighteenth-Century Studies* 11 (Spring 1988): 1–17.

————. "The Lilliputian Utopia: A Revised Focus." *Swift Studies* 2 (1987): 67–76.

Philmus, Robert M. "The Language of Utopia." *Studies in the Literary Imagination* 6 (Fall 1973): 66–74.

Pyle, Fitzroy. "Yahoo: Swift and the Asses." *Ariel* 3, no. 2 (1972): 64–69.

Radner, John B. "The Struldbruggs, the Houyhnhnms, and the Good Life." *Studies in English Literature, 1500–1900* 17 (Summer 1977): 419–433.

Reichert, John F. "Plato, Swift, and the Houyhnhnms." *Philological Quarterly* 47 (April 1968): 179–192.

Remington, Thomas J. " 'The Mirror up to Nature': Reflections of Victorianism in Samuel Butler's *Erewhon.*" In *No Place Else,* 33–55.

Renaker, David. "Swift's Laputians as a Caricature of the Cartesians." *PMLA* 94 (October 1979): 936–944.

Samuel, Irene. "Swift's Reading of Plato." *Studies in Philology* 73 (October 1976): 440–462.

Schakel, Peter J. "Big Men and Little Men, Houyhnhnms and Yahoos: Structural Parallels and Meaning in *Gulliver's Travels*." In *Approaches to Teaching Swift's Gulliver's Travels*, 30–36.

Seelye, John D. "Hobbes' *Leviathan* and the Giantism Complex in the First Book of *Gulliver's Travels*." *Journal of English and Germanic Philology* 60 (April 1961): 228–239.

Sherburn, George. "Errors Concerning Houyhnhnms." *Modern Philology* 56 (November 1958): 92–97.

Steele, Peter. "Terminal Days Among the Houyhnhnms." *Southern Review (University of Adelaide, Australia)* 4 (1971): 227–236.

Stringfellow, Frank Hargrave, Jr. "Verbal Irony in Literature: A Psychoanalytic Investigation." Ph.D. diss., Cornell University, 1988.

Suits, Conrad. "The Role of the Horses in a Voyage to the Houyhnhnms." *University of Toronto Quarterly* 34 (January 1965): 118–132.

Sullivan, E. E. "Houyhnhnms and Yahoos: From Technique to Meaning." *SEL* 24 (Summer 1984): 497–511.

Thomas, W. K. "*Brave New World* and the Houyhnhnms." *Revue de l'Université Ottawa* 37 (October-December 1967): 686–696.

Torchiana, Donald T. "Jonathan Swift, the Irish, and the Yahoos: The Case Reconsidered." *Philological Quarterly* 54 (Winter 1975): 195–212.

Vickers, Brian. "The Satiric Structure of *Gulliver's Travels* and More's *Utopia*." In *The World of Jonathan Swift*, 240–257.

Voigt, Milton. "*Gulliver's Travels* in a Utopian-Dystopian Course." In *Approaches to Teaching Swift's Gulliver's Travels*, 117–120.

Washington, Gene. "Natural Horses—the Noble Horse—Houyhnhnms." *Swift Studies* 3 (1988): 91–95.

———. "Swift's *Gulliver's Travels*, Book 2, Chapter 1; Book 4, Chapter 1." *Explicator* 46 (Fall 1987): 8–10.

Williams, Kathleen M. "Gulliver's Voyage to the Houyhnhnms." *ELH* 18 (September 1951): 275–286.

Zimansky, Curt A. "Gulliver, Yahoos, and Critics." *College English* 27 (October 1965): 45–49.

SWIFT, MORRISON ISAAC

A League of Justice

Parrington, Vernon Louis, Jr. *American Dreams,* 131, 132, 134.

Rooney, Charles J., Jr. *Dreams and Visions,* 106, 197.

TARDE, GABRIEL DE

Underground Man

Ross, Harry. *Utopias Old and New,* 101–117.

Wells, H. G. Preface. *Underground Man.* By Gabriel Tarde. Translated by Cloudesley Brereton. Westport, CT: Hyperion Press, 1974.

THOM, ROBERT

Wild in the Streets

Berger, Harold L. *Science Fiction and the New Dark Age,* 135–138.

THOMAS, CHAUNCEY

The Crystal Button

Neustadter, Roger. "Mechanization Takes Command: The Celebration of Technology in the Utopian Novels of Edward Bellamy, Chauncey Thomas, John Jacob Astor, and Charles Caryl." *Extrapolation* 29 (Spring 1988): 21–33.

Parrington, Vernon Louis, Jr. *American Dreams,* 64–68.

Roemer, Kenneth M. *The Obsolete Necessity,* 66–67.

TIBBLES, T. H. and BEATTIE, ELIA M.

The American Peasant

Rooney, Charles J., Jr. *Dreams and Visions,* 11, 70, 148, 198.

TILLYARD, AELFRIDA

Concrete, A Story of Two Hundred Years Hence

Albinski, Nan Bowman. "Thomas and Peter: Society and Politics in Four British Utopian Novels." *Utopian Studies* 1 (1987): 11–22.

———. *Women's Utopias in British and American Fiction,* 79–80, 86, 87, 104.

Garrett, J. C. *Utopias in Literature Since the Romantic Period,* 56.

TINCKER, MARY AGNES

San Salvador

Albinski, Nan Bowman. *Women's Utopias in British and American Fiction,* 49, 60, 73.

Pfaelzer, Jean. *The Utopian Novel in America, 1886–1896,* 76.

TIPTREE, JAMES, JR.
(SHELDON, ALICE HASTINGS)

General Criticism

Hayler, Barbara J. "The Feminist Fiction of James Tiptree, Jr.: Women and Men as Aliens." *Spectrum of the Fantastic,* edited by Donald Palumbo, 127–132. Westport, CT: Greenwood Press, 1988.

Heldreth, L. M. " 'Love is the Plan, the Plan is Death': The Feminism and Fatalism of James Tiptree, Jr." *Extrapolation* 23 (Spring 1982): 22–30.

Seal, Julie Luedtke. "James Tiptree, Jr.: Fostering the Future, Not Condemning it." *Extrapolation* 31 (Spring 1990): 73–82.

"Houston, Houston, Do You Read"

Albinski, Nan Bowman. *Women's Utopias in British and American Fiction*, 164–165, 167, 169–170, 172, 184.

Pei, Lowry. "Poor Singletons: Definition of Humanity in the Stories of James Tiptree, Jr." *Science-Fiction Studies* 6 (November 1979): 276–277.

Siegel, Mark. *James Tiptree, Jr.* San Bernardino, CA: Borgo Press, 1986, p. 41–43.

TOLSTOI, ALEXEI NIKOLAEVICH

Aelita

Gakov, V. "Laser Ray in 1926: Alexei Tolstoy's Science Fiction." *Soviet Literature* 1 (1983): 161–169.

Striedter, Jurij. "Three Post Revolutionary Russian Utopian Novels." In *The Russian Novel from Pushkin to Pasternak*, 177–201.

Yershow, Peter. *Science Fiction and Utopian Fantasy in Soviet Literature*, 19–21.

TOURGÉE, ALBION WINEGAR

A Fool's Errand: By One of the Fools

Dibble, Roy F. *Albion W. Tourgée.* New York: Lemcke & Buechner, 1921, pp. 59–71.

Gross, T. L. *Albion W. Tourgée*. New York: Twayne, 1963, pp. 58–86.

Olsen, Otto H. *Carpetbagger's Crusade: The Life of Albion Winegar Tourgée*. Baltimore: Johns Hopkins Press, 196, pp. 221, 223, 241.

Sommer, Robert F. "The Fool's Errand in Albion W. Tourgée's Reconstruction Novels." *Mid-Hudson Language Studies* 5 (1982): 71–79.

TROLLOPE, ANTHONY

The Fixed Period

Letwin, Shirley Robin. *The Gentleman in Trollope: Individuality and Moral Conduct*. Cambridge, MA: Harvard University Press, 1982, pp. 179–183.

Murdoch, W. *72 Essays: A Selection*. Sydney: Angus & Robertson, 1947, pp. 332–336.

Pollard, Arthur. *Anthony Trollope*. London: Routledge & Kegan Paul, 1978, pp. 165–166.

Skilton, David. "*The Fixed Period*: Anthony Trollope's Novel of 1980." *Studies in the Literary Imagination* 6 (Fall 1973): 39–50.

Tracy, Robert. *Trollope's Later Novels*. Berkeley: University of California Press, 1978, pp. 284–294.

TUCKER, GEORGE

A Voyage to the Moon

McLean, Robert Colin. *George Tucker: Moral Philosopher and Man of Letters*. Chapel Hill, NC: University of North Carolina Press, 1961, pp. 90–94.

Parrington, Vernon Louis, Jr. *American Dreams,* 13–16.

TWAIN, MARK (CLEMENS, SAMUEL LANGHORNE)

General Criticism

Khouri, Nadia. "The Other Side of Otherness: Forms of Fictional Utopianism in the U.S.A. from Mark Twain to Jack London."

Salomon, Roger Blaine. "Mark Twain's Conception of History." Ph.D. diss., University of California, Berkeley, 1957.

"Captain Stormfield's Visit to Heaven"

Bellamy, Gladys. *Mark Twain as a Literary Artist,* 368–370.

Browne, Ray. "Mark Twain and Captain Wakeman." *American Literature* 33 (November 1961): 320–329.

————. Introduction. *Mark Twain's Quarrel with Heaven: 'Captain Stormfield's Visit to Heaven' and other Sketches.* By Mark Twain. New Haven, CT: College & University Press, 1970. 11–32.

Budd, Louis. *Mark Twain: Social Philosopher.* Bloomington: Indiana University Press, 1962, pp. 189–190.

Canby, Henry Seidel. *Turn West, Turn East: Mark Twain and Henry James.* Boston: Houghton Mifflin, 1951, pp. 243–244.

Cox, James M. *Mark Twain and the Fate of Humor.* Princeton, NJ: Princeton University Press, 1966, pp. 291–293.

Gibson, William M. *The Art of Mark Twain.* New York: Oxford University Press, 1976, pp. 83–89.

Rees, Robert A. " 'Captain Stormfield's Visit to Heaven' and *The Gates Ajar.*" *English Language Notes* 7 (March 1970): 197–202.

Wecter, Dixon. *Report from Paradise.* New York: Harper, 1952, pp. 1x–xxv.

Wilson, James D. *A Reader's Guide to the Short Stories of Mark Twain.* Boston: G. K. Hall, 1987, pp. 83–92.

A Connecticut Yankee in King Arthur's Court

Allen, Gerald. "Mark Twain's Yankee." *New England Quarterly* 39 (December 1966): 435–446.

Anderson, Kenneth. "The Ending of *A Connecticut Yankee in King Arthur's Court.*" *Mark Twain Journal* 14 (Summer 1969): 21.

Armytage, W. H. G. *Yesterday's Tomorrows,* 81–82.

Baetzhold, Howard G. "The Autobiography of Sir Robert Smith of Camelot: Mark Twain's Original Plan for *A Connecticut Yankee.*" *American Literature* 32 (January 1961): 456–461.

————. "The Course of Composition of *A Connecticut Yankee*: A Reinterpretation." *American Literature* 33 (May 1961): 195–214.

————. "Mark Twain: England's Advocate." *American Literature* 28 (November 1956): 328–346.

Baldanza, Frank. *Mark Twain: An Introduction and Interpretation.* New York: Barnes & Noble, 1961, pp. 74–79.

Bellamy, Gladys. *Mark Twain as a Literary Artist,* 311–316.

Berkove, Lawrence I. "The Reality of the Dream: Structural and Thematic Unity in *A Connecticut Yankee.*" *Mark Twain Journal* 22 (Spring 1984): 8–14.

Canby, Henry Seidel. "Hero of the Great Know-How: Mark Twain's Machine-Age Yankee." *Saturday Review of Literature* 34 (October 20, 1951): 7–8, 40–41.

Cotora, Craig. "Mark Twain's Literary Offenses; or the Revenge of Fenimore Cooper." *Mark Twain Journal* 21 (Spring 1983): 19–20.

Cox, James M. "*A Connecticut Yankee in King Arthur's Court*: The Machinery of Self-Preservation." *Yale Review* 50 (Autumn 1960): 89–102.

Fetterley, Judith. "Yankee Showman and Reformer: The Character of Mark Twain's Hank Morgan." *Texas Studies in Literature and Language* 14 (Winter 1973): 667–679.

Foner, Philip S. *Mark Twain: Social Critic.* New York: International Publishers, 1958, pp. 103–115.

Gardiner, Helen Jane. "American Utopian Fiction, 1885–1910."

Goldman, Liela. " 'A Giant Among Pygmies.' " *Mark Twain Journal* 21 (Fall 1983): 14–17.

Guttman, Allen. "Mark Twain's *Connecticut Yankee*: Affirmation of the Vernacular Tradition." *New England Quarterly* 33 (June 1960): 232–237.

Hansen, Chadwick. "The Once and Future Boss: Mark Twain's Yankee." *Nineteenth-Century Fiction* 28 (June 1973): 62–73.

Henderson, Harry. *Versions of the Past: The Historical Imagination in American Fiction.* New York: Oxford University Press, 1974, pp. 175–197.

Hoben, John B. "Mark Twain's *A Connecticut Yankee*: A Genetic Study." *American Literature* 18 (November 1946): 197–218.

Holmes, Charles S. "*A Connecticut Yankee in King Arthur's Court*: Mark Twain's Fable of Uncertainty." *South Atlantic Quarterly* 61 (Autumn 1962): 462–472.

Jones, Joseph. "Utopias as Dirge." *American Quarterly* (Fall 1950): 214–226.

Ketterer, David. "Epoch-Eclipse and Apocalypse: Special 'Effects' in *A Connecticut Yankee.*" *PMLA* 88 (October 1973): 1,104–1,114.

McKee, John Dewitt. "*A Connecticut Yankee* as a Revolutionary Document." *Mark Twain Journal* 11 (Summer 1960): 18–20, 24.

Maynard, Reid. "Mark Twain's Ambivalent Yankee." *Mark Twain Journal* 14 (Winter 1968): 1–5.

Michaels, Walter Benn. "An American Tragedy; or, The Promise of American Life: Classes and Individuals." *Representations* 25 (Winter 1989): 71–98.

Pratter, Frederick E. "The Mysterious Traveler in the Speculative Fiction of Howells and Twain." In *America as Utopia,* 78–90.

Reiss, Edmund. Afterword. *A Connecticut Yankee in King Arthur's Court.* By Mark Twain. New York: New American Library, 1963. 321–331.

Robinson, Douglas. "Revising the American Dream: *A Connecticut Yankee.*" In *Mark Twain,* edited by Harold Bloom, 183–206. New York: Chelsea House, 1986.

Sanford, Charles L. "Classics of American Reform Literature." *American Quarterly* 10 (Fall 1958): 302–305.

————. *The Quest for Paradise,* 187–190.

Sewell, David R. "Hank Morgan and the Colonization of Utopia." *American Transcendental Quarterly* 3 (March 1989): 27–44.

Shanley, Mary Lyndon, and Peter Stillman. "Mark Twain: Technology, Social Change, and Political Power." In *The Artist and Political Vision,* edited by Benjamin Barber and Michael McGrath, 267–289. New Brunswick, NJ: Transaction, 1982.

Simonson, Harold R. *The Closed Frontier: Studies in American Literary Tragedy.* New York: Holt, Rinehart and Winston, 1970, pp. 129–133.

Smith, Henry Nash. *Mark Twain's Fable of Progress: Political and Economic Ideas in 'A Connecticut Yankee.'* New Brunswick, NJ: Rutgers University Press, 1964.

Spofford, William. "Mark Twain's Connecticut Yankee: An Ignoramus Nevertheless." *Mark Twain Journal* 15 (Summer 1970): 15–18.

Tower, Tom. "Mark Twain's *Connecticut Yankee*: The Trouble in Camelot." *Challenges in American Culture,* edited by Ray Browne, Larry Landrum, and William Bottorff, 190–198. Bowling Green, OH: BG University Popular Press, 1970.

Trainor, Juliette A. "Symbolism in *A Connecticut Yankee in King Arthur's Court.*" *Modern Language Notes* 66 (June 1951): 382–385.

Warren, Robert Penn. "Bearers of Bad Things: Writers and the American Dream." *New York Review of Books* 22 (March 20, 1975): 12–19.

Wiggins, Robert. *Mark Twain: Jackleg Novelist.* Seattle: University of Washington Press, 1964, pp. 72–82.

Williams, James D. "Revision and Intention in Mark Twain's *A Connecticut Yankee.*" *American Literature* 36 (November 1964): 288–297.

———. "The Use of History in Mark Twain's *A Connecticut Yankee.*" *PMLA* 80 (March 1965): 102–110.

Wilson, James D. "Hank Morgan, Philip, Traum, and Milton's Satan." *Mark Twain Journal* 16 (Summer 1973): 20–21.

Winters, Donald E. "The Utopianism of Survival: Bellamy's *Looking Backward* and Twain's *A Connecticut Yankee.*" *American Studies* 21, no. 1 (1980): 23–28.

"Curious Republic of Gondour"

Bulger, Thomas. "Mark Twain's Ambivalent Utopianism." *Studies in American Fiction* 17 (Autumn 1989): 235–242.

Ferguson, John. "Mark Twain's Utopia." *Mark Twain Journal* 19, no. 3 (1979): 1–2.

Parrington, Vernon Louis, Jr. *American Dreams,* 47–50.

TYSSOT DE PATOT, SIMON

General Criticism

Minerva, Nadia. "L'Utopiste et le Péché: À Propos de Quelques Utopies de la 'Fruhaufklarung.' " In *Requiem pour l'Utopie?,* 73–91.

UPDIKE, JOHN

The Poorhouse Fair

Campbell, Jeff H. *Updike's Novels: Thorns Spell a Word.* Wichita Falls, TX: Midwestern State University Press, 1987, pp. 45–65.

Detweiler, Robert. *John Updike.* New York: Twayne, 1972, pp. 31–46.

Doyle, Paul A. "Updike's Fiction: Motifs and Techniques." *Catholic World* 199 (September 1964): 356–358.

Galloway, David. *The Absurd Hero in American Fiction.* Austin: University of Texas Press, 1966, pp. 21–50.

Greiner, Donald J. *John Updike's Novels.* Athens: Ohio University Press, 1984, pp. 3–29.

Hamilton, Alice, and Kenneth Hamilton. *The Elements of John Updike.* Grand Rapids, MI: Eerdmans Publishing Co., 1970, pp. 119–136.

————. *John Updike: A Critical Essay.* Grand Rapids, MI: Eerdmans Publishing Co., 1967, pp. 12- 22.

Markle, Joyce B. *Fighters and Lovers: Theme in the Novels of John Updike.* New York: New York University Press, 1973, pp. 13–36.

Newman, Judie. *John Updike.* New York: St. Martin's Press, 1968, pp. 8–12.

Rupp, Richard H. "John Updike: Style in Search of a Center." In *John Updike,* edited by Harold Bloom, 20. New York: Chelsea House, 1987.

Samuels, Charles Thomas. *John Updike.* Minneapolis: University of Minnesota Press, 1969, p. 34.

Searles, George J. "*The Poorhouse Fair*: Updike's Thesis Statement." In *Critical Essays on John Updike,* edited by William MacNaughton, 231–236. Boston: G. K. Hall, 1982.

Sy, Marieme. "John Updike: Face à l'Absurde." *University de Dakar Annales de la Faculte des Lettres and Sciences Humaines* 10 (1980): 221–241.

Taylor, Larry E. *Pastoral and Anti-Pastoral Patterns in John Updike's Fiction.* Carbondale, IL: Southern Illinois University Press, 1971, pp. 49–55.

Uphaus, Suzanne Henning. *John Updike.* New York: Ungar, 1980, pp. 10–18.

Vargo, Edward P. *Rainstorms and Fire: Ritual in the Novels of John Updike.* Port Washington, NY: Kennikat Press, 1973, pp. 28–50.

Ward, J. A. "John Updike's Fiction." *Critique* 5 (Spring-Summer 1962): 30–33.

Yates, Norris W. "The Doubt and Faith of John Updike." *College English* 26 (March 1965): 470–471.

VAIRAISSE, DENIS

General Criticism

Minerva, Nadia. "L'Utopiste et le Péché: À Propos de Quelques Utopies de la 'Fruhaufklarung.' " In *Requiem pour l'Utopie?*, 73–91.

L'Histoire des Sevarambes

Kuon, Peter. "L'Utopie Entre 'Mythe' et 'Lumières': La Terre Australe Connue. . . de Gabriel de Foigny et *L'Histoire des Sevarambes* de Denis Veiras." *Papers on French Seventeenth Century Literature* 14 (1987): 253–272.

Pellandra, Carla. "Transparences Trompeuses: Les Cosmogonies Linguistiques de Foigny et de Veiras." In *Requiem Pour l'Utopie?*, 55–71.

Sermain, Jean Paul. "La Langue de l'Utopie." In *Croisements Culturels*, 89–114.

Stockinger, Ludwig. " 'Realismus,' Mythos und Utopia: Denis Vairasse *L'Histoire des Sevarambes*." In *Literarische Utopien von Morus bis zur Gegenwart*, 73–94.

Swiggers, Pierre. "La Langue des Sevarambes." In *La Linguistique Fantastique*, edited by Sylvain Auroux *et al.*, 166–175. Paris: Ed. Denoel, 1985.

VERNE, JULES

General Criticism

Boia, Lucian. "L'Utopie Vernienne." *Synthesis* 8 (1981): 291–304.

Picot, Jean-Pierre. "Utopie de la Nort et Mort de l'Utopie Chez Jules Verne." *Romantisme* 18 (1988): 95–105.

Cinq Cents Millions de la Begum

Bailey, J. O. *Pilgrims Through Space and Time,* 54–55.

Chesneaux, Jean. "Jules Verne et la Tradition du Socialisme Utopique." *L'Homme et la Société* 4 (April-June 1967): 223–232.

Chevrel, Yves. "Questions de Méthodes et d'Idéologies Chez Verne et Zola: *Les Cinq Cents Millions de la Begum* et *Travail.*" *RLM* nos. 523–529 (April-June 1978): 69–96.

Jules-Verne, Jean. *Jules Verne.* Translated by Roger Greaves. New York: Taplinger Pub., 1976, pp. 56–58, 65.

Martin, Charles-Noel. Preface. *Cinq Cents Millions de la Begum . . .* By Jules Verne. Lausanne: Editions Rencontre, 1966, pp. 7–14.

Wagner, Nicolas. "Le Soliloqué Utopiste des *Cinq Cents Millions de la Begum.*" *Europe* 56 (November-December 1978): 117–126.

Mathias Sandorf

Chesneaux, Jean. "Jules Verne et la Tradition du Socialisme Utopique." *L'Homme et la Société* 4 (April–June 1967): 223–232.

VICO, GIAMBATTISTA

La Scienza Nuova

Aronovitch, Hilliard. "Vico and Marx on Human Nature and Historical Development." In *Vico,* Volume 2, 47–57.

Barnouw, Jeffrey. "The Critique of Classical Republicanism and the Understanding of Modern Forms of Polity in Vico's *New Science.*" *Clio* 9 (1980): 393–418.

Caponigri, A. Robert. *Time and Idea: The Theory of History in Giambattista Vico.* London: Routledge and Kegan Paul, 1953, pp. 29–31.

————. "The Timelessness of the *Scienza Nuova* of Giambattista Vico." In *Italian Literature: Roots and Branches,* edited by Giose Rimanelli and K. J. Atchity, 309–332. New Haven, CT: Yale University Press, 1976.

Flint, Robert. *Vico.* New York: Arno, 1979.

Horkheimer, Max. "Vico and Mythology." Translated by Fred Dallmayr. *New Vico Studies* 5 (1987): 63–76.

Lucente, Gregory L. "Vico's Notion of 'Divine Providence' and the Limits of Human Knowledge, Freedom, and Will." *Modern Language Notes* 97 (January 1982): 183–191.

Perkinson, Henry J. *Since Socrates: Studies in the History of Western Educational Thought.* New York: Longman, 1980, pp. 89–110.

Pompa, Leon. *Vico: A Study of the 'New Science.'* Cambridge, NY: Cambridge University Press, 1975.

Pons, Alain. "Vico, Marx, Utopia, and History." In *Vico and Marx,* 20–37.

Stone, Harold. "The Scientific Basis of Vico's *Scienza Nuova.*" In *Vico,* Volume 1, 117–126.

Tristram, Robert J. "Explanation in the *New Science*: On Vico's Contribution to Scientific Sociohistorical Thought." *History and Theory* 21 (1983): 146–177.

Vaughan, Frederick. *"The Political Philosophy of Giambattista Vico: An Introduction to 'La Scienza Nuova.' "* The Hague: Martinus/Nijhoff, 1972.

Verene, Donald Phillip. *Vico's Science of Imagination.* Ithaca, NY: Cornell University Press, 1981.

White, Hayden V. "The Tropics of History: The Deep Structure of the *New Science.*" In *Giambattista Vico's Science of Humanity,* edited by Giorgio Tagliacozzo and Donald Phillip Verene, 65–85. Baltimore: Johns Hopkins University Press, 1976.

Whittaker, Thomas. "Vico's New Science of Humanity." *Mind* 35 (1926): 59–71, 204–221, 319–336.

VIDAL, GORE

Messiah

Berger, Harold L. *Science Fiction and the New Dark Age,* 190–196.

White, R. L. *Gore Vidal.* New York: Twayne, 1968, pp. 89–94.

VINTON, ARTHUR DUDLEY

Looking Further Backward

Egbert, Nelson Norris. "Problems of Form and Content in Six Utopian Responses to Edward Bellamy's *Looking Backward: 2000–1887.*"

Parrington, Vernon Louis, Jr. *American Dreams,* 81–82.

Pfaelzer, Jean. *The Utopian Novel in America, 1886–1896,* 86–92.

VOLNEY, CONSTANTIN

The Ruins

Rigby, Brian. "Volney's Rationalist Apocalypse: *Les Ruines ou Méditations sur les Révolutions des Empires.*" In *1789: Reading, Writing, Revolution: Proceedings of the Essex Conference on the Sociology of Literature, July 1981,* edited by Francis Barker *et al.,* 22–37. Colchester, England: University of Essex, 1982.

VOLTAIRE, FRANÇOIS MARIE AROUET DE

Candide

Aldridge, A. Owen. *Voltaire and the Century of Light.* Princeton, NJ: Princeton University Press, 1975, pp. 250–260.

Barber, W. H. *Voltaire: Candide.* London: Edward Arnold, 1960.

Besterman, Theodore. *Voltaire.* Oxford: Basil Blackwell, 1969, pp. 429–436.

Bonneville, Douglas A. "*Candide* as Symbolic Experience." *Studies on Voltaire and the Eighteenth Century* 76 (1970): 7–14.

Bottiglia, William F. "Candide's Garden." *PMLA* 66 (September 1951): 718–733.

———. "The Eldorado Episode in *Candide*." *PMLA* 73 (September 1958): 339–347.

Brandes, Georg. *Voltaire.* New York: Albert and Charles Boni, 1930, pp. 143–146.

Dalnekoff, Donna Isaacs. "The Meaning of Eldorado: Utopia and Satire in *Candide*." *Studies on Voltaire and the Eighteenth Century* 127 (1974): 41–59.

Francis, R. A. "Prevost's *Cleveland* and Voltaire's *Candide*." *Studies on Voltaire and the Eighteenth Century* 191 (1980): 671–672.

Haac, O. A. "*Candide*: Or Comedy in Utopia." In *Approaches to Teaching Voltaire's 'Candide,'* edited by Renee Waldinger, 172–175. New York: MLA, 1987.

Havens, George R. "The Compositon of Voltaire's *Candide*." *Modern Language Notes* 47 (April 1932): 225–234.

Kahn, Ludwig W. "Voltaire's *Candide* and the Problem of Secularization." *PMLA* 67 (September 1952): 886–888.

Knowlson, James. "Voltaire, Lucian and *Candide*." *Studies on Voltaire and the Eighteenth Century* 161 (1976): 149–160.

Krappe, Alexander H. "The Subterraneous Voyage." *Philological Quarterly* 20 (April 1941): 119–130.

Marsland, Amy L. "Voltaire: Satire and Sedition." *Romantic Review* 57 (February 1966): 37–40.

Mason, Haydn. *Voltaire,* 57–73.

Pappas, John N. "Voltaire and the Problem of Evil." *L'Ésprit Créateur* 3 (Winter 1963): 199–206.

Price, William Raleigh. *The Symbolism of Voltaire's Novels.* New York: AMS Press, 1966, pp. 1–21, 198–229.

Richter, D. H. *Fable'e End,* 22–60.

Richter, Peyton, and Ilona Ricardo. *Voltaire,* 412–419.

Suderman, Elmer F. "*Candide, Rasselas* and Optimism." *Iowa English Yearbook* 11 (1966): 37–43.

Temmer, Mark J. "*Candide* and *Rasselas* Revisited." *Revue de Littérature Comparée* 56 (April–June 1982): 176–193.

Topazio, Virgil W. *Voltaire,* 38–46.

Wade, Ira O. "Voltaire's Quarrel with Science." *Bucknell Review* 8 (December 1959): 297–298.

Micromegas

Bailey, J. O. *Pilgrims Through Space and Time,* 21–22.

Barber, W. H. "The Genesis of Voltaire's *Micromegas.*" *French Studies* 11 (January 1957): 1–14.

Havens, George R. "Voltaire's *Micromegas*: Composition and Publication." *Modern Language Quarterly* 33 (June 1972): 113–118.

Mason, Haydn. *Voltaire,* 48–52.

Nablow, Ralph Arthur. "Was Voltaire Influenced by Lucian in *Micromegas?*" *Romance Notes* 22 (Winter 1981): 186–191.

Richter, Peyton, and Ilona Ricardo. *Voltaire,* 126–131.

Smith, Peter Lester. "New Light on the Publication of *Micromegas.*" *Modern Philology* 73 (August 1975): 77–80.

Topazio, Virgil W. *Voltaire,* 35–38.

VONNEGUT, KURT

General Criticism

Bodtke, Richard. "Great Sorrows, Small Joys: The World of Kurt Vonnegut, Jr." *Cross Currents* 20 (Winter 1970): 120–125.

Bryant, Jerry H. *The Open Decision.* New York: Free Press, 1970, pp. 303–324.

Carson, Ronald. "Kurt Vonnegut: Matter-of-Fact Moralist." *Listening* 6 (Autumn 1971): 182–195.

Dunn, Thomas P., and Richard Erlich. "A Vision of Dystopia: Beehives and Mechanization." *Journal of General Education* 33 (Spring 1981): 45–57.

Vanderbilt, Kermit. "Kurt Vonnegut's American Nightmares and Utopias." In *The Utopian Vision,* 137–173.

Weales, Gerald. "What Ever Happened to Tugboat Annie?" *Reporter* 35 (December 1, 1966): 50, 52–56.

Player Piano

Allen, Rodney William. *Understanding Kurt Vonnegut.* Columbia: University of South Carolina Press, 1991.

Berger, Harold L. *Science Fiction and the New Dark Age,* 17–19, 65, 124.

Broer, Lawrence. "'Pilgrim's Progress: Is Kurt Vonnegut, Jr., Winning His War with Machines?" In *Clockwork Worlds,* 137–161.

Engel, David. "On the Question of Foma: A Study of the Novels of Kurt Vonnegut, Jr." *Riverside Quarterly* 5 (February 1972): 119–128.

Giannone, Richard. *Vonnegut, A Preface to His Novels.* Port Washington, NY: Kennikat, 1977, pp. 12–24.

Hillegas, Mark. "Dystopian Science Fiction: New Index to the Human Situation." *New Mexico Quarterly* 31 (Autumn 1961): 245–247.

Hoffman, Thomas P. "The Theme of Mechanization in *Player Piano.*" In *Clockwork Worlds,* 125–135.

Hughes, David. "The Ghost in the Machine: The Theme of *Player Piano.*" In *America as Utopia,* 108–114.

Kateb, George. *Utopia and Its Enemies.* Glencoe, NY: Free Press, 1963, pp. 187–189.

Lundquist, James. *Kurt Vonnegut.* New York: Ungar, 1977, pp. 22–26, 94–95.

Mustazza, Leonard. "The Machine Within: Mechanization, Human Discontent, and the Genre of Vonnegut's *Player Piano.*" *Papers on Language and Literature* 25 (Winter 1989): 99–113.

Reed, Peter J. *Kurt Vonnegut, Jr.* New York: Warner Paperback Library, 1972, pp. 24–56.

Reid, Susan. "Kurt Vonnegut and American Culture: Mechanization and Loneliness in *Player Piano.*" *Journal of the American Studies Association of Texas* 15 (1984): 46–51.

Rhodes, C. H. "Tyranny by Computer: Automated Data Processing and Oppressive Government in Science Fiction." In *Many Futures, Many Worlds,* 66–93.

Schatt, Stanley. *Kurt Vonnegut, Jr.* Boston: Twayne, 1976, pp. 16–30.

Schickel, Richard. "Black Comedy with Purifying Laughter." *Harper's* 232 (May 1966): 103–104.

Schriber, Mary Sue. "You've Come a Long Way, Babbitt: From Zenith to Ilium." *Twentieth Century Literature* 17 (April 1971): 101–106.

Segal, Howard P. "Vonnegut's *Player Piano*: An Ambiguous Technological Dystopia." In *No Place Else,* 162–181.

Tanner, Tony. "That Uncertain Messenger: A Study of the Novels of Kurt Vonnegut, Jr." *Critical Quarterly* 11 (Winter 1969): 297–315.

Walsh, Chad. *From Utopia to Nightmare,* 85–88.

Wymer, Thomas L. "Machines and the Meaning of Human in the Novels of Kurt Vonnegut, Jr." In *The Mechanical Gods,* 41–52.

WALLACE, IRVING

The Three Sirens

Leverence, John. *Irving Wallace: A Writer's Profile.* Bowling Green, OH: BG University Popular Press, 1974, pp. 127–129.

WARD, ELIZABETH STUART PHELPS. See PHELPS, ELIZABETH STUART

WARNER, REX

General Criticism

Johnstone, Richard. *The Will to Believe: Novelists of the Nineteen-Thirties.* New York: Oxford University Press, 1982, pp. 37–61.

The Professor

Lamont, Daniel R. "*The Professor*: Intellect and Hubris." In *A Garland for Rex Warner,* 56–64.

The Wild Goose Chase

Armytage, W. H. G. *Yesterday's Tomorrows,* 120–122.

Atkins, John. "On Rex Warner." In *Focus One,* edited by B. Rajan and A. Pearse, 33–37. London: Denis Dobson, 1945.

Camp, Andrew. "*The Wild Goose Chase*: Theme, Symbol, Structure." In *A Garland for Rex Warner,* 19–31.

Churchill, Thomas. "Rex Warner: Homage to Necessity." *Critique* 10, no. 1 (1968): 40–44.

DeVitis, A. "Rex Warner and the Cult of Power." *Twentieth Century Literature* 6 (October 1960): 108–109.

Harris, Henry. "The Symbol of the Frontier in the Social Allegory of the 'Thirties,' " *Zeitschrift fur Anglistik und Amerikanistik (Leipzig)* 14 (1966): 127–140.

McLeod, A. L. *Rex Warner: Writer.* Sydney: Wentworth Press, 1960, pp. 10–18.

Tabachnick, Stephen E. "In Pursuit of *The Wild Goose Chase.*" In *A Garland for Rex Warner,* 77–88.

WAUGH, EVELYN

General Criticism

Doyle, Paul A. "The Politics of Waugh." *Renascence* 11 (Summer 1959): 171–174, 221.

Stinson, John J. "Waugh and Anthony Burgess: Some Notes Toward an Assessment of Influence and Affinities." *Evelyn Waugh Newsletter* 10, no. 3 (1976): 11–12.

Love Among the Ruins

Berger, Harold L. *Science Fiction and the New Dark Age,* 186–187.

Bradbury, M. *Evelyn Waugh.* London: Oliver & Boyd, 1964, pp. 103–104.

Carens, J. F. *Satiric Art of Evelyn Waugh.* Seattle: University of Washington Press, 1966, pp. 151–156.

Davis, Robert Murray. "Shaping a World: The Textual History of *Love Among the Ruins.*" *Analytical and Enumerative Bibliography* 1 (Spring 1977): 137–154.

Garrett, J. C. *Utopias in Literature Since the Romantic Period,* 55.

Miles, Peter. "Improving Culture: The Politics of Illustration in Evelyn Waugh's *Love Among the Ruins.*" *Trivium* 18 (1983): 7–38.

Stopp, F. J. *Evelyn Waugh: Portrait of an Artist.* Boston: Little, Brown, 1958, pp. 152–157, 189–190.

Walsh, Chad. *From Utopia to Nightmare,* 79–81.

Weinkauf, Mary. "The God Figure in Dystopian Fiction." *Riverside Quarterly* 4 (March 1971): 266–271.

WELCOME, S. BYRON

From Earth's Centre

Rooney, Charles J., Jr. *Dreams and Visions,* 22, 73, 113–114, 153, 199.

WELLS, H. G.

General Criticism

Aldridge, A. *The Scientific World View in Dystopia,* 19–32.

Armytage, W. H. G. *Yesterday's Tomorrows,* 95–101.

Asker, D. B. D. "H. G. Wells and Regressive Evolution." *Dutch Quarterly Review of Anglo-American Letters* 12, no. 1 (1982): 15–29.

Berneri, Marie Louise. *Journey Through Utopia,* 293–308.

Collins, Christopher. "Zamyatin, Wells and the Utopian Literary Tradition." *Slavonic and East European Review* 44 (July 1966): 351–360.

Crossley, Robert. "Famous Mythical Beasts: Olaf Stapledon and H. G. Wells." *Georgia Review* 36 (Fall 1982): 619–635.

Garrett, J. C. *Utopias in Literature Since the Romantic Period,* 52–55.

Gross, John. "The Road to Utopia." *New Statesman* 78 (July 25, 1969): 108–109.

Hertzler, Joyce Oramel. *The History of Utopian Thought,* 244–254.

Hillegas, Mark. "The Construction of the Future: H. G. Wells and Utopian Fantasy." In *H. G. Wells: Reality and Beyond,* edited by

Michael Mullin, 33–42. Champaign, IL: Champaign Public Library & Information Center, 1986.

————. *The Future as Nightmare,* 16–82.

Huntington, John. "H. G. Wells: Problems of an Amorous Utopian." *English Literature in Transition (1880–1920)* 30, no. 4 (1987): 411–422.

————. "Utopian and Anti-Utopian Logic: H. G. Wells and His Successors." *Science-Fiction Studies* 9 (July 1982): 122–146.

Leeper, Geoffrey. "The Happy Utopias of Aldous Huxley and H. G. Wells." *Meanjin* 24, no. 1 (1965): 120–124.

Leithauser, Brad. "A Peculiarly Dark Utopian: H. G. Wells." *New Criterion* 5 (November 1986): 13–23.

Parrinder, Patrick. "Imagining the Future: Zamiatin and Wells." In *H. G. Wells and Modern Science Fiction,* 126–143.

————. "Utopia and Meta-Utopia in H. G. Wells." *Utopian Studies* 1 (1987): 79–97.

Philmus, Robert M. "Utopias." *Science-Fiction Studies* 9 (July 1982): 117–121.

Ross, Harry. *Utopias Old and New,* 176–184.

Shelton, Robert Frederick. "Forms of Things Unknown."

Wagar, W. Warren. "Dreams of Reason: Bellamy, Wells, and the Positive Utopia." In *Looking Backward, 1988–1888,* 106–125.

Walsh, Chad. *From Utopia to Nightmare,* 52–54.

Woodcock, George. "Five Who Fear the Future." *New Republic* 134 (April 16, 1956): 17–19.

Zamyatin, Yevgeny. "H. G. Wells." *Midway* 10 (Summer 1969): 97–126.

First Men in the Moon

Sellin, Bernard. "Le Voyage Cosmique: H. G. Wells, David Lindsay, C. S. Lewis." In *Just the Other Day*, 235–248.

In the Days of the Comet

Hutchings, W. "Structure and Design in a Soviet Dystopia: H. G. Wells, Constructivism, and Yevgeny Zamyatin's *We*." *Journal of Modern Literature* 9, no. 1 (1981–1982): 81–102.

A Modern Utopia

Barnsley, John H. "Beguiling Visions: H. G. Wells's *A Modern Utopia* and *Men Like Gods*." *World Future Society Bulletin* 18 (September–October 1984): 27–40.

Berger, Harold L. *Science Fiction and the New Dark Age*, 17, 199–120.

Bleich, David. *Utopia*, 82–100.

Bloomfield, Paul. *Imaginary Worlds, or the Evolution of Utopia*, 198–219.

Christensen, Bryce J. *Utopia Against the Family*, 6–7.

Kumar, Krishan. *Utopia and Anti-Utopia in Modern Times*, 168–223.

Mumford, Lewis. *The Story of Utopia*, 183–189.

Parrinder, Patrick. "Utopia and Meta-Utopia in H. G. Wells." *Science-Fiction Studies* 12 (July 1985): 115–128.

––––––. "Wells and the Aesthetics of Utopia." *Caliban* 22 (1985): 19–27.

Schultze, Bruno. "Herbert George Wells: *A Modern Utopia*." In *Die Utopie in der Angloamerikanischen Literatur*, 161–175.

Russia in the Shadows

Prochazka, Martin, and Zdenek S. "A Vison of Soviet Russia: Wells's *Russia in the Shadows* as an Alternative in the Development of His Utopian Thought." *Philologica Pragensia* 30, no. 4 (1987): 183–193.

The Shape of Things to Come

Davis, Ken. "*The Shape of Things to Come*: H. G. Wells and the Rhetoric of Proteus." In *No Place Else*, 110–124.

Whitman, John Pratt. *Utopia Dawns*, 113–117.

"A Story of the Days to Come"

Philmus, Robert M. " 'A Story of the Days to Come' and *News From Nowhere*: H. G. Wells as a Writer of Anti-Utopian Fiction." *English Literature in Transition (1880–1920)* 30, no. 4 (1987): 450–455.

The Time Machine

Ash, Brian. *Faces of the Future*, 50–53.

Bellamy, William. *The Novels of Wells, Bennett, and Galsworthy, 1890–1910*. New York: Barnes & Noble, 1971, pp. 51–70.

Bergonzi, Bernard. *The Early H. G. Wells: A Study of the Scientific Romances*. Toronto: University of Toronto Press, 1961, pp. 46–61.

———. "The Logic of Prophecy in *The Time Machine*." In *H. G. Wells: A Collection of Critical Essays*, edited by Bernard Bergonzi, 39–55. Englewood Cliffs, NJ: Prentice-Hall, 1976, pp. 39–55.

———. "*The Time Machine*: An Ironic Myth." *Critical Quarterly* 2 (Winter 1960): 293–305.

Borrello, Alfred. *H. G. Wells: Author in Agony*. Carbondale, IL: Southern Illinois University Press, 1972, pp. 8–12, 54–56.

Braybrooke, Patrick. *Some Aspects of H. G. Wells*. London: Daniel, 1928, pp. 13–18.

Connelly, Wayne C. "H. G. Wells's *The Time Machine*: Its Neglected Mythos." *Riverside Quarterly* 5 (1972): 178–191.

Costa, Richard H. *H. G. Wells*. New York: Twayne, 1967, pp. 31–35.

Dickson, Lovat. *H. G. Wells: His Turbulent Life and Times*. New York: Atheneum, 1969, pp. 62–64.

Gill, Stephen. *Scientific Romances of H. G. Wells.* Cornwall, Canada: Vesta, 1975, pp. 32–41.

Harris, Mason. "Science Fiction as Dream and Nightmare of Progress: Thoughts on the Theory of Science Fiction." *West Coast Review* 9 (April 1975): 6–9.

Hillegas, Mark. "Cosmic Pessimism in H. G. Wells' Scientific Romances." *Papers of the Michigan Academy of Science, Arts and Letters* 46 (1961): 655–663.

———. *The Future as Nightmare,* 25–34.

Ketterer, David. "Oedipus as Time Traveller." *Science-Fiction Studies* 9 (November 1982): 340–341.

MacKerness, E. "Zola, Wells, and 'The Coming Beast.' " *Science-Fiction Studies* 8 (July 1981): 143–148.

Parrinder, Patrick. "Science Fiction as Truncated Epic." In *Bridges to Science Fiction,* 91–106.

———. *H. G. Wells.* Edinburgh, Scotland: Oliver and Boyd, 1970, pp. 16–23.

———. *H. G. Wells: The Critical Heritage.* London: Routledge and Kegan Paul, 1972, pp. 33–42.

Philmus, Robert M. "Revisions of the Future: *The Time Machine.*" *Journal of General Education* 28 (Spring 1976): 23–30.

———. "*The Time Machine*: Or, the Fourth Dimension as Prophesy." *PMLA* 84 (May 1969): 530–535.

Sedlak, Werner. "Utopie und Darwinismus." In *Alternative Welten,* 216–238.

Seeber, Hans Ulrich. "Utopien und Biologen: Zu H. G. Wells' *The Time Machine* und *A Modern Utopia.*" In *Literarische Utopien von Morus bis zur Gegenwart,* 172–190.

Suvin, Darko. "A Grammar of Form and a Criticism of Fact: *The Time Machine* as a Structural Model for Science Fiction." In *H. G. Wells and Modern Science Fiction,* 90–115.

———. *"The Time Machine* Versus *Utopia* as a Structural Model for Science Fiction." *Comparative Literature Studies* 10 (1973): 334–357.

Williamson, Jack. *H. G. Wells: Critic of Progress.* Baltimore: Mirage, 1973, pp. 51–55.

Woodcock, George. "The Darkness Violated by Light: A Revisionist View of H. G. Wells." *Malahat Review* 26 (April 1973): 144–160.

When the Sleeper Awakes

Aldridge, A. "Origins of Dystopia: *When the Sleeper Awakes* and *We.*" In *Clockwork Worlds,* 63–84.

Bailey, J. O. *Pilgrims Through Space and Time,* 307–310.

Mullen, Richard D. "H. G. Wells and Victor Rousseau Emanuel: *When the Sleeper Wakes* and *The Messiah of the Cylinder.*" *Extrapolation* 8 (May 1967): 31–63.

Staiger, Janet. "Future *Noir*: Contemporary Representations of Visionary Cities." *East-West Film Journal* 3 (December 1988): 20–44.

WERFEL, FRANZ

Star of the Unborn

Arlt, Gustave O. "Franz Werfel and America." *Modern Language Forum* 36 (March-June 1951): 4–7.

Doxiadis, Constantinos. *Between Dystopia and Utopia,* 17.

Jungk, Peter Stephan. *Franz Werfel: A Life in Prague, Vienna, and Hollywood.* Translated by Anselm Hollo. New York: Grove Weidenfeld, 1990, pp. 222–232.

Klarmann, Adolf. "Franz Werfel's Eschatology and Cosmogony." *Modern Language Quarterly* 7 (December 1946): 385–410.

Parrington, Vernon Louis, Jr. *American Dreams,* 214–216.

Puttkamer, Annemarie von. *Franz Werfel: Wort und Antwort.* Würzburg, Germany: Werkbund-Verlag, 1952, pp. 115–149.

Rolleston, J. L. "The Usable Future: Franz Werfel's *Star of the Unborn* as Exile Literature." In *Protest—Form—Tradition: Essays on German Exile Literature,* edited by J. Strelka, R. Bell, and E. Dobson, 57–80. Tuscaloosa, AL: University of Alabama Press, 1979.

Schoy-Fischer, Irene, and Heino Haumann. "Zukenftsvorstellung in Franz Werfels *Stern der Ungeborenen.*" *Text & Kontext* 12, no. 2 (1984): 304–314.

Steiman, Lionel B. *Franz Werfel: The Faith of an Exile.* Waterloo, Ontario, Canada: Wilfrid Laurier University Press, 1985, pp. 152–160.

Walsh, Chad. *From Utopia to Nightmare,* 90–91.

WHEELER, DAVID HILTON

Our Industrial Utopia

Pfaelzer, Jean. *The Utopian Novel in America, 1886–1896,* 95.

WILBRANDT, CONRAD

Mr. East's Experiences in Mr. Bellamy's World

Parrington, Vernon Louis, Jr. *American Dreams,* 82–84.

Walsh, Chad. *From Utopia to Nightmare,* 75.

WILSON, COLIN

The Mind Parasites

Bendau, Clifford P. *Colin Wilson: The Outsider and Beyond.* San Bernardino, CA: Borgo Press, 1979, pp. 43–44.

Berger, Harold L. *Science Fiction and the New Dark Age,* 111–113.

Bergstrom, K. *An Odyssey to Freedom: Four Themes in Colin Wilson's Novels.* Uppsala: Acta Universitatis Upsaliensis, 1983, pp. 122–139.

De Bolt, Joe, and John Pfeiffer. "Wilson, Colin. *The Mind Parasites.*" In *Anatomy of Wonder: A Critical Guide to Science Fiction,* 2nd edition, edited by Neil Barron, 299–300. New York: Bowker, 1981.

Dillard, R. "Toward an Existential Realism: The Novels of Colin Wilson." *Hollins Critic* 4 (October 1967): 1–12.

Dossor, Howard. *Colin Wilson: The Man and His Mind.* Longmead, Shaftesbury, Dorset: Element Books, 1990, pp. 274–275, 278–279, 315–316.

Tredell, Nicolas. *The Novels of Colin Wilson.* Totowa, NJ: Barnes and Noble, 1982, pp. 97–106.

Weigel, J. *Colin Wilson.* Boston: Twayne, 1975, pp. 90–94.

WINSTANLEY, GERRARD

General Criticism

Aylmer, G. E. "The Religion of Gerrard Winstanley." In *Radical Religion in the English Revolution,* edited by J. McGregor and B. Reay, 91–119. New York: Oxford University Press, 1984.

The Law of Freedom in a Platform

Berneri, Marie Louise. *Journey Through Utopia,* 145–173.

Davis, J. C. *Utopia and the Ideal Society,* 169–203.

Eurich, Nell. *Science in Utopia,* 167–168.

Farr, James. "Technology in the Digger Utopia." *Dissent and Affirmation: Essays in Honor of Mulford Q. Sibley,* edited by Arthur Kalleberg, Donald Moon, and Daniel Sabia, 118–131. Bowling Green, OH: BG University Press, 1983.

Hayes, T. Wilson. *Winstanley the Digger: A Literary Analysis of Radical Ideas in the English Revolution.* Cambridge, MA: Harvard University Press, 1979, pp. 210–218.

Lutaud, Oliver. *Winstanley: Socialisme et Christianisme sous Cromwell.* Paris: Didier, 1976, pp. 335–355.

Sabine, George. Introduction. *The Works of Gerrard Winstanley.* By Gerrard Winstanley. Ithaca, NY: Cornell University Press, 1941, pp. 58–70.

WITTIG, MONIQUE

General Criticism

Wenzel, Helene Vivienne. "The Text as Body/Politics: An Appreciation of Monique Wittig's Writings in Context." *Feminist Studies* 7 (Summer 1981): 264–287.

Wittig, Monique. "The Category of Sex." *Feminist Issues* 2 (Fall 1982): 63–68.

———. "Paradigm." In *Homosexualities and French Literature,* edited by George Stambolian and Elaine Marks, 114–121. Ithaca, NY: Cornell University Press, 1979.

Les Guérillères

Arbour, Kathryn Mary. "French Feminist Re-visions."

Bartkowski, Frances. "Toward a Feminist Eros."

Crowder, Diane Griffin. "The Semiotic Functions of Ideology in Literary Discourse." *Bucknell Review* 27, no. 1 (1982): 157–168.

Durand, Laurag. "Heroic Feminism as Art." *Novel* 8 (Fall 1974): 71–77.

Ostrovsky, Erika. "A Cosomogony of 0: Wittig's *Les Guérillères*." In *Twentieth-Century French Fiction: Essays for Germaine Bree,* edited by George Stambolian, 241–251. New Brunswick, NJ: Rutgers University Press, 1975.

Peel, Ellen Susan. "Utopian Feminism, Skeptical Feminism, and Narrative Energy." In *Feminism, Utopia, and Narrative,* 41–48.

Porter, Lawrence M. "Writing Feminism: Myth, Epic and Utopia in Monique Wittig's *Les Guérillères*." *L'Esprit Createur* 29 (Fall 1989): 92–100.

Rosenfeld, Marthe. "Language and the Vision of a Lesbian-Feminist Utopia in Wittig's *Les Guérillères.*" *Frontiers* 6 (Spring-Summer 1981): 6–9.

Waelti-Walters, Jennifer. "Circle Games in Monique Wittig's *Les Guérillères.*" *Perspectives on Contemporary Literature* 6 (1980): 59–64.

WOLFE, BERNARD

General Criticism

Galloway, David. "An Erratic Geography: The Novels of Bernard Wolfe." *Critique* 7 (Spring 1964): 75–86.

Limbo

Berger, Harold L. *Science Fiction and the New Dark Age,* 65–67, 181–182, 185.

Geduld, Carolyn. *Bernard Wolfe.* New York: Twayne, 1972, pp. 37–74.

Walsh, Chad. *From Utopia to Nightmare,* 149–150.

WORLEY, FREDERICK U.

Three Thousand Dollars a Year

Rooney, Charles J., Jr. *Dreams and Visions,* 21, 60, 108, 109, 199–200.

WOUK, HERMAN

The 'Lomokome' Papers

Beichman, Arnold. *Herman Wouk.* New Brunswick, NJ: Transaction, 1984, pp. 69–70.

Berger, Harold L. *Science Fiction and the New Dark Age,* 177–181.

WRIGHT, AUSTIN TAPPAN

Islandia

Flieger, Verlyn. "Wright's *Islandia*: Utopia with Problems." In *Women and Utopia,* 86–107.

Oliver, Kenneth. "*Islandia* Revisited." *Pacific Spectator* 9 (Spring 1955): 178–182.

Parrington, Vernon Louis, Jr. *American Dreams,* 208–210.

Powell, Lawrence Clark. *The Islandian World of Austin Wright.* Los Angeles, CA: Horace F. Turner, 1957.

———. *Passion for Books.* Cleveland: World Publishing, 1958, pp. 97–111.

WRIGHT, FRANCES

General Criticism

Follis, Jane Thompson. "Frances Wright: Feminism and Literature in Antebellum America." Ph.D. diss., University of Wisconsin-Madison, 1982.

Heineman, Helen. *Restless Angels: The Friendship of Six Victorian Women.* Columbus, OH: Ohio University Press, 1983, pp. 1–21.

Tyler, A. F. *Freedom's Ferment: Phases of American Social History to 1860.* Minneapolis: University of Minnesota Press, 1944, pp. 196–224.

A Few Days in Athens

Perkins, A. J. G., and Theresa Wolfson. *Frances Wright Free Enquirer: The Study of a Temperament.* New York: Harper and Brothers, 1939, pp. 19, 74.

WYLIE, PHILIP

The Disappearance

Amis, Kingsley. *New Maps of Hell,* 88–89.

Bendau, Clifford P. *Still Worlds Collide,* 44–47.

Keefer, Truman Frederick. *Philip Wylie,* 121–124.

Los Angeles, A. D. 2017

Barshay, Robert Howard. *Philip Wylie: The Man and His Work.* Washington, DC: University Press of America, 1979, pp. 64–65.

Bendau, Clifford P. *Still Worlds Collide,* 59.

Keefer, Truman Frederick. *Philip Wylie,* 151–152.

WYNDHAM, JOHN

Re-birth

Berger, Harold L. *Science Fiction and the New Dark Age,* 181, 184–185.

XENOPHON

General Criticism

Guilhamet, L. "*Gulliver's Travels* I, vi Reconsidered." *English Language Notes* 21 (March 1984): 44–53.

Cyropaedia

Farber, J. J. "*Cyropaedia* and Hellenistic Kingship." *American Journal of Philology* 100 (Winter 1979): 497–514.

O'Sullivan, J. N. "On Xenophon *Cyropaedia* 6.4.11." *American Journal of Philology* 97 (Summer 1976): 117–118.

YOUNG, MARGUERITE

General Criticism

Fuchs, Miriam. "Margarite Young's Utopias: 'The Most Beautiful Music [They] Had Never Heard.' " *Review of Contemporary Fiction* 9 (Fall 1989): 166–176.

YOUNG, MICHAEL

The Rise of the Meritocracy

Berger, Harold L. *Science Fiction and the New Dark Age,* 78, 82–84.

Walsh, Chad. *From Utopia to Nightmare,* 152–154.

YOUNGHUSBAND, SIR FRANCIS EDWARD

The Coming Country

Seaver, George. *Francis Younghusband: Explorer and Mystic.* London: John Murray, 1952, p. 330.

ZAMIATIN, EVGENII IVANOVICH

General Criticism

Dunn, Thomas P., and Richard Erlich. "A Vision of Dystopia: Beehives and Mechanization." *Journal of General Education* 33 (Spring 1981): 45–57.

We

Ainsa, Fernando. "Antes de *1984.*" *Plural* 15 (May 1986): 37–41.

Aldridge, A. "Myths of Origin and Destiny in Literature: Zamiatin's *We.*" *Extrapolation* 19 (December 1977): 68–75.

———. "Origins of Dystopia: *When the Sleeper Awakes* and *We.*" In *Clockwork Worlds,* 63–84.

————. *The Scientific World View in Dystopia,* 33–44.

————. *Scientising Society: The Dystopian Novel and the Scientific World View.* Ann Arbor, MI: UMI Research Press, 1984.

Alexandrova, Vera. *A History of Soviet Literature, 1917–1964: From Gorky to Solzhenitsyn.* Translated by Mirra Ginsburg. Garden City, NJ: Doubleday, 1963, pp. 97–111.

————. " 'In Every Herd There Is Some Restive Steer': An Enduring Theme." *Survey* 24 (April-June 1958): 74–75.

Angeloff, Alexander. "The Relationship of Literary Means and Alienation in Zamiatin's *We.*" *Russian Language Journal* 23 (June 1969): 3–9.

Armytage, W. H. G. *Yesterday's Tomorrows,* 148–149.

Barker, Murl G. "Onomastics and Zamiatin's *We.*" *Canadian-American Slavic Studies* 11 (Winter 1977): 551–560.

Barnsley, John H. "Two Lesser Dystopias: *We* and *A Clockwork Orange.*" *World Future Society Bulletin* 18 (January-February 1984): 1–10.

Barratt, Andrew. "The First Entry of *We*: An Explication." In *Structural Analysis of Russian Narrative Fiction,* edited by Joe Andrew and Christopher Pike, 96–114. Keele, England: Keele University Press, 1984.

————. "Revolution as Collusion: The Heretic and the Slave in Zamyatin's *My.*" *Slavonic and East European Review* 62 (July 1984): 344–361.

————. "The X-Factor in Zamyatin's *We.*" *Modern Language Review* 80 (July 1985): 659–672.

Baruch, E. H. " 'The Golden Country': Sex and Love in 1984." In *1984 Revisited; Totalitarianism in Our Century,* edited by Irving Howe, 47–56. New York: Harper, 1983.

Bayler, John. "Them and Us." *New York Review of Books* 29 (October 19, 1972): 18–21.

Beauchamp, Gorman. "Cultural Primitivism as Norm in the Dystopian Novel." *Extrapolation* 19 (December 1977): 88–96.

―――. "Future Words: Language and the Dystopian Novel." *Style* 8 (1974): 462–476.

―――. "Man as Robot: The Taylor System in *We*." In *Clockwork Worlds*, 85–93.

―――. "Of Man's Last Disobedience: Zamiatin's *We* and Orwell's *1984*." *Comparative Literature Studies* 10 (December 1973): 289–293.

―――. "Utopia and its Discontents." *Midwest Quarterly* 16 (January 1975): 161–174.

―――. "Zamiatin's *We*." In *No Place Else*, 56–77.

Beaujour, Elizabeth Klosty. "Zamiatin's *We* and Modernist Architecture." *Russian Review* 47 (January 1988): 49–60.

Beehler, Michael. "Yevgeny Zamyatin: The Essential, the Superfluous, and Textual Noise." *Sub-Stance* 15, no. 2 (1986): 48–60.

Berger, Harold L. *Science Fiction and the New Dark Age*, 100–102.

Berneri, Marie Louise. *Journey Through Utopia*, 313–317.

Billington, James H. *The Icon and the Axe: An Interpretive History of Russian Culture*. New York: Knopf, 1966, pp. 504–518.

Borman, G. "New Look at Eugene Zamiatin's *We*." *Extrapolation* 24 (Spring 1963): 57–65.

Brown, E. J. *'Brave New World,' '1984' and 'We.'*

―――. *Major Soviet Writers: Essays in Criticism*. New York: Oxford University Press, 1973, pp. 202–220.

―――. "Zamjatin and English Literature." In *American Contributions to the Fifth International Congress of Slavists, Sofia 1963*, Volume 2, 21–39. The Hague: Mouton & Co., 1963.

Browning, Gordon. "Toward a Set of Standards for [Evaluating] Anti-Utopian Fiction." *Cithara* 10 (December 1970): 18–32.

———. "Zamiatin's *We*: An Anti-Utopian Classic." *Cithara* 7 (May 1968): 13–20.

Carden, P. "Utopia and Anti-Utopia: Aleksei Gastev and Evgeny Zamyatin." *Russian Review* 46 (January 1987): 1–18.

Chang, Hui-Chuan. "City of Cats & Anti-Utopia: A Generic Investigation." *Tamkang Review* 19 (Autumn 1988-Summer 1989): 573–589.

Christensen, Bryce J. *Utopia Against the Family,* 8–12.

Collins, Christopher. *Evgenji Zamjatin: An Interpretative Study.* The Hague: Mouton, 1973.

———. "An Interpretive Study of the Major Fiction of Evgenij Zamjatin." Ph.D. diss., Indiana University, 1968.

———. "Zamyatin, Wells and the Utopian Literary Tradition." *Slavonic and East European Review* 44 (July 1966): 351–360.

———. "Zamjatin's *We* as Myth." *Slavic and East European Journal* 10 (Summer 1966): 125–133.

Connors, J. "Zamyatin's *We* and the Genesis of *1984.*" *Modern Fiction Studies* 21 (Spring 1975): 107–124.

Cowan, S. A. "The Crystalline Center of Zamyatin's *We.*" *Extrapolation* 29 (Summer 1988): 160–178.

Deutscher, Isaac. *Heretics and Renegades and Other Essays,* 35–50.

———. *Russia in Transition: And Other Essays.* New York: Coward-McCann, 1957, pp. 230–245.

Doyle, Peter. "Zamyatin's Philosophy, Humanism, and *We*: A Critical Appraisal." *Renaissance and Modern Studies* 28 (1984): 1–17.

Dyck, J. W. "Nietzsche's Last Man and Zamiatin's Society of Numbers." *Germano-Slavica* 3 (Spring 1981): 331–339.

Eastman, Max. *Artists in Uniform: A Study of Literature and Bureaucratism.* New York: Knopf, 1934, pp. 82–93.

Edwards, T. *Three Russian Writers and the Irrational,* 36–86.

Ehre, Milton. "Zamjatin's Aesthetics." *Slavic and East European Journal* 19 (Fall 1975): 288–296.

Elliott, Robert C. *The Shape of Utopia,* 84–101.

Evans, Robert O. "The *Nouveau Roman,* Russian Dystopias, and Anthony Burgess." In *British Novelists Since 1900,* 253–266.

Fondaneche, Daniel. "*La Ville Incertaine,* une Contre-Utopie Libértaire." *Cahiers due Centre d'Études et de Récherches sur les Littéraires de l'Imaginaire* 9 (1984): 99–107.

Gregg, Richard. "Two Adams and Eve in the Crystal Palace: Dostoevsky, the *Bible* and *We.*" *Slavic Review* 24 (December 1965): 680–687.

Grossman, Kathryn M. "Satire and Utopian Vision in Hugo, Dickens, and Zamiatin." *Journal of General Education* 37, no. 3 (1985): 177–188.

Gurewich, David. "Zamyatin: A Heretic for all Times." *New Criterion* 7 (December 1988): 21–34.

Heller, Leonid. "Zamjatin: Prophete ou Temoin? *Nous Autres* et les realités de son Époque." *Cahiers due Monde Russe et Sovietique* 22 (April-September 1981): 137–165.

Hillegas, Mark. *The Future as Nightmare,* 99.

Howe, Irving. *The Decline of the New.* New York: Harcourt Brace and World, 1970, pp. 66–74.

———. "The Fiction of Anti-Utopia." *New Republic* 146 (April 23, 1962): 13–16.

Huerta, Alberto. "Politica Apocaliptica: Zamjatin, Koestler, Orwell y Milosz." *Religion y Cultura* 30 (July-October 1984): 141–142.

Huntington, John. "Utopian and Anti-Utopian Logic: H. G. Wells and His Successors." *Science-Fiction Studies* 9 (July 1982): 122–146.

Hutchings, W. "Structure and Design in a Soviet Dystopia: H. G. Wells, Constructivism, and Yevgeny Zamyatin's *We*." *Journal of Modern Literature* 9, no. 1 (1981–1982): 81–102.

Jackson, Robert L. *Dostoevsky's Underground Man in Russian Literature*, 150–157.

Kern, Gary. "Zamyatin's Epitaphs." *Russian Literature Triquarterly* 7 (1973): 427–429.

Kerstan, Beate. "Vision und Wirklichkeit: Evgenij Zamjatins Roman *My*." *Wissenschaftliche Zeitschrift Der Friedrich-Schiller-Universitat Jena* 38, no. 1 (1989): 55–58.

Kolodziej, Jerzy. "Rereading Zamjatin's *We*: A Cultural Perspective." Ph.D. diss., Indiana University, 1984.

Kramer, Leonie. "Utopia as Metaphor." In *Utopias*, 133–143.

LaBossiere, Camille R. "Zamiatin's *We*: A Caricature of Utopian Symmetry." *Riverside Quarterly (University of Saskatchewan)* 5 (1973): 40–43.

Leatherbarrow, W. J. "Einstein and the Art of Yevgeny Zamyatin." *Modern Language Review* 82 (January 1987): 142–151.

Lebeau, Cecilia H. "The World Behind the Wall." *Doris Lessing Newsletter* 1 (Fall 1977): 7, 10.

McCarthy, Patrick A. "Zamyatin and the Nightmare of Technology." *Science-Fiction Studies* 11 (July 1984): 122–129.

Macey, Samuel L. "The Role of Clocks and Time in Dystopias: Zamyatin's *We* amd Huxley's *Brave New World*." In *Explorations*, 24–43.

McClintock, James. "United States Revisited: Pynchon and Zamiatin." *Contemporary Literature* 18 (Autumn 1977): 475–490.

Makinen, Robert S. "Doestoevsky's Underground Man in Zamjatin's Single State." Ph.D. diss., University of Pittsburgh, 1974.

Maslen, Elizabeth. "One Man's Tomorrow Is Another's Today: The Reader's World and Its Impact on *Nineteen Eighty-Four.*" In *Storm Warnings,* 146–158.

Mazer, Charles Litten. "Orwell's Oceania, Zamyatin's United States, and Levin's Unicomp Earth: Socially Constructed Anti-Utopias." Ph.D. diss., Texas Technological University, 1975.

Meckier, Jerome. "Poetry in the Future, the Future of Poetry: Huxley and Orwell on Zamyatin." *Renaissance and Modern Studies* 28 (1984): 18–39.

Mihailovich, Vasa D. "Critics on Evgeny Zamiatin." *Papers on Language and Literature* 10 (Summer 1974): 317–334.

Mikesell, Margaret Lael, and Jon Christian Suggs. "Zamyatin's *We* and the Idea of the Dystopic." *Studies in Twentieth Century Literature* 7 (Fall 1982): 89–102.

Mikhailov, Oleg. "Antiutopiia Evgeniia Zamiatina." *Literaturnaia Gazeta* 21 (May 25, 1988): 4.

Moody, C. "Zamyatin's *We* and English Antiutopian Fiction." *UNISA English Studies* 14 (April 1976): 24–33.

Muhlheim, Ulrike. "Utopie, Anti-Utopie and Science Fiction." In *Alternative Welten,* 315–328.

Myers, Alan. "Evgenii Zamiatin in Newcastle." *Slavonic and East European Review* 68 (January 1990): 91–99.

Orwell, George. "Freedom and Happiness." *Tribune (London)* 471 (January 4, 1946): 15–16.

Parrinder, Patrick. "Imagining the Future: Zamyatin and Wells." In *H. G. Wells and Modern Science Fiction,* 126–143.

Parrott, Ray. "The Eye in *We.*" *Russian Literature Triquarterly* 16 (1979): 59–72.

Pitcher, E. W. R. "That Web of Symbols in Zamyatin's *We.*" *Extrapolation* 22 (Fall 1981): 252–261.

Proffer, Carl R. "Notes on the Imagery in Zamjatin's *We*." *Slavic and East European Journal* 7 (Fall 1963): 269–278.

Reszler, Andre. "Man as Nostalgia: The Image of the Last Man in Twentieth-Century Postutopian Fiction." In *Visions of Apocalyps*, 196–215.

Rhodes, C. H. "Frederick Winslow Taylor's System of Scientific Management in Zamiatin's *We*." *Journal of General Education* 28 (Spring 1976): 31–42.

Richards, D. "Four Utopias." *Slavonic and East European Review* 40 (1962): 220–228.

———. *Zamyatin: A Soviet Heretic*. London: Bowes & Bowes, 1962, pp. 54–69.

Rosenshield, Gary. "The Imagination and the 'I' in Zamjatin's *We*." *Slavic and East European Journal* 23 (Spring 1979): 51–62.

Russell, Robert. "Literature and Revolution in Zamyatin's *[We]*." *Slavonic and East European Review* 51 (January 1973): 36–46.

Scheck, Frank Rainer. "Augenschein und Zukunft: Die Antiutopische Reaktion: Samjatins *Wir*, Huxleys *Schone Neue Welt*, Orwells *1984*." In *Science Fiction: Theorie und Geschichte*, edited by Eike Barmeyer, 259–275. Munich: Fink, 1972.

Schwartz, Johathan Matthews. "Two (Possible) Soviet Antecedents to Orwell's *1984*: Chayanov's *Peasant Utopia* and Zamiatin's *We*." In *George Orwell and 1984*, 73–81.

Shane, Alex M. *The Life and Works of Evgenij Zamjatin*. Berkeley: California University Press, 1968.

———. "Zamjatin's Prose Fiction." *Slavic and East European Journal* 12 (Spring 1968): 14–26.

Shklovsky, Viktor. "Evgeny Zamyatin's Ceiling." Translated by Gary Kern. In *Zamyatin's 'We': A Collection of Critical Essays*, edited by Gary Kern, 49–50. Ann Arbor, MI: Ardis, 1988.

Sicher, Efraim. "By Underground to Crystal Palace: The Dystopian Eden." *Comparative Literature Studies* 22 (Fall 1985): 377–393.

————. "Hard Times in Paradise: An Example of an Inverted Biblical Pattern." In *Biblical Patterns in Modern Literature,* edited by David Hirsch and Nehama Aschkenasy, 165–172. Chico, CA: Scholars, 1984.

Stenbock-Fermor, Elizabeth. "A Neglected Source of Zamiatin's Novel *We.*" *Russian Review* 32 (April 1973): 187–188.

Striedter, Jurij. "Three Post Revolutionary Russian Utopian Novels." In *The Russian Novel from Pushkin to Pasternak,* 177–201.

Struve, Gleb. *Russian Literature Under Lenin and Stalin, 1917–1953.* Norman, OK: University of Oklahoma Press, 1971, pp. 434–50.

Suvin, Darko. "Russian SF and Its Utopian Tradition." *Modern Language Review* 66 (January 1971): 139–159.

Swanson, Roy Arthur. "Love Is the Function of Death: Forster, Lagerkvist, and Zamyatin." *Canadian Review of Comparative Literature* 3 (Spring 1976): 197–211.

Thiry, A. "Zamjatins *Wij* als Model voor A. Huxley en G. Orwell." *Dietsche Warande en Belfort* 122 (1977): 508–521.

Thomson, Boris. *The Premature Revolution: Russian Literature and Society.* London: Weidenfeld & Nicolson, 1972, pp. 16–20.

Ulph, Owen. "I-330: Reconsiderations on the Sex of Satan." *Russian Literature Triquarterly* 9 (Spring 1974): 262–274.

Voronsky, A. "Evgeny Zamyatin." Translated by Paul Mitchell. *Russian Literature Triquarterly* 2 (Winter 1972): 153–175.

Walker, Jeanne, Murray. "Totalitarian and Liminal Societies in Zamyatin's *We.*" *Mosaic* 20 (Winter 1987): 113–127.

Walsh, Chad. *From Utopia to Nightmare,* 98–103.

Warrick, Patricia. "The Sources of Zamyatin's *We* in Doestoevsky's *Notes from Underground.*" *Extrapolation* 17 (December 1975): 63–77.

Watt, Alan. "George Orwell and Yevgeny Zamyatin." *Quadrant* 28 (July–August 1984): 110–111.

Weber, Eugene. "The Anti-Utopia of the Twentieth Century." *South Atlantic Quarterly* 58 (Summer 1959): 440–447.

White, John J. "Mathematical Imagery in Musil's *Young Torless* and Zamyatin's *We*." *Comparative Literature* 18 (Winter 1966): 71–78.

Woodcock, George. "Utopias in Negative." *Sewanee Review* 64 (Winter 1956): 81–97.

Yarwood, Edmund. "A Comparison of Selected Symbols in *Notes from the Underground* and *We*." In *Proceedings: Pacific Northwest Conference on Foreign Languages, Twenty-First Annual Meeting, April 3–4, 1970*, edited by Ralph Baldner, 144–149. Victoria, B. C.: University of Victoria, 1970.

Yershov, Peter. *Science Fiction and Utopian Fantasy in Soviet Literature*, 33–35.

Zilboorg, Gregory. Foreword. *We*. By Eugene Zamiatin. Translated by Gregory Zilboorg. New York: Dutton, 1924, xiii-xviii.

ZOLA, ÉMILE

General Criticism

Cosset, Evelyne. "L'Éspace de l'Utopie: Nature et Fonction Romanesque des Utopies dans *Le Ventre de Paris, Germinal, La Terre*, et *L'Argent*." *Les Cahiers Naturalistes* 63 (1989): 137–147.

Nelson, Brian. *Zola and the Bourgeoisie*. London: Macmillan Press, 1983.

L'Argent

Hemmings, F. W. J. *Émile Zola*, 225–227, 268–270.

Nelson, Brian. "Energy and Order in Zola's *L'Argent*." *Australian Journal of French Studies* 17 (September-December 1980): 275–300.

Germinal

Bellos, David. "From the Bowels of the Earth: An Essay on *Germinal*." *Forum for Modern Language Studies* 15 (January 1979): 35–45.

Bennetton, Norman A. "Social Thought in Émile Zola." *Sociology and Social Research* 13 (1928–1929): 375–376.

Blankenagel, John C. "The Mob in Zola's *Germinal* and in Hauptmann's *Weavers.*" *PMLA* 39 (September 1924): 705–721.

Cirillo, N. R. "Marxism as Myth in Zola's *Germinal.*" *Comparative Literature Studies* 14 (September 1977): 244–255.

Evenhuis, A. J. "Zola as Myth-Maker in *Germinal.*" *Journal of the Australasian Universities Language and Literature Association* 64 (November 1985): 101–111.

Goldberg, M. A. "Zola and Social Revolution: A Study of *Germinal.*" *Antioch Review* 27 (Winter 1967–1968): 491–507.

Grant, Richard B. "Zola's *Germinal.*" *Explicator* 18 (March 1960): Item 37.

Hemmings, F. W. J. *Émile Zola,* 175–199.

Howe, Irving. "Zola: The Poetry of Naturalism." In *Critical Essays on Émile Zola,* 111–112, 114–124.

King, Graham. *Garden of Zola.* London: Barrie & Jenkins, 1978, pp. 176–196.

Knapp, Bettina L. *Émile Zola.* New York: Ungar, 1980, pp. 98, 101–109.

Mackerness, E. D. "Zola, Wells, and 'The Coming Beast.' " *Science-Fiction Studies* 8 (July 1981): 143–148.

Mitterand, Henri. "Ideology and Myth: *Germinal* and the Fantasies of Revolt." Translated by Janice Best. In *Critical Essays of Émile Zola,* 124–130.

Pasco, Allan H. "Myth, Metaphor, and Meaning in *Germinal.*" *French Review* 46 (March 1973): 739–749.

Smethurst, Colin. *Émile Zola: Germinal.* London: Edward Arnold, 1974.

Walker, Philip. "Prophetic Myths in Zola." *PMLA* 74 (September 1959): 447–451.

La Terre

Grant, Elliott. *Émile Zola*. New York: Twayne, 1966, pp. 137–145.

Harvey, Lawrence. "The Cycle Myth in *La Terre* of Zola." *Philological Quarterly* 38 (January 1959): 89–95.

Richardson, Joanna. *Zola*. New York: St. Martin's Press, 1978, pp. 118–123.

Travail

Chevrel, Yves. "Questions de Méthodes et d'Idéologies chez Verne et Zola: *Les Cinq Cents Millions de la Begum* et *Travail*." *La Revue des Lettres Modernes* nos. 523–529 (April-June 1978): 69–96.

Hemmings, F. W. J. *Émile Zola*, 282–286.

Nelson, Brian. "Zola's Ideology: The Road to Utopia." In *Critical Essays on Émile Zola*, 168–171. Boston: G. K. Hall, 1986.

Zilli, Luigia. "La Citta Ideale di E. Zola, Ovvero la Saturazione del Senso." *Studi di Letteratura Francese* 11 (1985): 101–113.

Le Ventre de Paris

Gerhardi, Gerhard C. "Zola's Biological Vision of Politics: Revolutionary Figures in *La Fortune des Rougon* and *Le Ventre de Paris*." *Nineteenth-Century French Studies* 2 (Spring-Summer 1974): 164–180.

Lapp, John C. *Zola Before the Rougon-Macquart*. Toronto: University of Toronto Press, 1964, pp. 41–46.

Schor, Naomi. *Zola's Crowds*. Baltimore: Johns Hopkins University Press, 1978, pp. 21–34.

APPENDIX

Aaron, Daniel. *Men of Good Hope: A Story of American Progressives.* New York: Oxford University Press, 1951.

Action and Conviction in Early Modern Europe: Essays in Memory of E. H. Harbison, edited by Theodore Rabb and Jerrold Seigel. Princeton, NJ: Princeton University Press, 1969.

Acts of Interpretation: The Text in Its Contexts, 700–1600: Essays on Medieval and Renaissance Literature in Honor of E. Talbot Donaldson, edited by Mary Carruthers and Elizabeth Kirk. Norman, OK: Pilgrim, 1982.

Adams, John R. *Edward Everett Hale.* Boston: Twayne, 1977.

Albinski, Nan Bowman. *Women's Utopias in British and American Fiction.* London: Routledge, 1988.

Alcorn, John. *The Nature Novel from Hardy to Lawrence.* New York: Columbia University Press, 1977.

Aldridge, A. *The Scientific World View in Dystopia.* Ann Arbor, MI: UMI Research Press, 1984.

Alternative Welten, edited by Manfred Pfister. Munich: Fink, 1982.

America as Utopia, edited by Kenneth Roemer. New York: Franklin, 1981.

Amis, Kingsley. *New Maps of Hell: A Survey of Science Fiction.* New York: Harcourt, Brace and Co., 1960.

Anderson, David D. *Ignatius Donnelly.* Boston: Twayne, 1980.

Approaches to Teaching Swift's Gulliver's Travels, edited by Edward Rielly. New York: MLA, 1988.

Arbour, Kathryn Mary. "French Feminist Re-visions: Wittig, Rochefort, Bersianik, and D'Eaubonne Re-write Utopia." Ph.D. diss. University of Michigan, 1984.

Arbur, Rosemarie. *Marion Zimmer Bradley.* San Bernardino, CA: Borgo Press, 1985.

Armytage, W. H. G. *Yesterday's Tomorrows: A Historical Survey of Future Societies.* Toronto: University of Toronto Press, 1968.

The Art of Walker Percy: Stratagems for Being, edited by Panthea Broughton. Baton Rouge: Louisiana State University Press, 1979.

Arthur C. Clarke, edited by Joseph Olander and Martin Greenberg. New York: Taplinger, 1977.

Ash, Brian. *Faces of the Future—Lessons of Science Fiction.* London: Elek/Pemberton, 1975.

Autour de l'Idée de Nature: Histoire des Idées et Civilisation: Pédagogie et Divers. Paris: Didier, 1977.

Bailey, J. O. *Pilgrims Through Space and Time: Trends and Patterns in Scientific and Utopian Fiction.* New York: Argus Books, 1947.

Barr, Narleen. *Suzy McKee Charnas.* San Bernardino, CA: Borgo Press, 1986.

Bartkowski, Frances. "Toward a Feminist Eros: Readings in Feminist Utopian Fiction." Ph.D. diss., University of Iowa, 1982.

Bellamy, Gladys. *Mark Twain as a Literary Artist.* Norman, OK: University of Oklahoma Press, 1950.

Bendau, Clifford. *Still Worlds Collide: Philip Wylie.* San Bernardino, CA: Borgo Press, 1980.

Berdyaev, Nicholas. *Dostoevsky: An Interpretation.* Translated by Donald Attwater. Cleveland: World, 1957.

Berger, Harold L. *Science Fiction and the New Dark Age.* Bowling Green, OH: Bowling Green State University Popular Press, 1976.

Berger, Morroe. *Real and Imagined Worlds: The Novel and Social Science.* Cambridge, MA: Harvard University Press, 1977.

Berman, Marshall. *All that Is Solid Melts into Air: The Experience of Modernity.* New York: Simon and Schuster, 1982.

Berneri, Marie Louise. *Journey Through Utopia.* Boston: Beacon Press, 1950.

Between Dream and Nature: Essays on Utopia and Dystopia, edited by Dominic Baker-Smith and C. C. Barfoot. Amsterdam: Rodopi, 1987.

Bleich, David. "Utopia: The Psychology of a Cultural Fantasy." Ph.D. diss., New York University, 1968.

Bloomfield, Paul. *Imaginary Worlds, or the Evolution of Utopia.* London: Hamish Hamilton, 1932.

Bowering, Peter. *Aldous Huxley: A Study of the Major Novels.* New York: Oxford University Press, 1969.

Bradford, Richard. *Kingsley Amis.* London: Edward Arnold, 1989.

Brander, Laurence. *Aldous Huxley: A Critical Study.* Lewisburg, PA: Bucknell University Press, 1970.

Bridges to Science Fiction, edited by George Slusser, George Guffey, and Mark Rose. Carbondale, IL: Southern Illinois University Press, 1980.

British Novelists Since 1900, edited by Jack Biles. New York: AMS, 1987.

Brown, E. J. *Brave New World, 1984 and We: An Essay on Anti-Utopia.* Ann Arbor, MI: Ardis, 1976.

Calder, Jenni. *Chronicles of Conscience: A Study of George Orwell and Arthur Koestler.* Pittsburgh: University of Pittsburgh Press, 1968.

The Character of Swift's Satire: A Revised Focus, edited by Claude Rawson. Newark, DE: University of Delaware Press, 1983.

Christensen, Bryce J. *Utopia Against the Family: The Problems and Politics of the American Family.* San Francisco: Ignatius Press, 1990.

Clipper, Lawrence J. *G. K. Chesterton.* New York: Twayne, 1974.

Clockwork Worlds: Mechanized Environments in SF, edited by Richard Erlich and Thomas Dunn. Westport, CT: Greenwood, 1983.

Coates, John. *Chesterton and the Edwardian Cultural Crisis.* Hull, England: Hull University Press, 1984.

Colmer, J. *Coleridge to Catch-22: Images of Society.* New York: St. Martin's Press, 1978.

Contemporary Chicano Fiction: A Critical Survey, edited by Vernon Lattin. Binghamton, NY: Bilingual, 1986.

Coordinates: Placing Science Fiction and Fantasy, edited by George Slusser, Eric Rabkin, and Robert Scholes. Carbondale, IL: Southern Illinois University Press, 1983.

Cranny-Francis, Anne. *Feminist Fiction.* New York: St. Martin's Press, 1990.

Critical Essays on Anthony Burgess, edited by Geoffrey Aggeler. Boston: G. K. Hall, 1986.

Critical Essays on Émile Zola, edited by David Baguley. Boston: G. K. Hall, 1986.

Critical Essays on John Fowles, edited by Ellen Pifer. Boston: G. K. Hall, 1986.

Croisements Culturels, edited by Andre Tournon. Ann Arbor: Dept. of Romance Languages, University of Michigan, 1987.

Dante in America: The First Two Centuries, edited by A. Giamatti. Binghamton, NY: Medieval and Renaissance Texts and Studies, 1983.

Dante in the Twentieth Century, edited by Adolph Caso. Boston: Dante University of America Press, 1982.

Davis, J. C. *Utopia and the Ideal Society: A Study of English Utopian Writing, 1516–1700.* New York: Cambridge University Press, 1981.

Death and the Serpent: Immortality in Science Fiction and Fantasy, edited by Carl Yoke and Donald Hassler. Westport, CT: Greenwood Press, 1985.

Dedmond, Francis B. *Sylvester Judd.* Boston: Twayne, 1980.

Deutscher, Isaac. *Heretics and Renegades and Other Essays.* London: H. Hamilton, 1955.

Doris Lessing: The Alchemy of Survival, edited by Carey Kaplan and Ellen Rose. Athens: Ohio University Press, 1988.

Dover, K. J. *Aristophanic Comedy.* Berkeley: University of California Press, 1972.

Downs, R. B. *Molders of the Modern Mind: 111 Books that Shaped Western Civilization.* New York: Barnes and Noble, 1961.

Doxiadis, Constantinos. *Between Dystopia and Utopia.* London: Faber & Faber, 1966.

Duran, Juan Guillermo. "Literatura y Utopia en Hispanoamerica." Ph.D. diss. Cornell University, 1972.

Edwards, T. *Three Russian Writers and the Irrational: Zamyatin, Pil'nyak, and Bulgakov.* New York: Cambridge University Press, 1982.

Egbert, Nelson Norris. "Problems of Form and Content in Six Utopian Responses to Edward Bellamy's *Looking Backward: 2000- 1887.*" Ph.D. diss. State University of New York at Albany, 1979.

Elliot, Robert C. *The Shape of Utopia.* Chicago: University of Chicago Press, 1970.

The End of the World, edited by Eric Rabkin, Martin Greenberg, and Joseph Olander. Carbondale, IL: Southern Illinois University Press, 1983.

Erotic Universe: Sexuality and Fantastic Literature, edited by Donald Palumbo. New York: Greenwood, 1986.

Essays from Oceania and Eurasia: George Orwell and 1984, edited by Benoit Suykerbuyk. Antwerp: Universite Instelling Antwerpen, 1984.

Estudios en honor de Rololfo Oroz. Santiago: Universidad de Chile, 1985.

Eurich, Nell. *Science in Utopia: A Mighty Design.* Cambridge, MA: Harvard University Press, 1967.

Explorations: Essays in Comparative Literature, edited by Makoto Ueda. Lanham, MD: University Press of America, 1986.

The Feminine Eye: Science Fiction and the Women Who Write It, edited by Tom Staicar. New York: Ungar, 1982.

Feminism, Utopia, and Narrative, edited by Libby Jones and Sarah Goodwin. Knoxville: University of Tennessee Press, 1990.

Feminist Re-Visions: What has Been and Might Be, edited by Vivian Patraka and Louise Tilly. Ann Arbor, MI: Women's Studies Program, University of Michigan, 1983.

Firchow, Peter E. *Aldous Huxley: Satirist and Novelist.* Minneapolis: University of Minnesota Press, 1972.

France and North America: Utopias and Utopians, edited by Allain Mathé. Lafayette, LA: Center for Louisiana Studies, University of Southwestern Louisiana, 1978.

Frederick, John T. *William Henry Hudson.* New York: Wayne, 1972.

Fullbrook, Kate. *Free Women: Ethics and Aesthetics in Twentieth-Century Women's Fiction.* Philadelphia: Temple University Press, 1990.

Furbank, P. *Samuel Butler.* Cambridge, England: Cambridge University Press, 1948.

Future Females: A Critical Anthology, edited by Marleen Barr. Bowling Green, OH: Bowling Green State University Popular Press, 1981.

Garden Cities of To-Morrow. By Ebenezer Howard. London: Faber and Faber, 1946.

Gardiner, Helen Jane. "American Utopian Fiction, 1885–1910: The Influence of Science and Technology." Ph.D. diss. University of Houston, 1978.

A Garland for Rex Warner: Essays in Honour of His Eightieth Birthday, edited by A. McLeod. Mysore, India: Literary Half-Yearly Press, 1985.

Garrett, J. C. *Utopias in Literature Since the Romantic Period.* Christchurch, New Zealand: University of Canterbury, 1968.

George Orwell, edited by Courtney Wemyss and Alexej Ugrinski. Westport, CT: Greenwood, 1987.

George Orwell and 1984: Six Essays, edited by Michael Skovmand. Aarhus, Denmark: Seklos, Dept. of English, University of Aarhus, 1984.

Granderoute, Robert. *Le Roman Pédagogique de Fénelon à Rousseau.* Geneve: Slatkine, 1985.

H. G. Wells and Modern Science Fiction, edited by Darko Suvin. Lewisburg, PA: Bucknell University Press, 1977.

The Happening Worlds of John Brunner: Critical Explorations in Science Fiction, edited by Joe De Bolt. Port Washington, NY: Kennikat Press, 1975.

Hard Science Fiction, edited by George Slusser and Eric Rabkin. Carbondale, IL: Southern Illinois University Press, 1986.

Harsh, Philip Whaley. *A Handbook of Classical Drama.* Stanford, CA: Stanford University Press, 1944.

Havens, George R. *Jean-Jacques Rousseau.* Boston: Twayne, 1978.

Hemmings, F. W. J. *Émile Zola.* Oxford, England: Clarendon Press, 1953.

Hertzler, Joyce Oramel. *The History of Utopian Thought.* New York: Macmillan Co., 1923.

Hillegas, Mark. *The Future as Nightmare: H. G. Wells and the Anti-Utopians.* New York: Oxford University Press, 1967.

Hogan, Robert. *Eimar O'Duffy.* Lewisburg, PA: Bucknell University Press, 1972.

Hollow, John. *Against the Night, the Stars: The Science Fiction of Arthur C. Clarke.* San Diego, CA: Harcourt Brace Jovanovich, 1983.

Holmes, Charles M. *Aldous Huxley and the Way to Reality.* Bloomington, IN: Indiana University Press, 1970.

Hudson, William Henry. *Rousseau and Naturalism in Life and Thought.* New York: Scribner's, 1903.

Isaac Asimov. New York: Taplinger Publishing, 1977.

Issues in Russian Literature before 1917, edited by J. Douglas Clayton. Columbus, OH: Slavica, 1989.

Ivanov, Vyacheslav. *Freedom and the Tragic Life: A Study in Dostoevsky.* New York: Noonday, 1952.

Jackson, Robert L. *Doestoevsky's Underground Man in Russian Literature.* The Hague: Mooton & Co., 1958.

Jean-Jacques Rousseau, edited by Harold Bloom. New York: Chelsea, 1988.

Johnson, Wayne L. *Ray Bradbury.* New York: Ungar, 1980.

Jones, Malcolm V. *Doestoyevsky: The Novel of Discord.* New York: Barnes and Noble, 1976.

Just the Other Day: Essays on the Suture of the Future, edited by Luk de Vos. Antwerp, Belgium: EXA, 1985.

Kaufmann, M. *Utopias; or Schemes of Social Improvement.* London: Kegan Paul, 1879.

Keefer, Truman Frederick. *Philip Wylie.* Boston: Twayne, 1977.

Kessler, Carol Farley. *Elizabeth Stuart Phelps.* Boston: Twayne, 1982.

Ketterer, David. *New Worlds for Old: The Apocalyptic Imagination, Science Fiction, and American Literature.* Bloomington, IN: Indiana University Press, 1974.

Khouri, Nadia. "The Other Side of Otherness: Forms of Fictional Utopianism in the U. S. A. from Mark Twain to Jack London." Ph.D. diss., McGill University, 1983.

Kubal, David L. *Outside the Whale: George Orwell's Art and Politics.* Notre Dame, IN: University of Notre Dame Press, 1972.

Kumar, Krishan. *Utopia and Anti-Utopia in Modern Times.* Oxford, England: Basil Blackwell, 1987.

Kvindestudier V: Utopi og Subkultur, edited by Nynne Koch. Copenhagen, Denmark: Delta, 1981.

Laidler, Harry Wellington. *Social-Economic Movements: An Historical and Comparative Survey of Socialism, Communism, Co-operation, Utopianism, and other Systems of Reform and Reconstruction.* New York: Crowell, 1944.

Lane, Ann J. *To Herland and Beyond: The Life and Work of Charlotte Perkins Gilman.* New York: Pantheon Books, 1990.

Leddy, Annette Cecille. "Swift, Carroll, Borges: A History of the Subject in Dystopia." Ph.D. diss., University of California, Los Angeles, 1986.

Lee, Robert E. *Orwell's Fiction.* Notre Dame, IN: Notre Dame University Press, 1969.

Levene, Mark. *Arthur Koestler.* New York: Ungar, 1984.

Lewis Carroll: A Celebration, edited by Edward Guilano. New York: Potter, 1982.

La Linguistique Fantastique, edited by Jean-Claude Chevalier, Nicole Jacques-Chaquin, and Christiane Marchello-Nizia. Paris: Ed. Denoel, [1985].

Literarische Utopien von Morus bis zur Gegenwart, edited by Klaus Berghahn and Ulrich Seeber. Konigstein/Ts.: Athenaum, 1983.

Looking Backward, 1988–1888: Essays on Edward Bellamy, edited by Daphne Patai. Amherst, MA: University of Massachusetts Press, 1988.

McEvoy, Seth. *Samuel R. Delany.* New York: Ungar, 1984.

Machiavelli Attuale/Machiavel Actuel, edited by Georges Barthouil. Ravenna, Italy: Longo, 1982.

Man, God, and Nature in the Enlightenment, edited by Donald Mell, Theodore Braun, and Lucia Palmer. East Lansing, MI: Colleagues, 1988.

Many Futures, Many Worlds: Theme and Form in Science Fiction, edited by Thomas Clareson. Kent, OH: Kent State University Press, 1977.

Margaret Atwood: Visions and Forms, edited by Kathryn Van Spanckeren and Jan Castro. Carbondale, IL: Southern Illinois University Press, 1988.

Mason, Haydn. *Voltaire.* London: Hutchinson, 1975.

Mason, Ronald. *The Spirit Above the Dust: A Study of Herman Melville.* London: John Lehmann, 1951.

Masso, Gildo. *Education in Utopias.* New York: AMS, 1972.

The Mechanical God: Machines in Science Fiction, edited by Thomas Dunn and Richard Erlich. Westport, CT: Greenwood, 1982.

Missions in Conflict: Essays on U.S.-Mexican Relations and Chicano Culture, edited by Renate von Bardeleben, Dietrich Briesemeister, and Juan Bruce-Novoa. Tubingen: Narr, 1986.

Mogen, David. *Ray Bradbury.* Boston: Twayne, 1986.

More's Utopia and Its Critics, edited by Ligeia Gallagher. Glenview, IL: Scott, Foresman, 1964.

Moylan, Tom. *Demand the Impossible: Science Fiction and the Utopian Imagination.* New York: Methuen, 1986.

Mumford, Lewis. *The Story of Utopias.* New York: Boni and Liveright, 1922.

Murray, Gilbert. *Aristophanes: A Study.* Oxford, England: Clarendon Press, 1933.

Mylne, Vivienne. *The Eighteenth-Century French Novel: Techniques of Illusion.* Manchester, England: Manchester University Press, 1965.

Newquist, Roy. *Counterpoint.* New York: Rand McNally, 1964.

Nineteen Eighty-Four in 1984: Autonomy, Control and Communication, edited by Paul Chilton and Crispin Aubrey. London: Comedia, 1983.

No Place Else: Explorations in Utopian and Dystopian Fiction, edited by Eric Rabkin, Martin Greenberg, and Joseph Olander. Carbondale, IL: Southern Illinois University Press, 1983.

Nydahl, Joel. Introduction. *An Experiment in Marriage.* By Charles Bellamy. Delmar, NY: Scholar's Facsimiles and Reprints, 1977.

Old Lines, New Forces, edited by Robert Morris. Cranbury, NJ: Associated University Press, 1976.

The Orwellian Moment: Hindsight and Foresight in the Post-1984 World, edited by Robert L. Savage, James Combs, and Dan Nimmo. Fayetteville: University of Arkansas Press, 1989.

Oxley, B. T. *George Orwell.* New York: Arco, 1969.

Pachmujss, Temira. *F. M. Dostoevsky: Dualism and Synthesis of the Human Soul.* Carbondale, IL: Southern Illinois University Press, 1963.

Parrington, Vernon Louis, Jr. *American Dreams: A Study of American Utopias.* Providence, RI: Brown University Press, 1947.

Patrouch, Joseph F., Jr. *The Science Fiction of Isaac Asimov.* Garden City, NY: Doubleday, 1974.

Patterns of the Fantastic, edited by Donald Hassler. Mercer Island, WA: Starmont House, 1983.

Peel, Ellen Susan. "Both Ends of the Candle: Feminist Narrative Structures in the Novels by Stael, Lessing, and Le Guin." Ph.D. diss., Yale University, 1983.

Pfaelzer, Jean. *The Utopian Novel in America, 1886–1896.* Pittsburgh: University of Pittsburgh Press, 1984.

Philosophers Look at Science Fiction, edited by Nicholas Smith. Chicago: Nelson-Hall, 1982.

Pickering, Jean. *Understanding Doris Lessing.* Columbia: University of South Carolina Press, 1990.

Popular Fiction and Social Change, edited by Christopher Pawling. New York: St. Martin's, 1984.

Proceedings of the Xth Congress of the International Comparative Literature Association/Actes du X Congres de L'Association Internationale de Litterature Comparee, New York, 1982, edited by James Wilhelm *et al.* New York: Garland, 1985.

Rabkin Eric S. *Arthur C. Clarke.* West Linn, OR: Starmont House, 1979.

Ray Bradbury, edited by Martin Greenberg and Joseph Olander. New York: Taplinger, 1980.

Reappraisals of Rousseau: Studies in Honour of R. A. Leigh, edited by Simon Harbey *et al.* Totowa, NJ: Barnes & Noble, 1980.

Reckford, Kenneth J. *Aristophanes' Old-and-New Comedy: Six Essays in Perspective.* Chapel Hill, NC: University of North Carolina Press, 1987.

Reflections on the Fantastic, edited by Michael Collings. New York: Greenwood, 1986.

Requiem pour l'Utopie? Tendances autodestructives du Paradigme Utopique, edited by Carmelina Imbroscio. Paris: Nizet, 1986.

Richter, D. H. *Fable'e End: Completeness and Closure in Rhetorical Fiction.* Chicago: University of Chicago Press, 1974.

Richter, Peyton, and Ilona Ricardo. *Voltaire.* Boston: Twayne, 1980.

Rideout, Walter B. *The Radical Novel in the United States, 1900–1954.* Cambridge, MA: Harvard University Press, 1956.

Roemer, Kenneth M. *The Obsolete Necessity: America in Utopian Writings, 1888–1900.* Kent, OH: Kent State University Press, 1976.

Rooney, Charles J., Jr. *Dreams and Visions: A Study of American Utopias, 1865–1917.* Westport, CT: Greenwood Press, 1985.

Ross, Harry. *Utopias Old and New.* Norwood, PA: Norwood Editions, 1978.

Rubenstein, Roberta. *The Novelistic Vision of Doris Lessing: Breaking the Forms of Consciousness.* Urbana, IL: University of Illinois Press, 1979.

The Russian Novel from Pushkin to Pasternak, edited by John Garrard. New Haven, CT: Yale University Press, 1983.

Sade: Écrire la Crise, edited by Michel Camus and Philippe Roger. Paris: Belford, 1983.

Saldivar, Ramon. *Chicano Narrative: The Dialectics of Difference.* Madison, WI: University of Wisconsin Press, 1990.

Sanford, Charles L. *The Quest for Paradise: Europe and the American Moral Imagination.* Urbana, IL: University of Illinois Press, 1961.

Scharnhorst, Gary. *Charlotte Perkins Gilman.* Boston: Twayne, 1985.

Science Fiction Dialogues, edited by Gary Wolfe. Chicago: Academy Chicago, 1982.

Science Fiction Writers: Critical Studies of the Major Authors from the Early Nineteenth Century to the Present Day, edited by B. Bleiler. New York: Scribner's, 1982.

Sedgwick, William Ellery. *Herman Melville: The Tragedy of Mind.* Cambridge, MA: Harvard University Press, 1944.

Selected Proceedings of the 1978 Science Fiction Research Association National Conference, edited by Thomas Remington. Cedar Falls: University of Northern Iowa, 1979.

Shelton, Robert Frederick. "Forms of Things Unknown: The Alien and Utopian Visions of Wells, Stapledon, and Clarke." Ph.D. diss. University of California, Berkeley, 1982.

Singleton, Mary Ann. *The City and the Veld: The Fiction of Doris Lessing.* Lewisburg, PA: Bucknell University Press, 1977.

Skerl, Jennie. *William S. Burroughs.* Boston: Twayne, 1985.

Spann, E. K. *Brotherly Tomorrows: Movements for a Cooperative Society in America, 1820–1920.* New York: Columbia University Press, 1989.

Spatz, Lois. *Aristophanes.* Boston: Twayne, 1978.

Spivack, Charlotte. *Ursula K. Le Guin.* Boston: Twayne, 1984.

Stern, Milton R. *The Fine Hammered Steel of Herman Melville.* Urbana, IL: University of Illinois Press, 1957.

Stillman, Clara G. *Samuel Butler: A Mid-Victorian Modern.* New York: Viking Press, 1932.

Stinson, John J. *Anthony Burgess Revisited.* Boston: Twayne, 1991.

Storm Warnings: Science Fiction Confronts the Future, edited by George Slusser, Colin Greenland, and Eric Rabkin. Carbondale, IL: Southern Illinois University Press, 1987.

Strauss, Leo. *Socrates and Aristophanes.* Chicago: University of Chicago Press, 1966.

Studies in Eighteenth-Century Culture, edited by O. Brack, Jr. Madison: Published for the American Society for Eighteenth-century Studies by the University of Wisconsin Press, 1985.

Topazio, Virgil W. *Voltaire: A Critical Study of His Major Works.* New York: Random House, 1967.

The Transcendent Adventure: Studies of Religion in Science Fiction/ Fantasy, edited by Robert Reilly. Westport, CT: Greenwood, 1985.

Trousson, R. *Voyages aux Pays de Nulle Part: Histoire Littéraire de la Pensée Utopique.* Brussels: Éditions de L'Université de Bruxelles, 1975.

Ursula K. Le Guin, edited by Joseph Olander and Martin Greenberg. New York: Taplinger, 1979.

Ursula K. Le Guin: Voyager to Inner Lands and to Outer Space, edited by Joe De Bolt. Port Washington, NY: Kennikat, 1979.

Ursula K. Le Guin's 'The Left Hand of Darkness,' edited by Harold Bloom. New York: Chelsea House, 1987.

Utopian Thought in American Literature, edited by Arno Heller, Walter Holbling, and Waldemar Zacharasiewicz. Tubingen, Germany: G. Narr, 1988.

The Utopian Vision: Seven Essays on the Quincentennial of Sir Thomas More, edited by E. D. S. Sullivan. San Diego, CA: San Diego State University Press, 1983.

Utopias, edited by Eugene Kamenka. Melbourne: Oxford University Press, 1987.

Utopias and Utopian Thought, edited by Frank Manuel. Boston: Houghton Mifflin, 1966.

De l'Utopie à l'Uchronie: Formes, Significations, Fonctions, edited by Hinrich Hudde and Peter Kuon. Tubingen, Germany: Gunter Narr Verlag, 1988.

Die Utopie in der Angloamerikanischen Literatur: Interpretationen, edited by Harmut Heuermann and Bernd-Peter Lange. Dusseldorf, Germany: Bagel, 1984.

Utopieforschung: Interdisziplinare Studien zur Neuzeitlichen Utopie, edited by Wilhelm Vosskamp. Stuttgart: Metzler, 1982.

Vico: Past and Present, edited by Giorgio Tagliacozzo. Two Volumes Bound as One. Atlantic Highlands, NJ: Humanities Press, 1981.

Vico and Marx: Affinities and Contrasts, edited by Giorgio Tagliacozzo. London: Macmillan, 1983.

Visions of Apocalypse: End or Rebirth?, edited by Saul Friedlander *et al.* New York: Holmes, 1985.

Voyages: Recits et Imaginaire, edited by Bernard Beugnot. Paris: Papers on French Seventeenth Century Literature, 1984.

Vulliamy, C. E. *Rousseau.* Port Washington, NY: Kennikat Press, 1972.

Walsh, Chad. *From Utopia to Nightmare.* London: Geoffrey Bles, 1962.

War and Peace: Perspectives in the Nuclear Age, edited by Ulrich Goebel and Otto Nelson. Lubbock, TX: Texas Tech University Press, 1988.

Watts, Harold H. *Aldous Huxley.* New York: Twayne, 1969.

Weedman, Jane Branham. *Samuel R. Delany.* Mercer Island, WA: Starmont House, 1982.

Westmeyer, R. E. *Modern Economic and Social Systems.* New York: Farrar, 1940.

White, Frederic R. *Famous Utopias of the Renaissance.* New York: Hendricks House, 1946.

Whitman, John Pratt. *Utopia Dawns.* Boston: Utopia Publishing Co., 1934.

William Golding: Some Critical Considerations, edited by Jack Biles and Robert Evans. Lexington: University Press of Kentucky, 1978.

Winwar, Frances. *Jean-Jacques Rousseau: Conscience of an Era.* New York: Random House, 1961.

Women and Utopia, edited by Marleen Barr and Nicholas Smith. Lanham, MD: University Press of America, 1983.

Women Worldwalkers: New Dimensions of Science Fiction and Fantasy, edited by Jane Weedman. Lubbock: Texas Tech Press, 1985.

The World of Jonathan Swift: Essays for the Tercentenary, edited by Brian Vickers. Oxford: Blackwell, 1968.

A Yearbook of Studies in English Language and Literature 1985/86, edited by Otto Rauchbauer. Vienna: Braumuller, 1986.

Yershov, Peter. *Science Fiction and Utopian Fantasy in Soviet Literature.* New York: Research Program on the U.S.S.R. Mimeographed Series no. 62, 1954.

Young, S. *The Women of Greek Drama.* New York: Exposition Press, 1953.

Zaki, Hoda M. *Phoenix Renewed*. Mercer Island, WA: Starmont House, 1988.

Ziemba, Margaret Mary. "Contrasting Social Theories of Utopia: An Analysis of *Looking Backward* and *Walden Two*." Ph.D. diss., American University, 1977.

TITLE INDEX

CRITIC INDEX

ABOUT THE AUTHOR

PAUL G. HASCHAK (M.L.S., Louisiana State University) is Night Reference Librarian and Assistant Professor of Library Science at Southeastern Louisiana University, Hammond, Louisiana. He became interested in the creative process in general, and utopian literature in particular, while working on his undergraduate degree in English Literature at Cleveland State University.